Reminiscences of a Bungle

Western Canada Reprint Series

Reminiscences of a Bungle

by
One of the Bunglers

■

and Two Other
Northwest Rebellion Diaries

Edited and with an
introduction by
R.C. Macleod

Western Canada Reprint Series
The University of Alberta Press

First published by
The University of Alberta Press
450 Athabasca Hall
Edmonton, Alberta,
Canada T6G 2E8

Copyright © The University of Alberta Press 1983

ISBN 0–88864–077–3

Canadian Cataloguing in Publication Data
Main entry under title:

Reminiscences of a bungle, by One of the Bunglers, and two other
   Northwest Rebellion diaries

(Western Canada reprint series, ISSN 0820–9561 ; 3)
Diaries of Lewis Redman Ord, Richard Scougall Cassels, and
Harold Penryn Rusden.
   ISBN 0–88864–077–3

1. Riel Rebellion, 1885–Personal narratives. I. Macleod, R.C.,
1940– II. Ord, Lewis Redman, 1856–1942, III. Cassels, R.S.
(Richard Scougall) IV. Rusden, Harold Penryn. V. Series.

Typesetting by Solaris Press, Inc., Rochester, Michigan
Printed by McNaughton & Gunn, Ann Arbor, Michigan, U.S.A.

For Elaine
who knows that I eventually get things right

Contents

ACKNOWLEDGMENTS

The original suggestion for this volume came from Rudy Wiebe, who had been entertained by *Reminiscences of a Bungle* while doing research for *The Temptations of Big Bear*. Noel Parker-Jervis, as chairman of the Western Canadian Publications Project Committee, provided the drive and enthusiasm to get the project off the ground.

I took advantage of the good natures of many of my colleagues and friends to discuss the work. John Foster, Doug Owram, Olive Dickason, and David Hall were always particularly helpful. Bob Beal accompanied me on a memorable tour of the battle sites in May 1982.

My secretary, Sharon MacKenzie, did her usual superb job of typing the manuscript.

Elaine, Laura, and Daphne provided support and encouragement and, best of all, a reason for doing the work.

The staffs of Public Archives Canada, the Glenbow-Alberta Institute, and the Saskatchewan Archives were most helpful.

I am grateful to the Clifford E. Lee Foundation for financial support. This work is published in cooperation with the Western Canadiana Publications Project Committee of the University of Alberta, with the assistance of a grant from the University of Alberta Alma Mater Fund.

Introduction

The motives that drive men to record their experiences are almost infinitely varied and complex. Leaving aside those who describe events professionally — journalists and writers of all manner of official reports make up the great bulk of this group — the rest fall into two broad categories; those who write because they are convinced of their personal uniqueness and those who write because they are ordinary people who have participated in extraordinary events. The accounts of the 1885 rebellion in this volume clearly belong in the latter group. They are vastly different from the diary of William Lyon Mackenzie King or the countless other political and literary memoirs that fill library shelves. These are the words of modest individuals who, had they not been uprooted from their daily routines and marched off to war, would certainly not have committed any part of their lives to paper. The two for whom biographical information is available, Ord and Cassels, lived interesting and productive lives for half a century after 1885 and never wrote another work. Cassels even went out of his way to avoid appearing in print.

Ord, Cassels, and Rusden all began to record their experiences the moment they decided to participate in the rebellion. *Reminiscences of a Bungle* and *Notes on the Suppression of the Northwest Insurrection*, although written after the fact, are quite apparently based on diaries. The day-by-day structure and the amount of detail devoted to the joining up, getting organized, and travelling to the scene of the fighting make this a certainty. Clearly the sense of taking part in unique and important events, of making history, is the primary motivating factor in these accounts. Fear of death in battle and the accompanying desire to leave some memorial behind do not seem to have figured largely for any of the three. Each saw it rather as the adventure of a lifetime, not to be forgotten in later years when memory might prove false. "I am very lucky to have the chance to go," Cassels wrote, "change is pleasant and one is sure to see something worth seeing." Ord and Rusden were wary of official and journalistic versions of events and sought to set the record straight. Rusden's papers contain a copy of Middleton's dispatch summarizing the campaign that appeared in the London *Gazette* on 7 August 1885. There is a marginal note in Rusden's handwriting: "General Middleton's dispatch is in many places entirely wrong as in many cases the troops were not placed in the position stated in his dispatch."[1]

The theme of war as adventure is, of course, persistent in military literature throughout the ages. Even in a conflict as squalid and unpopular as the Viet Nam war, there were many volunteers attracted by the prospect of danger and excitement in an exotic location. Interestingly, none of the three accounts in this volume shows any evidence that patriotism was an important reason for enlisting. Ord, Cassels, and Rusden did not see themselves as defending the Canadian way of life nor did they consider the rebellion a serious threat to the integrity of the country. The Indians and Métis were in their eyes, a rather contemptible lot. The government had mismanaged the native population to the point of revolt and it was the diarist's good fortune in each case to have the opportunity to see the West at public expense while helping to administer the necessary chastisement. The justice of the cause was never in doubt but the cause was a thoroughly Victorian conception of the majestic and inevitable progress of civilization rather than Canadian nationalism or manifest destiny.

The theme of disillusionment in the later parts of the diaries is almost as pervasive as that of adventure at the beginning. Initial anticipation and enthusiasm are rapidly eroded by boredom, bad food, and the death and mutilation of friends. War, as always, turned out to be mostly endless red tape, guard duty in the cold and wet, and mile after mile of apparently aimless marching. "It was not the sort of fighting we expected at all," Rusden said, unwittingly echoing the soldier's complaint since the beginning of organized warfare. There is disillusionment, too, with the leadership. Brought up on a steady diet of Anglophilia and countless reminders of British military prowess, Canadians expected a standard of perfection in the art of war that no mortal could have achieved, much less the British commander of the Canadian militia, General Middleton. The streets in Ontario towns named after Napoleonic or Crimean war battles, popular literature of the *Boy's Own Paper* variety, and newspaper accounts of distant victories in India or the Sudan conveyed nothing of the inevitable waste, confusion, and misery of war. The reality of the campaign, mild though it was by the standards of most wars, quickly eliminated much of the supposed glory for the participants and made them examine their experience with new and critical eyes. Middleton's pomposity and ill-concealed distrust of Canadians did nothing to improve the situation. Some Canadians like Charles A. Boulton, who had professional experience in the British army, were less inclined to make harsh judgments. In his autobiographical account, *Reminiscences of the North-West Rebellions*, Boulton praises Middleton's performance. The standard British army textbook on how to deal with minor colonial insurrections, Colonel C.E. Callwell's *Small Wars: Their Principles and Practice*, published in 1899, also refers to Middleton's leadership in favorable terms.[2]

II

The Northwest Rebellion was a very minor affair compared to the mass slaughters of the twentieth century. Total casualties for both sides amounted to about 110 dead and perhaps 300 wounded. Barely thirty years later, well within the active lifetimes of the diarists in this volume, the Canadian army would lose 7,000 men in a single day in the assault on Vimy Ridge and count it a victory lightly won. But even compared with the other small colonial conflicts that abounded in the nineteenth century, this was a modest war, indeed. It lacked the uninhibited ferocity that too often characterized those clashes between widely different cultures. The reader who looks for the sort of atrocities on both sides that occurred during the Indian Mutiny, the Zulu War, or the conflicts in the American West will be disappointed. The 1885 rebellion was a modest and moderate kind of war, a very Canadian affair in all respects.

The rebellion had its origin in the plight of the Métis people living in the Saskatchewan River valley in the early 1880s. The Métis were a unique people, a cultural group distinct from both the European and native stocks from which they sprang.[3] A product of the peculiar social and economic circumstances of the Canadian fur trade, both the livelihood and group identity of the Métis were defined by their relations with the fur companies until the 1860s. The settlement at Red River was their metropolis and cultural center. There they had begun to practice, to some degree by the middle of the nineteenth century, a rudimentary agriculture on their long, narrow farms stretching back from the banks of the Red and Assiniboine rivers. The mainstay of their economy, however, and the primary focus of their yearly cycle remained the buffalo hunt. The market for the produce of the hunt was the Hudson's Bay Company, which needed tons of pemmican each year to maintain its scattered posts in the fur-rich but food-poor North.

From a global or even a continental perspective the fur trade economy of the Canadian West was rapidly becoming a marginal endeavor by the 1860s. The trade in beaver pelts, for almost two centuries the only economically viable export of the region, was about to be displaced by a new staple product with drastic consequences for the Métis. The Métis were not, like their Indian cousins, totally without means of effectively responding to the coming revolution that large-scale agricultural settlement would bring. The Roman Catholic church at Red River, in particular, had foreseen the inevitability of change and had taken what steps it could to prepare its Métis adherents. Farming had been encouraged and some of the more promising Métis youth had been educated beyond minimum levels of literacy.

Among the latter group was Louis Riel, the individual whose personality was to dominate the Canadian West from 1869 to 1885. Louis Riel, aged twenty-five in 1869, first demonstrated his abilities by leading the resistance at Red River to the transfer of the Hudson's Bay Company's territories to Canada. All negotiations for the transfer had taken place in London without any thought of consulting the inhabitants of the region. The Métis, understandably, were not prepared to take the Canadian government on trust. Their successful resistance and subsequent negotiation of terms of entry with the Canadian government was a remarkably intelligent and skilful exercise in leadership by Riel. The Métis achieved their aims almost without bloodshed and saw their demands embodied in the Manitoba Act of 1870.

Although armed conflict was averted in 1870, the larger problem of increasing economic marginality for the Métis was less easily solved. They had been given 1.4 million acres of land, initially in the immediate vicinity of Red River Settlement, under the terms of the Manitoba Act. Within a few years, partly because the Métis showed no inclination to set up farms away from the river banks on the allotted blocs of land, and partly because the government wanted the land for incoming settlers, the system was changed. Under the new plan, each eligible Métis was given scrip entitling him to choose a farm anywhere in Manitoba or the Northwest Territories. The scrip, which was negotiable, quickly passed into the hands of white traders for small sums in cash or goods. Most of the Métis drifted west and north to the area around the junction of the North and South Saskat-chewan rivers. Here it was easier to pursue the diminishing buffalo herds. Here, also, there was unoccupied river bank land on which to establish the traditional Quebec-style farms. In the new com-munities of St. Laurent and Batoche, the Métis were able to postpone their confrontation with the nine-teenth century for another decade.

The leader who had made possible this reprieve was less fortunate than his people for the next decade and a half. Excluded from the general amnesty granted to participants in the uprising, Riel was forced to flee to the United States. This marked the begin-ning of his semi-permanent exile, which ended with his death on the Regina gallows in 1885. The stress of living in constant fear of arrest or assassination, com-bined with repeated expulsions from his seat in Par-liament, finally began to affect Riel's mental balance.

His friends and relatives were forced to commit him to an asylum where he remained for two years before recovering sufficiently to be released.

From 1880 onward Riel lived in Montana, and was marginally associated with the substantial community of Métis buffalo hunters who had drifted south of the border to pursue the rapidly vanishing beasts. Although he became an American citizen in 1883 and took an active part in Montana politics, Riel remained faithful to his people north of the border. Employment as a school teacher at a Catholic mission along with his marriage and the birth of his two children seem to have merely postponed Riel's effort to put into practice his grand design for the Métis. In his years of exile, Riel had elaborated a vision of the future in which the Métis were to be the new "chosen people," selected by God to redeem the world.[4] They would form the core of an independent theocratic republic in the Northwest. There were too few mixed-bloods to form a purely Métis nation, but Riel believed his vision could be accomplished by incorporating the Indians as well as selected immigrants from the Catholic countries of Europe.

An effort by Riel in 1879–80 to organize a native confederacy as a first step in his plan had failed.[5] He also canvassed for support among the Fenian Brotherhood in the United States without success. But if opportunity was lacking, the dream remained, and an increasingly concrete and elaborate sense of mission dominated Riel's thought during his last years. In June of 1884, when a delegation from Batoche arrived to

invite him back to lead the Métis in a new confrontation with the Canadian government, Riel was not surprised. He was convinced that through him the destiny of his people would finally be fulfilled.

The ferment in the valley of the Saskatchewan that
led to Riel's invitation had been brewing since the
beginning of the decade. All three of the groups that
made up the population of the area were seriously
discontented by 1884. The Plains Cree bands, many
of whom had accepted the treaty signed in 1876 with
great reluctance, were, three years later, beginning to
feel the full impact of the disappearance of the buffalo.
The Indian Affairs department was obligated to pro-
vide food in time of need under the terms of both
Treaties Six and Seven, which encompassed most of
the southern prairies. How much food and on what
terms, however, remained at the discretion of the
government. After some years of allowing the situation
to drift, the government found itself facing dangerously
large numbers—up to 7000—of half-starved Indians
congregating around the Mounted Police post at Fort
Walsh in the Cypress Hills. Here, within striking distance of the few remaining buffalo herds south of the
49th parallel, the Indians clung grimly to the remnants
of their traditional way of life, subsisting on the mini-
mal rations doled out by the police.

The most important Cree leaders who held out,
Big Bear, Little Pine, and Piapot, were not just stubborn old men clinging blindly to the past. They had
all recognized early in the 1870s that their people
would have to change and that agriculture represented

their only prospect of survival. But unlike those chiefs who accepted the treaties as they were offered by Ottawa, these three held out for better terms. In particular, they sought more generous food rations, more farm instructors, and a contiguous bloc of reserves, preferably in the Cypress Hills. As far as Ottawa was concerned, the first two points were negotiable, the third definitely was not. Government policy was firmly based on keeping reserves well separated and north of the Canadian Pacific Railway main line.

In 1879 when the disappearance of the buffalo from their last Canadian refuge in the Cypress Hills created a food crisis, the government used it as a lever to try to enforce its policy of small, widely scattered reserves. The culmination of this policy came in 1883 when Fort Walsh was closed down and the distribution of rations there halted. At the same time, the men in charge of Indian Affairs in the West, Hayter Reed and Edgar Dewdney, managed to increase rations somewhat and arranged for a few more farm instructors. Big Bear and the other recalcitrant chiefs reluctantly abandoned the Cypress Hills and moved north. But they did not abandon their demand for contiguous reserves, a virtual "Indian Nation," perhaps near Poundmaker's reserve close to Battleford, perhaps farther west in the vicinity of Buffalo Lake.

The careful and, on the whole, sensible policy pursued by Reed and Dewdney was sabotaged in 1884 by a combination of circumstances, natural and manmade. The Deputy Superintendent General of Indian

Affairs, Lawrence Vankoughnet, visited the West that year and, impatient with the slow progress in settling the Cree, decided that a cutback in spending on rations would speed the process. In fact, it had the opposite effect. The Mounted Police reported that many Indians were living on gophers and that even chiefs like Poundmaker, who had always been co-operative with the government, could not control their people. The winter of 1883–84 saw a series of thefts of food and assaults on government farm instructors. The situation became so tense that late in 1884 the government relented and reversed its policy. By this time the damage had been done. Big Bear, Little Pine, and Piapot, although opposed to the government's policies, had no intention of risking armed conflict. Their actions were designed to put as much pressure on the government as possible, short of war. Vankoughnet's foolish policy of coercion upset the delicately calculated balance and undermined the authority of the older chiefs. By the end of 1884, Big Bear's control over his band was being seriously challenged by his son Imasees along with Little Poplar and Wandering Spirit. The exceptionally severe winter of 1884–85 worsened conditions to the point where many of the younger Cree were willing to ignore the older leaders and join an armed insurrection led by the Métis.

A few thousand settlers had established themselves in the Northwest Territories in the 1870s and early 1880s. Most of these pioneers had chosen to take up land in the North Saskatchewan valley. This was the part of the Territories best served by the existing transportation systems, river steamers, and Red River cart brigades. The valley was in the center of the area identified by the Palliser and Hind expeditions as the "fertile belt." Until 1881 it was universally expected that the transcontinental railway would follow this route to the west coast. When the Canadian Pacific Railway made its momentous decision in that year to move the main line 200 miles to the south, the settlers' hopes for an outlet for their crops were dashed. Bad weather and crop failures in 1883 and 1884 made even subsistence a desperate struggle. The settlers organized the first western agrarian association, the Manitoba and North West Farmers' Union, to seek government assistance.

To a considerable degree, the Métis suffered from the same problems that afflicted their white and Indian neighbors, as well as a number of unique dilemmas. Like the Indians, the Métis had been dependent upon the buffalo hunt, now gone forever. But unlike the Indians, the Métis were not included in the treaties and were not entitled to government rations. Like the whites, the Métis suffered crop failures, but unlike the settlers, they had no reserves of capital to see them through the hard times. The Métis were also deeply concerned about the question of title to their lands and how their narrow riverfront farms could be accommodated under the square survey system. Petitions to Ottawa brought no satisfactory response. The Prime Minister, Sir John A. Macdonald, was preoccupied with building the Canadian Pacific Railway, and was inclined to the view that Métis land claims had been fully and finally settled by the Manitoba Act of 1870.

With the memory of the successful resistance at Red River in 1869–70 still fresh in their minds, it is hardly surprising that both whites and Métis turned to Riel as a means of jolting Ottawa out of its complacency. It seems unlikely that any of those who invited Riel to lead their cause in the summer of 1884 believed that full-scale armed rebellion would be the result. This was clearly one of those situations — history abounds with them — in which moderates attempted to use a charismatic leader for their own limited purposes only to lose control of the situation almost at once. This is not to suggest that Riel was determined to provoke an armed uprising from the outset. It is quite evident from Thomas Flanagan's fine biography of the Métis leader that Riel's grandiose visions were in more or less constant conflict with day-to-day realities in his mind. It is not beyond the realm of possibility that the right gesture at the right time, such as appointing Riel to the North West Territories Council or giving him a sizable bribe disguised as payment for his claims, could have diverted him from his tragic course. No one on the government side had the imagination to make such an offer. Failure on the part of Ottawa to deal with Riel was crucial because he alone was in a position to avert the clash. No other leader had the complete confidence of the Métis and could offer them psychological reassurance that they had a future in western Canada.

Many historians have attempted to explain the rebellion in terms of the disastrous economic circumstances of the population of the region in the early 1880s and the inadequacy of the government's response. This explanation has very serious shortcomings because it does not take into account how the economic difficulties were perceived and interpreted by the three groups. Economic distress had different meanings for the whites, the Indians, and the Métis. Unless these differences are understood, it is impossible to account for the differences in participation. The settlers were certainly unhappy, but most of them undoubtedly saw their difficulties as a temporary setback in the process of building a new life in the West. At worst, they might have lost the time and money invested in their homesteads and have been forced to move elsewhere. The plight of the Indians was worse in that they faced the permanent loss of their traditional livelihood. By 1885 even the most optimistic Indian could no longer cherish the dream that the settlers would somehow disappear and the buffalo return. Through the treaties, however, the Indians were offered a future that, whatever its shortcomings, held out the prospect of survival with their identity as a people more or less intact. For the Indians, the treaties were of the utmost symbolic significance.[6]

The hard times of the 1880s had much more profound implications for the Métis. Like the Indians, the Métis faced the permanent loss of their traditional economy. Without treaties it was a choice between assimilation and starvation. The Métis could see no future for themselves *as a people* in the new agricultural West. Their cultural identity as a "new nation," a people distinct from both whites and Indians, had developed over the previous century and was heavily dependent on their economic role in the fur trade. The buffalo hunt defined the Métis to at least as great an extent as their language, their religion, or their ancestry. Métis social and political organization derived from the hunt. Their songs and poetry centered on that part of their experience. The end of that role meant not just the loss of livelihood, but the obliteration of almost everything that gave meaning to their lives. Fifteen years before, when they had faced a similar threat, Riel's leadership had given them the bargaining power that enabled them to wring concessions from a reluctant Ottawa. As a strategy for preserving Métis society, the Manitoba Act had turned out to be ineffectual, but this was not the lesson the Métis drew from the events of 1869–70. What they remembered was Riel's ability to influence the course of events. With the exercise of this kind of power there was always hope for the future. Hope has always been a far more potent motivator than individual considerations of loss or gain.

The Métis were not an aggressive people who went to war lightly. The celebrated military engagements in their tradition, Seven Oaks in 1817 and the battle of Grand Coteau in 1857, were, in their own eyes at least, strictly defensive. The Seven Oaks incident, in which the Métis were manipulated by the North West Company into attacking the Red River settlers, also illustrates the importance of leadership among the Métis in defining ambiguous situations. Riel certainly understood this but, unfortunately, no one on the government side did. Thomas Flanagan has argued that Ottawa responded to specific Métis demands about as effectively as any nineteenth-century government was able to do. This is probably true, but at the same time, it is not very relevant to an understanding of why the Métis were prepared to follow Riel into a war they could not hope to win. All the indications are that, given the misery of their circumstances in 1884 and their fears for an even darker future, the Métis would have been prepared to accept almost any direction Riel cared to give them. Therefore, when Riel's personal demands were rejected, armed conflict was inevitable.

III

The military resources at the disposal of the Canadian government in March 1885, when the Métis declared their provisional government, were not very impressive, even on paper. The permanent force of full-time soldiers numbered no more than 750 men, mainly artillery personnel manning the fortifications at Kingston and Quebec. Militia, varying enormously in training and experience from battalion to battalion, made up the great bulk of the country's defence force. The one quality that could be counted on in the militia was enthusiasm. Certainly they received the absolute minimum of encouragement from the government. When an outsider raised questions about discipline in the Queen's Own Rifles, Lieutenant Cassels reacted with indignation, "Our men are a fine willing lot of fellows and friends that one knows intimately are not to be ordered about like a parcel of slaves." Training was limited to twelve days a year, and the arms and equipment provided were obsolete, if provided at all. Support services of all kinds, from transportation to medical care, were lacking and had to be improvised. During the rebellion a third type of military unit, consisting of improvised bodies of volunteers, most of them with western experience, were employed as scouts.

At the time of the outbreak there were also some 500 North West Mounted Police scattered throughout the region. A number of factors prevented them from being used as an immediate counter to the insurrection. Most important was their dispersion in small contingents throughout the whole of the Northwest Territories. The greatest concentration of men was in the Lethbridge–Fort Macleod area, several hundred kilometers away from the outbreak. To pull the Mounted Police away from their duties elsewhere all at once would have been foolish and impractical. With great difficulty, Commissioner A.G. Irvine had managed to concentrate about 200 men in the affected region before Riel proclaimed his provisional government, but this proved insufficient to act as a deterrent. The opening skirmish at Duck Lake on 26 March, in which police and civilian volunteers were soundly defeated, clearly demonstrated the necessity to avoid direct confrontation and maintain a defensive posture until help could be sent from the East.

Once the magnitude of the uprising in the West became clear, the Canadian government reacted with uncharacteristic vigor. The commanding officer of the militia, Major General Frederick Middleton, had been ordered to Winnipeg several days before the events at Duck Lake. He arrived just as news of the engagement reached the city and realized immediately that an all-out military effort would be necessary. This meant arranging to bring west as many permanent force units as possible to form the nucleus of a force to defeat the rebels. The majority of the troops would be militia, drawn from those regiments considered to be most proficient. The urban Ontario battalions were the best organized and trained, so it is not surprising that Middleton preferred them. Several Quebec units and one from Halifax were also called up. As many local troops as possible were recruited in Manitoba and the Territories. They amounted to about a third of the total force.

After consulting with the Lieutenant-Governor of the Northwest Territories, Edgar Dewdney, Middleton made his basic strategic decision. Dewdney correctly believed that Riel's leadership was crucial to the rebellion. If he could be captured or put out of action the uprising would rapidly grind to a halt. The campaign must therefore aim at concentrating the maximum number of troops against the rebel headquarters at Batoche as quickly as possible. Getting the troops there in a hurry yet still in reasonable shape to fight was the biggest problem Middleton faced. With some improvisations, the railway could bring the soldiers from Ontario to the Northwest Territories. There were two possible ways to cover the remaining 300 kilometers from the main line to Batoche. The first was to leave the railway at Qu'Appelle and follow the old Carlton Trail northwest to Clarke's Crossing on the South Saskatchewan River, just north of where Saskatoon now lies. From that point a trail led north along the river to the Métis settlements. The river offered a second possibility since both the Hudson's Bay Company and the North West Coal and Navigation Company operated steamboats between Medicine Hat and Prince Albert in the summers. Troops and supplies could be unloaded from the trains at Swift Current and taken downriver to Batoche.

Both potential routes had drawbacks. The Carlton Trail was not particularly difficult, but all supplies would have to be carried by wagon. No grass for the horses would be available along the route until late May or early June. All fodder would have to be carried, which meant that to reach Batoche, fully half of each wagon load would be taken up by feed for the horses. The wagon train accompanying the troops would be large, expensive, and vulnerable to attack. Steamboat navigation, on the other hand, was marginal at best because of the shallowness of the river, and could not begin at all until the ice melted. In Middleton's original plan, the larger part of his force would go overland from Qu'Appelle. A smaller contingent under the command of Lieutenant Colonel

William Otter would leave the railway at Swift Current and proceed by steamboat to join the main force
as soon as navigation was possible.

The simplicity of Middleton's plan rested on the
assumption that the small groups of settlers scattered
throughout the region were in no immediate danger
from the rebels. News of the Frog Lake Massacre, in
which nine whites, including two priests and the Indian agent, were killed by members of Big Bear's
band, forced a fundamental change in Middleton's
strategy. The town closest to Frog Lake, Battleford,
seemed in most immediate danger and Otter's force
was diverted to go to the rescue. The Midland Battalion was the unit affected most dramatically by the
change in plans. The troops had detrained and were
marching through the streets of Winnipeg when new
orders arrived. Without even reaching the camp they
were turned around and marched back to the train.[8]
Occuring as it did far to the west of Batoche, Frog
Lake raised the prospect of the rebellion spreading
west to threaten Edmonton or even Calgary. A third
column known as the Alberta Field Force was therefore organized at Calgary under the command of a
retired British Army officer, General Thomas Bland
Strange. Strange was ranching near Calgary in 1885
and had commanded the artillery at Quebec earlier in
his career. Middleton distrusted French-Canadian
militia even more than their English-speaking com-
patriots. He took advantage of Strange's admiration
for French Canadians and sent the two largest Quebec
units, the 9th Voltigeurs and the 65th Mount Royal

Rifles, to join the Alberta Field Force. Strange was ordered north of Edmonton to show the flag and re-assure the panic-stricken inhabitants then he was to proceed eastward in pursuit of Big Bear.

On paper the picture of three columns converging on the valley of the Saskatchewan from different directions has a neat and logical appearance. But it is evident that Middleton was responding to pressures he would have preferred to ignore in the cases of Otter's column and the Alberta Field Force. Fortu-nately for Middleton, he had sufficient men that he could afford the luxury of detaching a few hundred in the interests of calming public fears. Events proved that the general's original instincts were correct. The two supplementary columns were sideshows and had no real effect on the outcome of the rebellion. Otter, in an act that came uncomfortably close to insubordi-nation, provoked a major and quite unnecessary bat-tle with Poundmaker's Cree at Cut Knife Creek. Up to this point (2 May), Poundmaker had made no aggressive moves, although some of his young men had been unable to resist the temptation to loot and burn a few abandoned houses in Battleford. In the tense months preceding the rebellion, Poundmaker had been firmly in the camp of the "government" In-dians. Otter's attack forced Poundmaker to abandon his precarious neutrality and join the rebel cause.

Otter's principal motive in attacking Poundmaker seems to have been a fear that his column would otherwise miss the fighting altogether. The trip from Swift Current to Battleford had been accomplished quickly and without incident. As soon as the troops arrived, the Cree withdrew from the vicinity of Battleford to Poundmaker's reserve fifty kilometers to the west. After a week at Battleford with no sign of movement from the Indians, Otter decided to take the initiative, ignoring a telegram from Middleton recommending that he stay in the town. On 1 May Otter led about 300 men in the direction of Poundmaker's reserve, apparently with the intention of forcing the Indians to surrender. After marching all night the force reached Cut Knife Hill, behind which the Cree were camped. Otter's force made their way to the top of the hill, a roughly circular treeless area about 1,000 meters in diameter, before the Indians reacted. As soon as the Cree began firing from the cover of the ravines around the summit, the position of the troops became extremely uncomfortable. Adding to their difficulties, their two ancient Mounted Police field guns soon broke down. By noon, with casualties mounting rapidly and facing the possibility of being surrounded, Otter decided to retreat. Had the Indians followed the retreating force they might easily have annihilated them, but Poundmaker's influence prevailed and they returned to Battleford without further fighting.

While Otter's force was thus occupied, General Strange's Alberta Field Force was struggling north to Edmonton, which they reached on 1 May. There a number of crude flatboats were hastily thrown together and the force proceeded down the North Saskatchewan in the direction of Frog Lake. When Strange finally arrived at the site of the massacre on 25 May, Big Bear and his followers had left. They had moved on to the North West Mounted Police post at Fort Pitt and burned it when the police abandoned it. When the Alberta Field Force reached Fort Pitt, the Cree were camped a few kilometers downstream on the north side of the river near a prominent landmark known as Frenchman Butte.[9] Big Bear had chosen the position well. The Cree were dug in at the top of a steep hill at the foot of which was a marshy creek bed that had to be crossed under fire before the hill could be climbed. On the morning of 28 May Strange's small force of just over 200 men and one field gun reached the creek and opened fire on the Cree at long range. Both sides were content not to press the engagement. Strange wisely decided that a frontal assault would be suicidal and he lacked sufficient men to outflank the position.

During the night, Big Bear retreated and moved off to the northeast. He was pursued by a small group under the command of Superintendent Sam Steele of the North West Mounted Police. There were two brief skirmishes before Steele was forced to abandon the chase at Loon Lake. He was running out of food and had several wounded men. The pursuit of Big Bear was temporarily abandoned until more resources were available.

While the sideshows under Strange and Otter were going on farther west, the main event was being played out along the South Saskatchewan. By 18 April Middleton had assembled about 800 men and four guns at Clarke's Crossing. He divided his force into two groups, one for each side of the river, and started off in the direction of Batoche on 23 April with a cable ferry to maintain communication between the two parts of his force. The decision to divide the troops effectively halved their strength should the enemy be encountered, but Middleton was supremely confident, and worried more about not being able to find the Métis than about being defeated by them. The Batoche settlement spanned the river and the rebels might be found on either side, although the odds favored the right bank.

For nearly a month after the initial confrontation at Duck Lake, the Métis had remained at Batoche. From their scouts, Riel and Dumont knew exactly where the government forces were from the moment they stepped off the train, but they made no move to try to stop the invaders until they were a few kilometers from Batoche. Nor did they interfere with Middleton's long and tenuous lines of communication; they could have cut the telegraph wires. The standard explanation for this baffling lack of activity has been that while Dumont wanted to carry out a campaign of harassment, he was restrained by Riel.[10] This explanation, which has been accepted quite uncritically by historians, relies solely on Dumont's own version of events, taken down four years after the fact.[11] One of the reasons it has been taken for granted is that to attack the lines of communication seems so obvious to anyone familiar with European concepts of warfare. There is absolutely no reason to assume that it would have been equally obvious to the Métis. In the years after the rebellion, however, Dumont had many opportunities to reflect on his actions and discuss them with others. For part of the time he was a featured performer with Buffalo Bill's Wild West Show. To appease the reporters who interviewed him in cities visited by the show, Dumont had to come up with an account of the rebellion that explained the military failure of the Métis yet preserved Dumont's personal image as a fighter. No doubt there was some truth to the assertion that Dumont was restrained by Riel, but as a complete explanation for Métis inactivity, it will not do.

The actions of the Métis do, however, fit into a logical and consistent pattern if considered in the light of their own military experience. Half a century or so before the rebellion, the Métis had been tactical innovators on the prairies. In their conflicts with the Sioux, which arose from the annual buffalo hunts, the Métis had overcome inferiority of numbers by making more effective use of guns.[12] Whereas the Sioux, like other plains Indians, used guns from horseback as they had used bows and arrows, the Métis developed the technique of encircling their camps with rifle-pits. Shooting from rest improved accuracy enormously, and by using tactics that took advantage of the greater range and hitting power of the gun, the Métis were able to inflict severe losses on their enemies. Great military successes, however, almost invariably bring conservatism in their wake. From 1857 onward, the Métis were unchallenged masters of the prairies. Without challenge there was no necessity to change.

In times of crisis a people's first instinct is to fall back on what has worked before. The Métis in 1885, Dumont included, were not about to experiment in the face of the threat posed by Middleton's force. Ignoring opportunities to go on the offensive in favor of digging entrenchments and rifle-pits around the settlement at Batoche makes perfect sense in the light of Métis military experience to that time. At the last moment, however, just as Middleton's troops were leaving Clarke's Crossing, Dumont moved south with about 200 men. His aim was not to attack the enemy's lines of communication. Instead Dumont established his men along a steep ravine created by Fish Creek running roughly at right angles to the Saskatchewan. The ravine was, in effect, an extension of the prepared positions at Batoche, a ready-made rifle-pit in which the Métis and Indians could wait unobserved. When the enemy was within range, they could fire from cover at the troops exposed on the open prairie.

After camping for the night a few miles south of Fish Creek, Middleton's force resumed their march on the morning of 24 April. As the scouts riding in advance of the main column approached, the rebels opened fire. A stalemate was quickly reached with the government forces pinned down and the rebels unable to drive them back. There was frantic activity to transfer the troops from the left bank of the river. The two field guns kept up a steady fire that frightened some of the Indians and Métis but injured few of them. The gunners, in turn, suffered heavy casualties in their exposed positions. After several hours both commanders decided to withdraw. Middleton was convinced that his raw soldiers were on the verge of panic. Dumont, on the other hand, had reason to be pleased with the outcome of the fighting. He had fought a classic Métis battle from concealment against substantial odds and had inflicted much heavier casualties than he had suffered. If the adversary had been the Sioux or some other traditional enemy, the fight would have been decisive and Batoche would have been safe for a season or more. But these were a new kind of opponents who, for all their clumsiness and inexperience, were formidable because they were prepared to accept substantial losses in the expectation of ultimate victory.

The fighting at Fish Creek had a remarkable effect on Middleton. Up to this point he had been consistently energetic, efficient, and confident. Getting the troops into position to fight so close to the Métis heartland and so far from the railway within a month of the outbreak of hostilities was an impressive achievement by any standard. During the battle, Middleton's personal disregard of danger impressed even his severest critics. But from this point on, Middleton's conduct of the campaign was marked by excessive caution and indecision. For two weeks after Fish Creek he kept his force in camp, waiting for the wounded to be evacuated. The list of excuses seemed endless. Middleton's frequently expressed contempt for the Métis as fighters had turned into an exaggerated fear of their potential.

Finally, after receiving some 400 reinforcements from the Midland Battalion, Middleton decided to move. The steamer *Northcote* had also arrived, bringing a Gatling gun under the supervision of an American employee of the manufacturers, Captain A.L. Howard. On 7 May the force broke camp and moved north toward Batoche. They camped that night a few miles south of the settlement without incident. The next day a cautious reconnaissance was carried out that revealed little of the rebels' dispositions. The Métis had fortified all approaches to Batoche with well-hidden entrenchments and rifle-pits.

The Batoche settlement occupied a roughly rectangular piece of land approximately two kilometers long by one kilometer deep created by a bend in the South Saskatchewan, where the land slopes gradually to within a short distance of the river, and then drops off abruptly. At the south end of this natural basin near a small ravine was a large church, a rectory, and a cemetery. About a kilometer further north lay the center of the settlement, consisting of the ferry crossing and a few houses and stores. Middleton's initial plan was to attack along the trail that followed the top of the river bank, starting at 9 A.M. on the morning of 9 May. The *Northcote*, hastily converted into a makeshift gunboat, would proceed downriver at the same time and attack from that direction. The plan could hardly have been simpler, but things began to go wrong almost at once. The *Northcote* left an hour too early and the rebels, undistracted by other attackers, gave the prairies' first warship a very hot time. Dumont had anticipated the move and had raised the ferry cable to stop the boat, but succeeded only in knocking off its mast and funnels. Riddled with bullets, the *Northcote* escaped downriver. It was ordered back into the fight, but its American civilian crew refused to risk their necks again.

Meanwhile, as Middleton's troops approached the church they came under heavy fire from the rebels in their well-prepared positions. Once again, as at Fish Creek and Cut Knife Creek, the soldiers found themselves pinned down by an invisible enemy, unable to take advantage of their superior numbers and gunpower. Although there is little indication that the troops were overly concerned about the check, the first day at Batoche was the low point of the campaign for Middleton. His state of mind can be gauged by his decision to send his chief of staff, Lord Melgund, back to Ottawa that day. Middleton believed that his little army might easily be wiped out and that Melgund should be available to lead a relief expedition of British troops. As the diaries in this volume reveal, Middleton's low opinion of his Canadian militia was not lost on officers and men.

By the evening of 9 May, Middleton was apparently planning to retreat all the way back to Fish Creek. Various individuals have taken credit for persuading him to change his mind. Regardless of who was responsible, Middleton did reconsider and chose instead to fortify the wagon park just south of the church. In this "zareba" the troops spent the night. In the morning they marched out and took up the previous day's positions. Much ammunition was expended on both sides with very little result, the total casualties on the government side being one killed and five wounded. While the foot soldiers were engaged along the river bank, French's Scouts explored northward and discovered that Batoche could also be approached from the east across an open, gradually sloping plain. Near the settlement, however, more of the ubiquitous rifle-pits concealed in a line of trees defended the position.

Monday, 11 May, saw a repetition of the previous day's fighting around the church with no apparent change in the stalemate. Casualties were again light and rather than becoming panicky as Middleton seems to have expected, the troops were increasingly restless and eager for a more aggressive approach to the battle. Middleton spent part of the day with his staff exploring the eastern approach to the village discovered by French's Scouts. As a result of what he saw, Middleton changed the plan for the following day. On 12 May he would lead a small diversionary attack from the east to draw off the rebel forces from their positions near the church. As soon as the Métis were committed to the eastern defences, a field gun would open fire, signalling the majority of the troops to attack the weakened positions along the river. This was a reasonable plan but it failed in the execution. The infantry at the church did not hear the field guns and remained in place until Middleton returned, furious at the lack of movement. The officers in charge of the infantry, Colonels Van Straubenzie, Williams, and Grasett, were severely reprimanded before the general stamped off to his lunch.

Having held their restless men in check for three days only to be criticized for not advancing, the three colonels can hardly be blamed for what happened next. Colonel Williams ordered his men of the Midland Battalion forward along the edge of the river to straighten out the line of attackers. This movement precipitated a general advance all along the line which, if not actually ordered, was certainly not discouraged by the colonels once it began. The Métis positions near the church that had held firm for three days were quickly overrun and the troops streamed toward the village without serious opposition. Ironically Middleton's plan had the desired effect in spite of the half-day's delay and the fact that the general was at lunch at the critical moment. Many of the defenders were in the rifle-pits facing east, including Dumont himself. By the time they realized what was happening it was too late to organize an effective resistance. The Métis and Indians who were not killed or captured on the spot scattered, never to regroup. The battle was lost and so, for all practical purposes, was the war. Dumont fled to the United States and on 15 May Riel surrendered.

Middleton and his column, after shipping Riel off to Regina to await trial, moved on to Prince Albert then by steamer to Battleford. Back in control of the situation once again, Middleton indulged himself in the pleasures of basking in the congratulations of the citizenry, accepting Poundmaker's surrender and, by no means least, pointing out to his subordinates their alleged shortcomings. Superintendent Irvine was reprimanded for staying at Prince Albert, Colonel Otter for disobeying instructions, and General Strange for failing to press the attack at Frenchman Butte. Finally on 3 June the pursuit of Big Bear was resumed. Four columns were sent north from Battleford in the general direction of Big Bear's last known position. Strange was sent to Beaver River, Otter to Turtle Lake, and Irvine to Green Lake. Middleton, with 400 men and a Gatling gun, headed for Loon Lake, the scene of Steele's last brush with the Cree. After taking nearly a week to reach Loon Lake, Middleton abruptly abandoned the pursuit without ever catching sight of Big Bear's people. The other columns fared no better.

About thirty kilometers south of Loon Lake, the country changes abruptly from rolling parkland to gloomy, featureless boreal forest. It must have seemed to Middleton that Big Bear could evade him indefinitely in this wilderness. In fact, Big Bear's following was disintegrating rapidly. He had released his white prisoners and when he got word of Riel's defeat at Batoche, surrendered voluntarily at Fort Carlton on 2 July. Big Bear's surrender brought the uprising to a definite end. Arrangements were quickly made to send the troops back and almost all of them were home by the end of July.

IV

The first of the diaries in this volume, *Reminiscences of a Bungle*, was published anonymously in Toronto in 1886. It has been long since out of print and its scarcity is one of the reasons for reprinting it. Perhaps a better reason is that it is the liveliest and least inhibited account of the rebellion by a participant. It is also the most biased, although not a great deal more than Middleton's official account.

The author of *Bungle*, Lewis Redman Ord, was born in Toronto in 1856. The family was reasonably prosperous and had close connections with the prominent Jarvis family. Ord was well educated and acquired a taste for English literature, particularly Shakespeare. His sixty-year career was launched in 1872 when at the age of sixteen he travelled to Edmonton as part of a survey party led by Colonel William B. Jarvis. Ord spent most of his time between 1872 and 1885 in the West, carrying out surveys all over the Territories from the international boundary to the North Saskatchewan. Although he was not yet thirty at the time he participated in the rebellion, Ord was certainly an expert on the subject of living and travelling in the Northwest. His scorn is most biting when describing Middleton's bumbling efforts at bush travel in pursuit of Big Bear.

In whatever wild and remote survey camp Ord found himself, he invariably carried with him the complete works of Shakespeare. He kept a diary for at least part of his life, some portions of which survive. At some point he wrote a rough draft of a family history, but *Reminiscences of a Bungle* was the only thing he ever published. This is a great pity; some of the comments in his letters and diaries about such things as land speculation are as acid as his opinions on Middleton.

The rebellion interrupted Ord's career only temporarily. From 1886 (presumably he spent the last half of 1885 putting together *Reminiscences of a Bungle*) to 1888 he carried out surveys for the Canadian Pacific Railway. Then he spend a decade in South America, mainly Argentina. From 1890 to 1912 he was back in western Canada engaged in the topographical survey. In 1921 he returned to Ontario where he lived and worked until his death in 1942.[13]

Richard Scougall Cassels, author of the second diary in this volume, was almost perfectly representative of the English-Canadian élite of his day. Born at Holland House near Quebec City in 1859, Cassels's early years in that province are almost the only features of his life that set him apart from his contemporaries. The family moved to Toronto some time during Cassels's early youth. He attended St. Andrew's school and the University of Toronto, graduating in 1879. The Cassels family was Presbyterian with vaguely Liberal sympathies rather than Anglican and Tory, but this had not been a social obstacle for at least two generations. Cassels's physical appearance certainly cannot have hindered his professional and social life. A photograph taken a few years after 1885 shows a slim, fair-haired, handsome young man. Another taken shortly before his death in 1935 reveals an aristocratic-looking elderly gentleman who has not lost a hair or gained a pound since his adventures at Cut Knife Creek fifty years before.

After leaving university, Cassels studied law at Osgoode Hall and articled with the city's leading

Liberal law firm, Blake, Kerr, and Lash. Cassels was called to the bar in 1882 and had just begun his practice when the rebellion erupted. For a young man of Cassels's station in life, a commission in a prestigious militia regiment was almost a social requirement. In Toronto in the early 1880s there could only be one choice, the Queen's Own Rifles, a battalion with the closest possible ties to the city's élite. The list of officers in 1885 reads like a branch of the University of Toronto alumni association or an Upper Canada College old boys' group. In 1891 Cassels left the Queen's Own Rifles, but only to help found the 48th Highlanders, another élite unit with Scottish and Presbyterian connections that presumably attracted him.

After the rebellion, Cassels returned to Toronto and a career of unblemished success and respectability. He became one of the leading corporation lawyers in the country and eventually founded his own law firm, which became Cassels, Brock, and Kelley. For much of his career he was counsel for the Presbyterian Church in Canada and was deeply involved in church affairs. His legal eminence was recognized with an appointment as King's Counsel in 1910.[14]

Cassels was an intensely private man, refusing even to have his name listed in *Who's Who*. This almost reclusive avoidance of publicity seems slightly at odds with the personality that emerges from the diary. Cassels was quite obviously an extrovert who enjoyed people and social contact. Indeed, his lengthy list of acquaintances in Winnipeg and elsewhere in the West provides a unique glimpse of the process by which the Ontario social and business élite extended itself across the country. Winnipeg may have been the metropolis of the Métis buffalo hunters fifteen years earlier, but in 1885 the young officers of the Queen's Own found it as familiar as Toronto, with many of its leading positions occupied by their school friends and business acquaintances.

Cassels's case is an excellent example of Middleton's talent for irritating his Canadian soldiers. The young lieutenant was the complete establishmentarian and the least likely person to be critical of authority. His diary at first contains no suggestion of discontent but by June, doubts had begun to set in. Cassels ends up almost as critical of the general as Ord, although his language is more moderate. This is partly a reaction to Middleton's abrasive personality, but it also reflects a different attitude to the war on the part of the Canadians. In current jargon they would be described as goal-oriented, willing to do whatever seemed necessary to accomplish the task at hand as rapidly and efficiently as possible.

The third diarist, Harold Penryn Rusden, has, regrettably, left behind no trace of his life either before or after the rebellion. One is left with the internal evidence of the diary itself, which is meager. The only certainty is that Rusden was living in Manitoba or the Northwest Territories, probably the latter, at the time the rebellion began. Rusden's unit, French's Scouts, were all recruited locally by Captain John French, an ex-Mounted Policeman who was ranching in the Qu'Appelle Valley when the rebellion began.

Introduction

The summary Rusden gives at the beginning of the diary of Riel's career and the causes of the uprising are exactly those one would expect from a habitual reader of an Ontario Liberal newspaper such as the Toronto *Globe*. Riel is the primary villain, closely followed by the incompetent and criminally indolent Conservative government and the Hudson's Bay Company. This suggests that Rusden had lived in Ontario before going west, but it is by no means a certainty. The numerous spelling and grammatical errors, along with the almost complete absence of punctuation, in Rusden's original manuscript (all of which have been corrected here for ease of reading) indicate that he had little formal education. His diary is interesting because it is one of the few participant accounts not written by an officer. For just that reason, however, it has proved impossible to find biographical details about the author.

March 1983   R.C. Macleod
University of Alberta

Notes

1. Public Archives of Canada, MG 29, E–64, Papers of Harold Penryn Rusden.

2. Charles A. Boulton, *Reminiscences of the North West Rebellion* (Toronto: Grip Printing, 1886). C.E. Callwell, *Small Wars: Their Principles and Practice* (London, H.M.S.O., 1899), p. 231.

3. See John E. Foster, "The Origins of the Mixed Bloods in the Canadian West," in L.H. Thomas, ed., *Essays on Western History* (Edmonton: University of Alberta Press, 1976) or George Woodcock, *Gabriel Dumont: The Metis Chief and his Lost World* (Edmonton: Hurtig, 1975).

4. Thomas Flanagan, *Louis 'David' Riel: 'Prophet of the New World'* (Toronto: University of Toronto Press, 1979).

5. Flanagan, *Riel*, pp. 105–8.

6. This analysis of the situation among the Cree is based largely on an unpublished paper by Professor John L. Tobias of Red Deer College entitled, "The Plains Cree Struggle for Autonomy, 1870–1885."

7. Cassels Diary, 16 April 1885.

8. Public Archives of Canada, MG 29, E–103, Lieutenant Charles A. Clapp. "Reminiscences of '85," p. 9.

9. Frenchman (not Frenchman's) Butte is the highest hill in the vicinity and was named for a trading post that had existed there at one time. The battle was actually fought on a slightly less prominent unnamed hill a few kilometers to the north.

10. Desmond Morton, *The Last War Drum: The North West Campaign of 1885* (Toronto: Hakkert, 1972), pp. 61–62.

11. B.A.T. de Montigny, *Biographie et récit de Gabriel Dumont sur les evenements de 1885* (Montreal, 1889) a translation by G.F.G. Stanley appeared in the *Canadian Historical Review* in 1949 under the title, "Gabriel Dumont's Account of the North-West Rebellion, 1885."

12. W.L. Morton, "The Battle at the Grand Coteau, July 13 and 14, 1851," *Papers Read Before the Historical and Scientific Society of Manitoba*, ser. 3, no. 16 (1961). Reprinted in D.W. Swainson, ed., *Historical Essays on the Prairie Provinces* (Toronto: McClelland and Stewart, 1970).

13. The biographical information on Ord is found in his obituary in the Association of Ontario Land Surveyors, *Annual Report*, 1943, p. iii. I have used additional information from notes of interviews with Ord's descendants carried out by Robert F. Beal.

14. C. Stewart Parker, *The Book of St. Andrew's* (Toronto: Centenary Committee of the Congregation of St. Andrew's Church, 1930), pp. 60–61; Ernest J. Chambers, *The Queen's Own Rifles of Canada* (Toronto, 1901), p. 154; K. Beattie, *The 48th Highlanders of Canada* (Toronto, 1932), p. 4; Obituary, Toronto *Star*, 18 July 1935.

Reminiscences
of a Bungle

■

by
One of the Bunglers

Lewis Redman Ord

To
The Everlasting Confusion
of
Red Tape,
These Pages are Hopefully
Inscribed

PREFACE

In writing the pages that follow, I occupy much the same position as that of the character in the "Impressions of Theophrastus Such," who attacks the scientific dissertations of a certain author and is promptly squelched by him; or else I imitate the example of Don Quixote in making a charge upon a windmill. The Northwest Rebellion and all connected therewith have been so puffed by pen and pencil, and the generalship and management so eulogized, that I feel no little diffidence in having a shot at so sacred an event, or attempting to ridicule the actors therein. But I have waited for a truthful and unvarnished account of the campaign, and as no abler hand seems willing to write it, I will give my idea of what I have called our "Bungle," only regretting my inability to do it justice.

THE AUTHOR

Chapter I

Before commencing the reminiscences that follow, it would perhaps be as well to give a short sketch of the forming of the corps of which I was a member, and I will therefore devote a few words to that purpose.

Several members of the Association of Dominion Land Surveyors were in Ottawa, seeking information regarding the probable surveys for the coming season of 1885 and employment thereon, when news of the outbreak and fight at Duck Lake, near Prince Albert, Northwest Territories, reached the capital and put an end to the hope of surveys for that year at least. At once the thought struck these gentlemen that men who knew the country in which the disturbance occurred would be of service to the government, and several of them waited upon the Minister of the Interior with a proposal to place a corps at the service of the general commanding. The minister gave us a letter to his colleague of Militia and Defence and, thus strengthened, we sent a committee to that gentleman with a memorandum of the following scheme. Each of ten surveyors was to be accompanied by four men who had been in his service in surveys in the Territories, were conversant with plains life, and accustomed to any amount of roughing it; the corps of fifty, armed and mounted on native horses, were to be used as one troop or divided among the different brigades, were to furnish information as to trails, etc., and generally to act as intelligence men, scouts, or mounted rifles as might be required. The Honorable Mr. Caron, now Sir Adolphe, also approving the scheme, directed us to elect a captain to take charge of financial matters, so a meeting was called and the post offered to Mr. Wheeler, and then to another member, but refused by both. It was then offered to Mr. J.S. Dennis,[1] who, being descended of martial ancestors, confident in his skill as a commander, without hesitation accepted the office. I write this to correct some reports that Mr. Dennis organized the Surveyors' Intelligence Corps, and to state that the evening of the meeting of which I have just spoken was his first appearance on the scene; whether the offer or its acceptance were wise I will leave the sequel to determine.

After a certain amount of red tape had been wound off the departmental reel, we got away from Ottawa, and travelling as civilians, proceeded by rail through the States to Winnipeg; again a few days' delay, and on April 14th, we reached Qu'Appelle, then the base of supplies, and going into camp, awaited the arrival of our horses and arms. More red tape, but at last the horses appear, and while waiting for arms and orders, our captain proceeds to put us through our drill.

The kyuses [*sic*], the local term for native horses, were a fair lot, considering how they had been scratched together, and as soon as each man was provided with a charger our first mounted parade was held. Many of us, I grieve to say, were not as familiar with the back of a broncho as could be wished, and when the order to saddle was given, some got into shape in tolerably quick time, whilst others seemed to have an infinite number of buckles and straps to arrange. However, we get the saddles on at last and are drawn up in line. More, we are drawn up in two lines, front and rear ranks, forsooth, somewhat of an innovation for mounted men, number off and dress from the left, but probably our captain, who, like Shakespeare's Parolles,[2] "was a gallant militarist, and had the whole theory of war in the knot of his scarf and the practice in the chape of his dagger," had some deeply hidden scheme in this that our uneducated eyes could not discover; indeed, throughout the whole campaign there was an amount of military science and skill displayed that was quite appalling to people accustomed only to common sense.

But I have left the survey corps standing waiting all this time, though doubtless there are still a few straps and stirrups to adjust; a little explanation as to the correct way to "climb onto the hurricane deck of your kyuse," as the boys put it, from Parolles, and the commands, "Pre-pare-to-mount! Mount!" are given, and the variety of attitudes assumed by our bold scouts when the last order is obeyed would give a caricaturist subjects for innumerable cartoons. Some of the troopers get up so rapidly that they fall over on the other side; some crawl up like a boy up a greased pole at a fair; here a horse stands as if he had taken root, another pivots round and round on his own axis, and many of them signify their distaste for their riders by bursting from the line like lightning from a cloud, indulging in the not ungraceful but all too energetic gambols peculiar to the broncho, known as "bucking," and alas for the riders of these latter: from embryo soldiers decked in all the pomp and paraphernalia of war they are transformed into roughriders, whose sole and only aim is to stick on. Carbines rattle, spurs jingle, yells of laughter, frantic curses. "Stick in your spurs" – "Hold his head up" – "Let him go, man" – "Stay with him, Billy" – "Freeze on to him" – "O-o-o-oh." Well for us there are no onlookers, for our trimness and discipline are fled and gone and we are about as disorderly a lot as one would care to see; but we pull ourselves together, try it again, and, after many efforts, manage to get into our saddles about the same time, and having mounted, to stay so, after which we are put through some cavalry manoeuvres that would astonish even Colonel Denniston[3] [*sic*] for their novelty. I do not include all of the corps in the above remarks, for some of them were really good riders and would have been a credit to any troop, one of them breaking in an old Mounted Police bucker and making an excellent troop horse of him; but a great many of our comrades would have felt much safer on the ground, where, indeed, several were violently deposited during the first tournaments with their chargers.

This sort of thing went on for some days and, added to the labor of evolving novel systems of drill, our transport caused poor Parolles a great deal of mental anxiety; having been once in the Rockies, and having there seen a man who knew another who had heard of someone else accustomed to that mode of travel, our captain determined upon carrying the tents and etcetera upon packhorses, and many and learned were the dissertations upon packsaddles, the diamond hitch, and all the rest of it; but long before he had decided upon the particular saddle to use, a telegram from the major-general commanding, who had been notified of our presence at Qu'Appelle, arrived, ordering us to proceed to Swift Current and report to General Laurie, who was in command at that point. Accordingly we embarked our outfit (anything from a wheelbarrow to a circus caravan is an outfit here) on the train, and had a pleasant little hour or two getting the ponies into the cars. Tom, the cook, was our first wounded man, being worsted in an encounter with an ill-tempered mare who struck several square inches of skin off his cheek with a well-directed blow of her fore hoof. Tom dodged a bit or she would have broken his skull.

Reaching Swift Current early on the morning of the 20th of April, we pitched our five tents a short distance from those of the Midland Battalion and practised our extraordinary cavalry exercises until further orders. One night some of the "new chums" discovered sundry suspicious characters on the hills down southward and an order was sent over for us to investigate. Not a man of the corps believed there was a suspicious character within some hundreds of miles, but in a few minutes three men armed with rifles and pistol were off at a swift canter, prepared to attack anything bigger than a gopher; that is, unless it was a redskin, and in such a case, why, our spurs were sharp, our horses swift, and discretion being, etc., etc., we were ready to retire at great speed—for reinforcements. However, we were much relieved, after a ride of a few miles, to find that the dusky warriors were only creations of the vivid imaginations of some of our brethren in uniform. I suppose I had better apologize here and say patrons in uniform, for we found ourselves looked upon as very small potatoes by the gold-laced and bedizened gentry of the militiah.

CHAPTER II

A few days at Swift Current to allow the regulation quantity of red tape to be unwound and General Laurie, who, I believe, is really a soldier, divided the troop into two portions, sending one half to the Elbow of the South Saskatchewan to await the arrival of the steamer, then on its way down the river conveying stores and ammunition, and protected by the Midland Battalion and a Gatling, and scout the country before it to Clarke's Crossing; whilst the other half was to convey wagons of supplies in the trail of Colonel Otter's column on its way to Battleford and, if possible, to overtake him. But before the latter division had left Swift Current twelve hours, an order from the major-general commanding, to whom General Laurie had reported his disposal of our little troop, reached us, ordering the formation of a line of pickets to patrol the country from Cypress Hills to Long Lake. The only wonder is that we were not ordered to patrol from Fort Macleod to Fort Qu'Appelle; that would have been one man to each ten miles of linear distance and, of course, the enemy we were to round up were expected to be in such a disorganized condition after the general had trounced them that one man could easily run in a legion.

So we turned off the Battleford trail and struck for the Elbow, with numerous curses at our ill luck in missing all the fun, for we wanted to overtake Colonel Otter and his flying column; and at noon on Friday,

April 24th, our first picket was placed at the lower crossing of Swift Current Creek, and two of us were sent forward with orders for the half-troop at the Elbow, nearly eighty miles northeast.

Our blankets are under the saddles, a feed of oats and a small tin "billy" tied on behind, a small package of tea, some hard tack, and corned beef in the canteeners, and we ride out of the valley at a trot. We grin at each other as we look at the sky, for we know that Parolles has not taken any wood on the carts and we remember what he has forgotten—that there is none on the trail nearer than the northern slope of the Vermilion Hills, forty miles away. The clouds gather and thicken, and half an hour out down comes the rain, changing into snow as the cold north wind sweeps over the plain and drives it into our faces. But we have no intention of camping, cold and fireless, in the open and, keeping the sturdy ponies' heads in the teeth of the blast, we push on at a pace that only varies from a trot to a canter over the gradually whitening prairie until the southern slopes of the Vermilions rise before us. The storm clears and in the fading light we see to the northwestward the tree tops in the ravines of the South Saskatchewan. The horses, feeling that there is rest before them, need the spur no longer—and before the darkness closes in we find the place we seek; dry wood, water, and grass in a sheltered coulee, where the ponies are picketed and fed. A glorious fire sends its sparks up into the clear cold air and we dry our soaking clothes before it, refreshing the inner man with draughts of that pleasant compound yclept, Johnston's Fluid Beef. And then to sleep, as only plainsmen can sleep after a day's ride. Fears of the enemy troubled not our dreams that night and sentry go was left to the horses, if they liked to keep awake, for we only moved to throw another log on the fire until early dawn sees us in the saddle and after a thirty-five-mile ride, we are ensconced in the camp at the Elbow.

Our comrades of the other half of the troop are here waiting for the steamer, and our dispatches elicit more groans of disgust at military discipline (?) and red tape, for this care about the protection of the rear is something new to us; but, live and learn. We had thought we knew something of the country and the people therein, but it now begins to dawn upon us that the resources of the rebels had been vastly under-rated and that they are really (?) about as formidable as all the Arabs in the Sudan put together: but perhaps our picket line was so disposed as to stand off Fenians from south of latitude 49°, who might be about to attack the general from that direction.

The morning after our arrival as we sit at breakfast, the sentry reports an antelope and, looking out, we see one a few hundred yards from camp. Now as everyone knows, antelope venison is remarkably good eating so Mac, as the best shot, is deputed to stalk and shoot it and after a cautious advance we see his hat rise about a knoll, a long aim taken, elbow on knee, a puff of smoke flashes out, and the game, with a little start, trots a few paces, slightly astonished but unhurt.

"Missed! — and at a hundred and fifty yards, too," — and half a dozen men, rifle in hand, join in the fun, for after one shot is fired sportsman's law says that an animal unhit is anyone's game. I ran up to the top of a hill and opened fire with my Winchester, while Mac attacked on the right and several others support us on the left. "Clink-clank" goes the lever and a cartridge flies into the chamber. "Bang!" and a yell of derision rises from the onlookers as "Cabri," startled by the whistling bullets, skips forward and stops again. "Crack! Crack! Crack!" go the rifles, now stirring the dust at his feet, now cutting the empty air above him, until the attacking column, with emptied magazines, retire in good order while the cause of the disturbance from a hill about half a mile distant looks back at the camp, tossing his graceful head in contempt of our marksmanship. Each man saunters into the tent as if his mouth were not fairly watering for antelope steak and continues his destruction of corned beef with the air of preferring it to any other delicacy.

"I was too far away!" "If I'd only had my own old gun!" "Oh, these rifles aren't sighted right!" in tones of disgust, show that as usual the weapons, and not the men, are to blame, until last in comes Mac with a frown on his noble brow, and, with an air of sublime resignation, lays down his rifle saying: "Next time an antelope comes near camp someone else can go out and shoot it, a fellow hasn't much chance when you chase the game away."

"We did it for your protection, Mac," says someone dryly. "Thought the infuriated animal might turn

on you." And there is a general laugh, for Mac's miss
was the worst of the lot, and with a good deal of reso-
lution to practise up for the "breeds," the remainder of
the meal is eaten in dignified silence.

On Monday the half-troop from Swift Current arrived, bringing with them news of an encounter between General Middleton and his forces and some
rebels under Gabriel Dumont at Fish Creek, a small
stream north of Clarke's Crossing. The troops were
said to have lost eight men killed, and forty wounded,
and the enemy, whose numbers run from 250 up-
wards, seven killed, wounded not known. We don't
know how much to believe, but I hear not a few
remarks, decidedly the reverse of complimentary,
from the boys upon his generalship's having been
"stood off" by a few breeds, and also a good deal of
bad language at the idea of our picket line, for now
the chances of our seeing fugitives are fainter than
ever. But, "obedience, etc.," and the next day the line
was completed, placed as follows:

Picket No. 1—Swift Current Creek, fifteen miles
from Swift Current, the base of supplies. Picket No.
2—Vermilion Hills, thirty-eight miles from No. 1.
Picket No. 3—Elbow of South Saskatchewan, thirty-
five miles from No. 2, this being headquarters camp
and on the Moosejaw and Clarke's Crossing via Saskatchewan trail. Picket No. 4—Plain sixteen miles east of
No. 3. Picket No. 5—Little Arm Creek, fifteen miles
east of No. 4, and the same distance west of Long Lake.

Riding from picket to picket daily, training horses,
now and then getting a shot at a cabri, sleeping, biting

our nails, and exhausting our vocabulary of English at red tape in general. A break in the monotony came on the 28th in the shape of a settler from Saskatoon wanting arms or men to guard the settlement, both of which our Parolles promptly refused him. He gave us more accounts of Fish Creek, painted in all the colors rumor could suggest, and departed with a dispatch for the general, being replaced later in the day by Captain Howard, the American officer instructing our artillerists in the use of the Gatling. This gentleman had left the steamer, slowly working its way down the river, much against the advice of the red tapists on board—in whose eyes every bush on the river bank was an armed and bloodthirsty savage—to pay us a visit, and stayed with us a day or two. He quite fraternized with us at first, not a little to our astonishment, for we were rather accustomed to be sat upon by the militia, our slouch hats and varied attire not showing off very well beside their new and gaudy uniforms, but we soon found that Gatling, as he was called, was anything but a military snob, and having seen some years of service in the Western States, possessed no small *savoir faire* and was a comrade after our own heart. He was in a state of fever at the delay, so anxious was he to get to the Front. Not that he was very bloodthirsty or that the rebels had ever done him any harm, but it was well known that White Cap's band of Sioux from the Moose Woods were with Riel and these gentry, now so warmly repaying us for our reception of them, being Indians from Minnesota and proud possessors of

16

scalps of American women and children, Gatling
desired no better fun than to "get a few turns of the
crank" at them and call it square.[4]

The gun could have reached Clarke's Crossing by
land in two days but the officer in command of the
steamer, having orders to take it down in that vessel,
appeared determined to carry out his instructions if it
took him all summer; and there seemed to be a chance
of a considerable part of the season slipping over, she
got along so slowly. The captains of the boat, old
river navigators both, then wished him to land a part
of the stores, leaving a guard over them, so as to
lighten the steamer, and guaranteed to take her down
to Clarke's Crossing in a very short time. But this
hardy (?) soldier aforesaid was either an extraordinary
slave of red tape, or afflicted with all of his senior's
caution (to put it mildly), and refused to be guided
by this sensible advice. How dare they advise him?

At last, from sandbar to sandbar, the vessel worked
her way down below the Elbow and as the river rose
made better progress, finally disappearing northward,
and our next visitors were a herd of cattle being
driven by the contractors to the Front to supply the
army with beef. One of the beeves was slain for our
use and two of the troop escorted the herders a few
miles north, returning to camp next day (Saturday),
May 2nd, which was marked by the advent of Dr.
Tom Roddick of Montreal and a number of assistants, hurrying to the Front to attend to the wounded.
He arrived late in the evening, and while sitting in
our tent waiting for the best our mess affords, the

doctor in him rises to the surface and, noticing the pale and languishing faces of the boys with his keen professional eye, he remarks that he must prescribe for us, and unslinging his water bottle, he passes it round the tent. The huge phial goes from hand to hand and as each patient takes it and raises it to his lips, instead of the grimace of nauseous "potions and notions," a pleasant smile shows the revivifying powers of this wonderful elixir. The head goes back and after the "glug, glug" of the liquor over the palate there comes an "ah–h–h" of gratitude—the wonderful tonic is excellent whisky, and the fact that the patients are surveyors explains their gusto, for ill-natured people say our affection for the fluid is as great as that of a Scotch parson.

Chapter III

On Sunday, May 3rd, long before dawn, our slumbers were disturbed by the sharp "Who goes there?" of the sentry, replied to by our friend, the Saskatoon settler, bringing dispatches from the general. He had handed our captain's message to the warrior, who showed his intimate acquaintance with the geography of the country and the retentiveness of his memory by demanding: "What are they doing there; do they expect an attack?" To which our messenger responds that he guesses we had orders to stay there, as indeed we had, our instructions being to run in all stray half-breeds and suspicious characters (he should have added tramps, organ-grinders, and confidence men, etc., etc., for we had seen as many of one as the other). The said halfbreeds were presumably fugitives whom the general had thrashed at Fish Creek (before he got there), he with the usual conceit of his kind expecting them to flee at the first sight of his Falstaffian figure; but, alas for human expectations and vanity, the mighty and glorious name of Middleton, "familiar in our mouths as households words," known wherever the flag of Britain spreads its folds to the breeze and used alike by Esquimaux and Maori to hush the restless infant, had not even been heard by these rude and ignorant sons of the plains, and his name being the only part of him that was awe-inspiring, they, in prairie parlance, stood him off, and now he wanted more men. Fortunately, our troop was the only one within reach, for the vast and stupendous intellect that had at last been penetrated with the idea that surely we were not required to protect a trail where cattle and unarmed settlers might pass unmolested, did not yet think it safe to leave his rear unprotected by bringing forward the Governor-General's Body Guard or Quebec Cavalry from the Qu'Appelle trail. However, if he could not send a request to Ottawa for "another ten thousand,"[5] our fifty were better than none, so his dispatch ordering us to the Front was handed over by our friend the settler.

All was bustle and excitement at the news—couriers started at once to call in the other pickets and as nearly all the carts were absent bringing up more supplies, it was noon on Thursday, May 7th, when we struck camp at the Elbow and set out for Clarke's Crossing, pickets nearly eighty miles away having been brought in in the interval.

The trip was uneventful and, had it not been for our cavalry drill, would have been monotonous, but as our captain was constantly introducing new manoeuvres, his inventive genius aided vastly in whiling away the time until we reached Saskatoon on Friday evening, where we met tangible evidence of the Fish Creek fight in the shape of a number of wounded. Some had their left arms amputated and the poor lads were quite proud of the loss, not thinking how deuced inconvenient it is to be literally single-handed in ordinary everyday life.

Next morning on our way to Clarke's Crossing, we met a settler driving a wagon, and were rather amused

at the doubtful compliment he paid our motley as-
sembly by hauling out a rifle as long as himself and in
the most businesslike manner loading her up to receive
us. He told us there had been another big fight but reports at the Crossing failed to confirm this, though the
two companies of the 40th London who were stationed here had heard the field guns the day before.

After leaving the Crossing, the precautions taken at
night were redoubled, for were we not in an enemy's
country? Sentries paced about the camp and an officer
kept at least one eye open all night, but as the orders
were that the horses should be fed and turned loose
at dawn I can scarcely see that such extreme vigilance
was thoroughly carried out, for one mounted man
could have stampeded every hoof and indeed when
the words to "saddle" was given on Sunday morning
there was the deuce to pay because several chargers
were missing.

A little search, however, discovered them among
the bluffs and proceeding toward the "seat of war," as
Kippen called it, shortly after striking camp, we
reached Fish Creek where we had an opportunity of
surveying the scene of the late encounter and thereat
were rather disappointed. Educated by the highly colored versions of the affair, our mind's eye had pictured a precipitous ravine lined with dense thickets
and filled with howling savages; but we find a
shallow valley, or coulee, drained by a small muddy
stream and crossed by the wagon trail. The gentle
slopes are wooded, it is true, but the innumerable
rifle-pits, boiled down, amount to only a very few,

and why the enemy were not driven out puzzles our unmilitary brains not a little. Accounts of the affair are many and conflicting and it is hard to fix upon the correct one. No doubt the official report as to how "I pushed forward my right" and "brought up my supports" and all the rest of it is very nice and interesting reading, but it is hardly reliable. That the men, raw soldiers though they were, behaved creditably all are agreed, and one cannot but admire their pluck and firmness when one reflects that, in addition to being almost surprised and suddenly placed in a trying position, the incompetence of their commander prevented them from doing more effective service. In fact, that august tactician was aghast at the temerity of these halfbreeds in daring to oppose him, and so nonplussed at the manner in which they carried out their opposition, that he seems to have lost his head completely. I don't mean that he was afraid, for as far as personal bravery goes I believe him to be fully endowed, but that the enemy should occupy a position in a hollow instead of on a hill completely paralyzed what inventive resource he possessed, and he did not know how on earth to get at them. Experience was at fault in this case. He made a few random efforts to dislodge the rebels and these failed. He kept his men under fire in a most disadvantageous position, that is, against a sky background and firing at short range into the bush in which the halfbreeds and Indians were concealed; he lost a number of men and toward evening he withdrew his troops; yet, he defeated the enemy, he says. I think most people are agreed that a dash by the volunteers would not only have determined the fortunes of the day, but have broken the back of the rebellion, and, with the loss of no more than actually fell at Fish Creek, would have spared all the lives that were spent afterward at Batoche. As a regular soldier, General Middleton may theorize as he pleases about the risk and danger of charging with raw troops and doubtless many wiseacres, whose opinion is as valuable as his own will support him, but common sense recommends that he should have charged, and for these reasons:

First—the enemy, with some very few exceptions, were not good marksmen, although it is generally supposed that they are dead shots. A number of years in the Northwest have shown me that those of them who shoot at all decently do so only at short distances, depending upon their skill in approaching game rather than on the accuracy of long shots; moreover, they were badly armed. General Middleton gave them every advantage and played directly into their hands by placing his men as he did, for the half-breeds used their skill as hunters in keeping concealed in the brush, while their inferior arms were equal to the rifle of the volunteers at the short range at which they were used. I do not think it necessary further to urge their bad marksmanship than to point out that, with all these odds in their favor, they hit so few of our men, and will maintain that they would have killed no more, if as many, of the troops had the latter charged them. Disciplined foes might have held

23

their ground, but even disciplined troops, unless very old campaigners, have nerves that would not draw as steady a bead at a line of bayonets advancing at a run, and, as for the undisciplined rebels, after a few shots they would have broken cover like rabbits.

Lastly, it was important in this first action that he should dishearten the rebels by gaining a swift and undoubted victory. But why argue the point? After defeating (?) the enemy at Fish Creek, instead of pushing his advantage, this mighty warrior proves how he deserves the encomiums lavished upon him by retiring a mile, going into camp, and remaining inactive for a fortnight. Waiting for the Gatling, say some; for ammunition, say others; couldn't leave the wounded and a host of other whys. But, meantime, the halfbreeds, who think they were victorious, are gaining courage, strengthening their position at Batoche, and patting each other on the back at having thrashed the "Shemōgonsūe" and their "Okeemāgh."[6]

It may be remembered that some little time after Fish Creek, Lord Melgund left the brigade and went eastward for some reason unknown. Possibly, that gentleman was disgusted at the inactivity of his commander, but one explanation I have heard given for his departure and the general's delay that is, perhaps, worthy of credence, is that the Big Gun, with a regular soldier's contempt for our volunteers, was convinced after his repulse that, with the latter alone, he could not cope with the rebels, and had sent Lord Melgund to use his influence with the governor-general to procure the services of regular British troops to crush the rebellion. That was his valuation of Canadians, then.

CHAPTER IV

From Fish Creek the trail northward runs through a beautiful prairie country, well wooded and watered, and rich and fertile, with sundry farms scattered through it, and on our march we passed a number of houses, now abandoned and many of them pretty thoroughly looted. Toward evening on Sunday we came to one that gave certain signs of life in the shape of sundry chickens around the door, and as a surveyor has rather a weakness for the fleshpots, the four who form the advance guard began to deliberate upon the advisability of placing some of the fowl in such shape as to fit them for chicken stew, when a dozen horsemen appeared about a house some three hundred yards further on and the small game was forgotten.

Were they the enemy or not? They looked quite ragged enough to be breeds, but we did not like the idea of firing in and dropping a few of them, so sent a man back to the troop and sat unperceived, rifle in hand, waiting for a shindy, of which we were disappointed as they proved to be Boulton's Mounted Infantry. So after a certain amount of fraternizing we proceeded onward to the brigade camp, where, even to our unsophisticated eyes, it was apparent that military science had been at work in the choice of the position.

A ploughed field had been chosen as a site for part of the corral, and the earth breastwork that partly surrounded it had been placed so low on the slopes that a man standing on the rising ground inside afforded a splendid mark for anyone a few hundred yards away down to the very soles of his boots. I think the hospital tent was almost unprotected, being near the crest of the hill. Westward of the camp about seven hundred yards, the wooden church of Batoche stood where the land fell off toward the river and in the slight depression between, an occasional puff of smoke rose from the brush, the clear crack that followed telling that someone had drawn a bead with more or less accuracy — generally less.

The southwest corner of the entrenchments was allotted to us and, after depositing our traps therein, we amused ourselves pottering about to get an idea of the position. First we went out to where two field guns were shelling some rifle-pits near the graveyard, and found a number of other men lying a hundred yards or so behind the artillery. As these latter were on a knoll so high that when walking erect among our recumbent comrades we could not even see the roof of the church, it was rather rich to be addressed first by one and then another son of Mars lying sprawling on his face and told we "were a d----d fool and had better keep out of that or lie down, they were not going to be shot for us," and as we could see no fun in embracing mother earth where only a falling star could hit one, we came away and, having recuperated exhausted nature with the evening ration of corned beef and hard tack and revived ourselves with tea, Wheeler suggested that we should go out and occupy one of the rifle-pits that had been dug along the top of the river bank a few yards from our corner of the entrenchments and, for want of better employment, we did so. The sun was setting and the firing of musketry had almost ceased, so we did not lie very close. Wheeler and a redcoat were sitting in the pit and the third man was lying behind it and all chatting comfortably when there came a sharp "pat" and "b-z-z-zng," a bullet flew past my ear, and the "crack" of a rifle rang out.

"Gad!" said Wheeler coolly, "there's a hit anyway," and turning round showed where the bullet had punched a hole through the muscles of his arm near the shoulder, fortunately not touching the bone; an excellent shot, too, for the marksman must have been full five hundred yards distant, and now that there was a bull's-eye we came away, everyone else lay very close, and Wheeler put himself in the hands of the surgeons. It began to grow dusk shortly after and, beyond a few shots fired into the corral, everything was quiet, these few shots proving the vantage and scientific nature of our position by wounding some of the horses. If the enemy had been more liberal with their ammunition, we should not have got off so easily. We turned in all standing and, except the sentries, were soon sound asleep, for most of us were tolerably accustomed to fitting our ribs into little inequalities of surface. My turn on guard came about midnight and I don't know that either Gore or myself kept a very sharp lookout for the enemy. Pacing up and down together I rather think the conversation turned more upon surveying instruments and fishing than "ambuscades, cannon and culverin"; for as Kippen used to say, "It is hard to realize, boys, that we are actually up here for the purpose of war"—so our beat was rapidly passed and we roused out our relief and turned in. One or two of the fellows were rather of the alarmist type and twice we were startled to our feet by hoarse whispering that a night attack was imminent, but in one instance it was only a few stray cattle and in the other the excited imagination of the guard had seen "men as trees walking," as the Parson put it. Who does not remember the Parson and his command of language, so extensive and fluent when he was riled, no broken disjointed utterance, but a steady roar increasing in volume like an avalanche poured upon the head of anyone unlucky enough to incur his wrath?

Early on Monday morning we turned out and were sent off with the Gatling and a nine-pounder and Boulton's troop to attack (?) the enemy's left, one of our carts accompanying us with ammunition for the "hurdy-gurdy," and Jack the teamster as driver. We rode in and out among the bluffs until we reached a small strip of prairie running north and south, the woods along whose western edge were faced with the enemy's rifle-pits. Howard and his gun were a little north of us and the two troops of horsemen were dismounted and directed to advance in skirmishing order to support the gun. Our boys were moved forward to the edge of the brush, but owing to some bungle on the part of the general, his aide, or Parolles, had not reached the crest of the hill in front of us and deuce a bit of the enemy could we see at all.

Along came the general, whose hair had been rubbed up the wrong way and wanted to know "why the devil we didn't advance to the top of the hill," whereupon Parolles, to show him the independence of the free-born Canuck, answered that we'd go and stand (dance—some of the boys heard it) on the top if he liked, which was to say the least of it a generous offer on his part to make. Then appeared one of Boulton's men, sent for the ammunition cart, riding at full speed along the open in so tempting a manner that several shots were fired at him without effect. Jack grimly cut a small poplar about five feet long, and as thick as a man's wrist, and when last seen he was kneeling in the front of the cart while the "whack! whack!" of the twig as his muscular arm plies it to old Baldy's ribs almost drowns the rattle of the Gatling.

Truth compels me to state that some of our troops were as verdant as many of our uniformed comrades, as the following incident proved. While advancing through the brush, Mac, in his ardor, got somewhat before the line and as Mac, like hairy-faced Dick in the ballad, is

> Swart of hue,
> Between a gingerbread nut and a Jew,

his glossy black hair and sun-browned neck showed to the excited vision of a comrade like those of a breed, though what the deuce a breed would be doing there with his back to us this deponent sayeth not, and the brilliant youth took a pot shot at him at about forty yards. But fortunately his aim was more nervous than his imagination and, beyond a certain number of naughty exclamations, no harm was done. A few shots were fired, but the boys never see any enemy to fire at, and then "the very model of a modern major-general" gets hungry and we returned to camp, where we attacked our midday meal with much greater effect, and probably with more spirit, than we did the enemy.

Our great Mogul appeared to think that if he got up early and pottered around a bit during the morning he had earned his day's pay, for in the afternoon he came forth resplendent in blue and braided toggery. Perhaps in the sultry climes where he has slain his tens of thousands it is so hot at noon that, like Hotspur,[7] he "kills me six or seven dozen at a breakfast," literally. Anyway, we all take it rather easy in the latter part of the day.

After lunch we took our rifles and sauntered down towards the hill where two of the field-pieces were having a little practice at a house over the river, and learned something more of the art of war. The house, about fifteen hundred yards distant, was supposed to be a rebel council chamber or other important post—at least there was a flag flying over it—and the two nine-pounders were turned loose upon it with shot and shell under the direction of all the military glory the camp could produce. "Bang!" goes a gun and the puff of smoke and answering report from the bursting shell comes back across the river. "Bang!" goes No. 2, with a like result—and so on.

Perhaps the battery men were anxious to spare life, for none of the shells hit the target and "Common shell! Percussion fuse! Load!" became rather monotonous after a bit. We began to think of going elsewhere for amusement. I have heard a great deal about that shooting, the battery men and others claiming that the practice was exceptionally accurate, and I admit that it might have been so and yet left a very large margin for improvement, for everything depends on one's standard of perfection. Not being an artillerist, I can only give my humble views and if it be true, as they maintain, that seventeen shells struck the house (with our glasses we saw them burst everywhere about it, though I really believe it was hit once), the battery must have been very well supplied with ammunition, for surely after the first bulls'-eye or two, no rebel would be such an ass as to stay inside of it.

After whiling away the afternoon in this fashion for some time, the keen sight of some of the decorated warriors descried a number of wagons moving up the trail from the ferry west of the river and a shell was fired in that direction. I won't say it was fired at them, for it hardly went into the same township, and as our field glasses showed the fugitives to be cattle quietly grazing up the slope, it is as well the shot went so wide. Then a new source of interest presented itself, for while we were all grouped about the guns intent upon the havoc and destruction they were causing, two rebels came out on the open road across a ravine between our position and the church and all who did not feel bound to stand up promptly assumed the horizontal. Had the enemy fired into the flock before they showed themselves they must have bagged someone in such a crowd, but our rapidity in executing this difficult manoeuvre was so great that their bullets only cut the empty air as they sung over us. The general, who swaggered about showing his rotund and rather corpulent figure, was quite indifferent whether they pinked him or not, but a number of the officers endeavored to reconcile the dignity of rank with a wholesale amount of discretion. It was rather ludicrous to see them standing in line one behind the other sheltered by a couple of very small poplars rather thicker than a man's arm. Determined to give us precept as well as moral courage, our commander, etc., etc., nerves himself for the occasion and shouts, "Don't look at the gun, men—watch the road—d--n it, men! don't look at the gun," rather unnecessarily, and rifles began to crack from our comrades in quite an alarming fashion, had their accuracy been reliable or the enemy in sight. This new arrival convinced our tacticians that the house had been hit, or ought to have been hit, for they limbered up the guns and went back to camp leaving us to do as we pleased about following. Two of us stayed with some dozen redcoats to interview our friends over the ravine and our comrades, having their pouches full of ammunition, fired innumerable shots at a dark object seen through the brush which they declared to be the rifle-pit sheltering two rebels (it afterward proved to be the body of an artillery horse that had been killed in the first day's action), but as I could not find any extra bullet holes in it and the rifle-pit was only about forty yards to one side, many of the bullets fired at the horse may have gone so close to the pit—so well did our men shoot, forty yards in a four-hundred-yard shot—as to be unpleasant to its occupants, for they did not fire very many in return. Others of the corps went down the slope of the hill with Colonel Williams and the Midland Battalion on the enemy's right flank, and one of them told me that he fancied that officer was putting out a feeler both for his own men and the enemy. His own idea was that we were able to stalk the enemy with as great caution as possible, so he was rather astonished at the noise that Colonel Williams encouraged and added to with his own voice during their advance, which was a short spurt made before the retire sounded, to try his supporters' and opponents' temper for future results.

As the sun set and the troops were recalled for the night, the great superiority of the civilized over the savage method of warfare was once more brought home to us. The camp, as I have said, was almost directly east of the church and in the morning, and in fact all day, the troops steadily worked their way toward the latter and the village of Batoche beyond it. The intervening ground being known to our men, and the enemy's rifle-pits being well constructed and carefully hidden by the brush, the advance in skirmishing order had to be made with caution, as the red and black tunics made very good marks for their keen-sighted opponents. Our boys would gain a certain amount of ground during the day and retire toward evening. Now, everyone who has ever tried to approach game knows the greater difficulty of retiring undiscovered than of approaching, and it may be easily imagined at what a disadvantage our brave lads in their bright tunics were placed when retiring rapidly and as rapidly followed by men as lightly clad as possible, skilled hunters who knew every inch of the ground. Add to this the fact that the sun was low and directly in our men's faces so that while they could see next to nothing, the enemy had every object thrown out in strong light. The fierce yells of the Sioux and their halfbreed allies as they followed our retreating men and the crackle of musketry tell us that the enemy feel their advantage, for Indians are not noisy unless successful. Only their bad marksmanship saved many of our men but on this evening Hardisty of the 90th was shot through the brain, proving that there were exceptions to the rule. How many casualties occurred I cannot say, but surely there was bad generalship displayed in taking positions at a disadvantage during the day, only to abandon them at a greater disadvantage at sundown. Indeed, it is well known that the troops were nearer the village of Batoche the first day than on any other until the "rush" was made, and I have heard that General Middleton was apparently so astonished at the warm reception given him that day that he wished to retire several miles, and was only dissuaded by the urgent request of his officers.

CHAPTER V

We spent another night in the dirt of the enclosure sleeping without disturbance, in the way of alarm, and on Tuesday again accompanied the Gatling and a nine-pounder to the enemy's left for another of those attacks (?) of ours. This time the field gun was close to us and, dismounting, we were ordered to advance extended and support it within a very short distance of our position of yesterday. The brush was thick and several of us walked up an old survey line cut through the bluff. Desirous of getting a sight of the enemy whom we expected to find across the little plain, we were walking nearly erect up the line and not knowing the ground before us must have shown our heads against the sky behind, when a dozen rifles cracked so close to us that the unpleasant "b-s-s-s-st" sounded simultaneously with the reports. It is rather absurd to drop at the whistle of a ball, when we think of it, for had the rifle that sped it been well aimed, one would never hear the sound, but we all did drop. Perhaps there is some sort of electric communication between a fellow's ear and the muscles of his knees causing them to contract, for down I went at once and then began to crawl up the slope, when Celluloid called out, "R——! Kippen is gone." "Badly hurt?," I asked, for I had not seen him fall. "I don't know, he is right behind you."

I crawled back at once and though the veriest tyro, a single glance showed me that all medical skill was useless here. Our poor comrade was lying in the old survey line on his right side. One hand grasped the rifle he had been about to use, his broad hat was still jauntily cocked on one side of his head and so calm was his face that, had it not been for the thin stream of blood flowing from his upper lip, one would have thought him asleep. The bullet had struck him just below the nose and passed directly through the brain producing instant death, so sudden, in fact, that he was dead before he fell and suffered no pain whatever. Word was passed along the line and the ambulance men were soon on the spot, but all they could do was carry him to the rear. The general, riding up, hears of the poor fellow's death and remarks, "What luck these men have, only a chance volley." His opinion apparently, but the fact is that as we had been brought to exactly the same locality as the day before, the enemy, accustomed now to our brilliant leader's method of attack, had quietly laid a little trap for us but, owing to hurry and bad shooting, had only killed one man. Some dozen or fifteen were lying down just beyond the ridge waiting for us and, as we made plenty of noise, they had warning of our approach, fired a volley into our ranks, and were seen to run across the open to their cover without a shot fired in return.

We were kept here for some time but, beyond the killing of a few cattle that we were ordered to shoot, I don't think we did much damage to the enemy and, having so got through our morning's duty, rode back to camp. We are a hard and careless lot as a rule, we surveyors; rough associates, hard work, and lack of women's society causes men to grow indifferent to the feelings of others, but I noticed that the troop was quiet and less joking carried on. The first gap had been made in our ranks and we could faintly imagine how he would be missed in the little home circle down in Eastern Canada. His quaint sayings and cheerful laugh are gone from No. 1 tent, yet, though he has fallen among us, in a week he will be almost forgotten and we cannot at all realize the sorrow of his parents when the first warning of their loss reaches them in the brief telegram, "A.W. Kippen, Surveyors' Corps, killed." We sympathize in some degree with his relatives, but I do not think much grief is felt for him; full of life, health, strength, and energy, prepared for all emergency, but untainted by a shade of fear, he meets a painless, instant death and is spared all misery and unhappiness that might befall him in later life. We do not pity him though we do miss him a little; he is only another victim of our bungle and we are fortunate in losing no more than one man.

After our return to camp we knocked about until shortly after noon when we sat down to lunch, rather a swell name to give the scramble for tea, corned beef, and hard tack eaten wherever a fellow could find space to sit down; it reminded one of our troopers of Dr. Watt's hymn:

> Whene'er I take my walks abroad,
> How many poor I see,

A'scoffin' pork without a fork,
What dirty beasts they be.

There is such a dearth of cutlery and he who does not carry his own fork must use his fingers; but a hungry man can worry his meal, fork or no fork, so we bolt our food and await further developments.

The day was bright and warm and were it not for the sight of the hospital tent and its wounded and the crack of the skirmishers' rifles near the church, we could almost think it a survey. No orders come and there are no prospects of any, so we stroll out to the top of the hill and watch the red tunics that show here and there among the brush, our attention being drawn to three of them who are lying on the river side of a narrow ridge they have gained and over which they are firing at the houses of Batoche, when sundry puffs of smoke rise in the timber and a volley is fired at these from over the river behind them. One man was hit and rolled down the slope; his comrades return the fire and then took cover and, as shot after shot was fired at the patch of scarlet lying motionless on the hillside, our rifles answer them and the reports come thick and fast. Colonel Williams with two of his companies was down beyond the graveyard at his position of yesterday afternoon, and near him a strong force of Grenadiers under Colonel Grasett and, probably feeling that now while his men were hot was the moment for the dash he had been longing for, he sent back to Colonel Grasett to ask that officer to support him and, calling to his own men, led the way. The fire grows hotter and a cheer goes up from the Midland, the 10th have caught the fever and take up the echoes with another shout and the Great I Am roused perhaps from his noonday snooze, wants to know—

"What's all that row about?"

"I think they're charging, sir," says an artillery officer standing on a gun near him.

"Who the devil told them to charge? I never told them to charge," remarks the irate warrior, and then mounts his horse and, followed by his staff, rides down to the field.

"Why in ──── don't he let us at them?" is in every man's mouth, and the astonishing variety of bad language would shock a mule driver. The crackle of rifles and hoarse cheering sets each of us on fire. This really looks like business, and excitement is at its height, when out of the corral comes Howard's "hurdy-gurdy" bouncing along like a featherweight behind the four powerful saddle horses, whilst a dozen yards in front sitting well down in his saddle rides the Yankee captain with blood in his eye and every line of his face meaning fight.

"Three cheers for Captain Howard," calls a voice, and before the echoes of the shouts have well died away, the rattle of the machine gun joins in the chorus. Another aide gallops into the enclosure and more red and black tunics go down to join the fun, and at last our troop is sent for to support Boulton's on the right, and we leg it down the trail near the church and are halted. "Front!"—our peculiar drill

39

puts us in such position that if we front, we get our backs to the enemy, and many of the troops do so, whereat the aide says to Parolles, "It is the other way I want you to go, captain." "Forward!"—the only command we require comes at last like the starter's "go" at a race. Let the strategic meaning of support be what it may, our rendition is that we are to get up alongside the others and as quickly as possible we proceed to do so. Where the deuce our commander wanders off to we don't know and do not care. We are just as well off without him and in open order, each man just feeling his next, we join in the rush. Boulton's troops seem as happy about tactics as we are and the two corps, indiscriminately mingled, begin to sweep the enemy out of the slopes before us.

Handicapped by our heavy boots and spurs and encumbered by our useless revolvers; cheering, laughing, swearing, keeping up an irregular fire into the bush, and yet advancing at a rapid run, we charge—if the rush of such a lot of undisciplined ragamuffins can be called a charge. Officers are needless for we are unanimous in our intentions; there is no red tape to hold us back, the boys have their heads now and an officer would have no breath for orders. The "crack, crack" of the repeaters come thick and fast and the whistle of bullets tell us the enemy are not idle; now and again the dull boom of a field gun sounds over the field followed by the echo of its bursting shell, whilst the terrible "skr-r-r-r" of the Gatling rings like music in our ears. We are not attacking our fellow-subjects, hardly our fellow-creatures;

we are attacking a set of scoundrelly Sioux and their allies whose fierce war-whoops when a wounded or dead man was brought in still echo about us. Knowing as we do that whatever few contemptible grievances the halfbreeds may have had, the Sioux had none and that only their love of blood and plunder brought them to Riel's camp, for us every man is an Indian, and we feel some of the hatred that animates Howard when we remember that these Sioux now opposed to us are refugees from Minnesota, and that not only white men but women and children had fallen their victims before we gave them protection. But they do not stand before us long. Their fire grows weaker under our own and distrusting the shelter of their rifle-pits, they seek that of flight. Not all of them get away, though. As we sweep through the brush and come upon an open stretch several of the enemy break cover before us, whether they were pluckier than the rest or only slower of foot no one stops to enquire, and the repugnance one might feel at killing a flying enemy dies when one thinks what the enemy is. They drop like partridges, only one of them escaping, but, as he had to run the gauntlet of some hundreds of bullets for as many yards and I noticed that he staggered twice, I fancy he carried away some little mementos the reverse of pleasant.

And now that the enemy are doing us very little damage, we begin to wish that we had red jackets to protect us from our own side, for the fighting fever has so possessed some of the uniforms on our near left that a number of them fire at us as we rise a gentle slope and our motley crew show against the hill. In fact, only the use of certain expletives in the plainest and most forcible English coupled with a threat to return their fire convince them, probably from our fluency, that we are friends. Our share of the work was over. We had driven the enemy out of the slopes of the hill along the front of their position before the redcoats had reached the houses and, as we lay on the ridges at what had been their left, we watched the advance of the uniforms over the open at our feet, covering their attack by using up our few remaining cartridges at the rifle-pits along the river bank.

Our own troop had suffered but little: Garden was hit in the left arm, Fawcett had a buckshot in the muscles of his chest, and there were some badly wounded hats and very ragged trousers among us. And now along came Wheeler who had helped Garden back to camp and then taken his rifle and followed, not that he could use the rifle, for his left arm was in a sling, but he was in the devil's own temper because he was a little late.

The uproar and stir and rattle of firearms gradually dies away, the sun gets low and the retire is sounded and, after killing a few chickens at a house on the hill, which house we are ordered (from—ahem!—strategical reasons) to burn, for we still feel that corned beef and glory are inferior to chicken and glory, we saunter back to Batoche where the infantry are throwing up earthworks, making loopholes, and otherwise carrying out the orders of the Great I Am, who, now that the place has been taken with scarce any help of his, begins to exercise his mighty intellect upon the correct way to prevent its being retaken by the enemy, who are, of course, very likely to attempt it, as with little ammunition and encumbered by women and children they scatter northward beyond harm's way. But it is military formula to observe such precautions, for if the enemy are not thinking of returning, they ought to be thinking of it, and so our comrades of the red jackets wield pick and spade while we irregulars walk quietly up to camp and turn in, thus ending May 12th, 1885.

Chapter VI

Call the affair a battle or not, it had the merit of breaking the back of the rebellion, and when one thinks of the number who are anxious to claim the whole credit of having ordered and organized the rush, one really fancies that this irregular attack of a lot of irregular soldiers is fit to be placed among most of the brilliant charges in history. Let us look at the affair as an outside observer would, and not claim any extra credit for the side I belonged to merely because I did belong to it.

The largest estimate of the enemy's strength that can be made places their number at about four hundred, and for my part I do not believe there were as many opposed to us. General Middleton, I have no doubt, in his reports, places them at half as many again and says he had the four hundred,[8] but I fancy that there were about seven hundred of us, besides teamsters who joined in just for the fun of the thing, and also two field guns and the Gatling, which latter, handled by the cool-headed artist, Howard, in supporting the advance, was worth just about two battalions of such marksmen as our average volunteer. So our victory was not such a creditable affair when all is said in point of numbers. Moreover, they were poorly armed, with one or two exceptions, with any sort of shooting iron from an old smooth-bore flintlock to a rim-fire Winchester repeater, whereas we had Sniders, improved Winchesters, and Martinis, and further, they were a half-hearted lot without sufficient grit to make a determined stand, although, owing to their success at Fish Creek and the general's senseless delay thereafter, they had plucked up a little spirit. A great deal has been said about the strength of the position at Batoche, "A veritable Sevastopol," one wisehead called it and so on, but I may say that all the sketches and maps, in which the number of rifle-pits has been vastly exaggerated as indeed they were in all the engagements, give one a very poor idea of its weakness.

Gabriel Dumont, who is said to have planned the defence, expected the attack on the old trail about the center of his position and made his pits strongest in that vicinity, protecting his north and south flanks by only a few scattered pits, and Colonel Williams and his men had worked their way in so far on the southern flank as to be really behind the main line of pits before the rush was made and, as the greater number of the rebels who occupied this main line were driven out by Boulton's Mounted Infantry and the Surveyors' Intelligence Corps, they probably fired only a few dozen shots at the troops before the rush of our scouts was on them and then they just skedaddled.

Of course, General Middleton, with characteristic modesty, takes all the credit of the direction of the rush and its success upon himself—how if it had not been successful?—although the brigade orders of that day say that it was entirely owing to the volunteer officers and men. And now he, no doubt, thinks the remark he is supposed to have made but never did

45

utter, of "There's death or victory in that charge, let them go," will be placed and perpetuated with the famous "England expects, etc." signal. I, for one, do not believe he had any idea the rush would be made and so far from ordering it, put not a little faith in the story that when he did reach the scene and the men had cleared out the first ravine, he ordered the "Cease firing" and "Retire" to be sounded and, when neither was obeyed, called out, "Why in God's name don't those men come back, they'll all be killed?" But they did not all come back, nor were they all killed, so he did the only thing he could do – supported them and now, *verb sap sat*, he has $20,000, a badge of knighthood, and some little kudos and all the credit of the charge as he has of putting down the disturbances in the Territories. As a writer in the Montreal *Star* put it: "Colonel Straubenzie as much deserves the credit of ordering the Batoche charge as General Middleton does the credit of the whole campaign." Quite so. I absolve E.J.C.[9] of all sarcasm, but I most sincerely agree with him – he does. But as General Middleton deserves no credit for the suppression of the rebellion and nothing but contempt for his management of the whole campaign, the few rags of credit that fall to the other officer will in no way lessen the praise due the better of both who originated and forced them to support him in the dash and, although the victory was not important enough to accord him any glory, yet had it not been for him we should have been kept for weeks at the work that cost the lives of Hardisty, Kippen, and others. And there is many a Canadian household that might today be mourning the loss of sons like them were it not for the pluck and energy of that better, the real leader of the rush, Lieutenant-Colonel Williams of the Midland Battalion.

Chapter VII

Wednesday, May 13th, was emblematic of the peace that had resulted from our successful arms, as the correspondents say, bright and fine. We could explore the field in an erect position without danger of coming in the track of a bullet, so took the opportunity of having a good bath in the Saskatchewan and felt like civilized men once more. The general had shut down on looting in the most effective manner by taking charge of a good many of the furs himself, and his zeal in this direction was imitated by so many of the officers that very few privates got a share.[10] What became of the furs afterward perhaps we had better not ask. They constituted about all the available plunder, for the lares and penates of either Sioux or halfbreed do not represent much that is lootable. I got one or two horn spoons in the Sioux camp, a new bath towel, and some bars of soap, and these, with a few forks and tin dishes for our mess, made up my booty. The soap was a boon, for our most excellent (?) transport service had cut us out of that luxury, and the towel was a blessing until some confounded teamster stole it out of my blankets a month afterward.

In the afternoon we paid our last poor marks of respect to Lieutenant Kippen, whose body, placed in a rough coffin, we followed down to the steamboat that had arrived the evening before. It was to be sent to his father's home in Perth for burial.

Thursday the whole brigade moved north to Gardepuy's Ferry thirteen miles down the river with our comrade Wheeler once more in the saddle, in despite of his wounded arm, and reached there somewhat late that night. I fancy that the generals, whose exploits in Latin and Greek were pounded into our heads at school, were lightning expresses to our commander's slow freight—stop, I'm wrong here—Zenophon[11] speaks of the "retreat of the 10,000." We were advancing this time, but later in the season when we were retreating from an enemy (that was going in the opposite direction), we moved about four times as fast as we advanced, and I will wager that in expediting (his own) retreat our general could utterly paralyze Zenophon. However, we got into camp at last and next day Boulton's troop, the Gatling, and the Survey Corps were sent out to round up fugitives.

We left camp early in the morning, travelling toward Batoche, and meeting numerous penitent rebels, found among them one who was willing to guide us out to where Riel and Dumont were concealed and, under his leadership, turned off eastward from the trail. The usual bungling was apparent here, for although there were several men in the column who knew Riel by sight, none of them had been placed in the advance guard, and to these latter and the scouts he was quite unknown. We met a number of halfbreeds without a speck of fight in them, disarmed and sent them into camp and, just as the bugle sounded a halt for lunch, two men leading their horses with a third man between them crossed the

49

*

foremost line of scouts. Knowing one of these men to
be Tom Hourie, the interpreter's son, we supposed
that he was bringing in a prisoner, and fancying that
he was attached to the column and would report to
Major Boulton, let him pass, one of the boys calling
out jokingly, "Well, Tom, have you got Riel?" little
thinking that the third man was the rebel chief.
Hourie crossed the line of scouts unchallenged, slipped
through the bluffs in front of the column until out of
reach, and took his prisoner into camp whilst we
went on scouring the country and our lariats hung
unstretched at the saddle bows. His reason for
avoiding us was that Riel was afraid the scouts would
shoot him, and Hourie wanted the imaginary reward
for himself.

Then we tumble off, picket the horses, and lunch
whilst Boulton and Parolles hold a council of war,
which results in a number of our men being sent on
under the guidance of the halfbreed to seek Gabriel
Dumont, the Gatling and Boulton's troop going back
to camp, while the rest of us wander on among the
bluffs till we strike a shanty whose owner is a French
Canadian with a Yankee wife. Gatling Howard and
this lady are natives of the same place and the two
persuade the husband to guide us to Riel's little
retreat, and as sundry shekels of silver are held out as
an inducement, and he may never get the chance to
fool such a crowd again, he consents. And off we
start with the Frenchman mounted on one of our
horses, Gatling Howard and Parolles in the van, and
the rest of the troop following like a flock of sheep.

Due south from the house we move among the ponds and bluffs at a brisk walk. The western sun gets round over our right eyes as we hold grimly on. We face it but the frown on our leader's brow tells us that no small obstacle shall hold us back. The beams of the setting sun fall on our left cheek, and we are travelling northward when we come on a last year's cart-track in the grass, which our guide assures us was made by Riel's cart. It crosses a long marsh with a boggy creek and even Parolles is not fool enough to follow there, so our Canadian, perhaps thinking there is a limit even to his imbecility, leads us northward again. And now old Sol throws out long shadows in front of us and we are eastward bound, but what are such trivial matters as points of the compass to men on such a quest as ours? Our captain is evidently bent on catching Riel if he describes all the figures of Euclid to do it, so we are not greatly astonished when we feel the sun on our right cheek again and, just before a long thick belt of poplar, willow, and the like, are informed that HERE is the hiding place of the arch rebel. Orders to draw carbines and, extended in skirmishing order, to advance straight through or over all obstacles quickly follow, and there is blood in our leader's eye as he spurs his charger and shouts "Forward!" I find my next man is Maddock and, as we pick our way through the brush, our rifles reposing quietly in their slings, I hear him call, "R-----! come here." A horrible thought flashes over my mind—was I wrong?—is the captain a confounded fool, or are all the troop?—is there really an enemy?—and I spur to the rescue.

"What?" in a hoarse whisper with carbine loaded (and in the holster).

"Look there." Visions of the remorse-smitten rebel weltering in his blood stiffen my hair as I see M——— standing afoot and gazing at something on the ground before him.

Horror! It is? It is? Joy! A duck's nest with six eggs in it and the revulsion of feeling from blood and carnage to wholesome edibles, added to the discovery that they are quite fresh, so unnerves us that we almost weep on each other's necks as we pack them in our holsters and remount.

On through break and bog once more till the open prairie stretches before us, and reunited after our hazardous but, alas, fruitless search, behold a sight that gladdens every heart, for there, straight on our path, directly south and scarce half a mile away, lies the cabin from which we set forth. Tears dim fierce revengeful eyes, bronzed cheeks are convulsed with emotion and exclamations burst from the stern men around; exclamations of delight too, for "Hell," "Damn fools," etc., show that the boys are evidently overjoyed at the feat we have just performed, *viz*., described a perfect circle of about a mile radius and come back to the point we started from. I tell you it takes an old plainsman to do that.

We reach the cabin and discover that the Yankee woman is not far behind the proverbial sharpness of her people, for while her husband has been making most egregious, I should say, gregarious fools of us, she has been baking cakes, which she now sells to the boys and rakes in coin therefor, and as we devour these delicacies, the mail courier going east with dispatches arrives and conveys the pleasing information that all the time we have been describing convolutions and curves, Riel is sitting in the general's camp fifteen miles away. So there is nothing to do but mount and jog thitherward, and during the march I notice that each individual trooper is so highly pleased with the success of our day's work that he fairly bubbles over with the expressions of satisfaction that seem peculiar to the country. And so ends another of our little bungles.

The next day was Sunday and, of course, military etiquette prescribed church parade, which ceremony was attended by most of the Survey Corps with the other troops. Three of us, however, being "little better than one of the wicked," and with our thoughts fixed more on the creature than on the spiritual comforts of this transitory existence, harnessed a horse in one of our carts, and sallied forth on a foraging expedition, examining with due care a number of houses on the trail northward, got sundry tin dishes and other useful articles, spent quite a pleasant morning and returned to camp with our spoils, foremost among them being several bags of potatoes found in a cellar, which, with half a keg of syrup, formed an addition to our diet for a few days.

Sundown found the greater part of the brigade on the west side of the Saskatchewan whence on Monday we start with rather more speed than customary for Prince Albert, reaching there the following day—a speed only explained by the fact that there are no foes between us and the people we have come to succor, and our general is anxious to pose as the Northwest Havelock delivering this beleaguered Lucknow. What a pity that, as we enter and receive the plaudits of the assembled multitudes (?), we cannot discover any sort of Jenny Campbell episode, and how we regret having no bagpipe or Jew's harp or other sweet-toned instrument to announce our arrival, for we have been so long on the way that one could almost work up a lot of heroics out of it. But alas! during these terrible and arduous marches, the strain upon physical energy had been so severe that the only music that disturbed the stillness of the night is the melodious snore of a major-general or other Great I Am, or the soothing voice of a transport mule calling to his mate. We have come, seen, conquered. Our deeds are chronicled as those of the mighty men of old, the glorious name of our gifted leader has burst forth in brightness now that Colonel Williams and the Canadian Volunteers have kicked over the bushel that enshrouded it, and, as we rest our war-worn limbs and sigh for more worlds to conquer, the sovereign of our country prepares to heighten the brilliancy of this farthing candle whose light is all of gravy, gravy, gravy. Congratulations from real soldiers pour upon him and while but little is said to those to whom credit is due, the well-meaning but unweighing and impetuous gentlemen who make our laws are even now about to tender a more substantial but undeserved token of appreciation to this modernized Major Monsoon.

Chapter VIII

The question now asked by the brigade who have
not yet had a surfeit of "guns and drums and
wounds, God save the mark," and are not yet convinced what an utter imbecile their commander is, is
whether Poundmaker and his Indians are going to
show fight or not, for we had heard so much of the
evil deeds of this particular band of Crees that we
looked upon them as real game. However, our Warrior somewhere in the recesses of his mighty brain
has stored the old whist player's maxim of when in
doubt play trumps, and the mountain called Poundmaker giving no sign of coming to Mohammed, that
gentleman decides upon going to the mountain. The
lesson he has learned from the halfbreeds at Fish
Creek and Batoche is not quite lost, for determined
that this rival star in the horizon of battle shall learn
something of his mighty name in arms, and aware of
the effect of a little preliminary bluster on an Indian,
he dispatches a note to the chief telling him that HE
has defeated Riel and will serve Poundmaker likewise
in short order if he does not come in and surrender.
Afterward, events prove that Poundmaker is fool
enough to believe the general will keep and can keep
his word, but the simplicity of the Indian is excusable
in one who knew so little of that officer when I recall
the fact that we ourselves, who knew him better, had
not quite divested ourselves of the idea that there
must be some determination in him.

Having sent his ultimatum (let us use polysyllables as befitting the pomposity of the sender), the general followed it in person on Friday, May 22nd, by steamer up the North Saskatchewan, guarded by the Midland Battalion and the Gatling and, as there was a possibility of the boat becoming stranded on the bars, he took Boulton's Mounted Infantry on board also, doubtless to haul the vessel up the river by horse power if she stuck fast or if her machinery gave out. I can find no other explanation for his thus moving mounted men. The remainder of the brigade awaited further orders at Prince Albert, and to kill time the following day, Saturday was observed as Her Majesty's birthday and celebrated in addition to the customary races and games by a few delicacies such as milk and butter for dinner. But the next day we donned our armor again and Grenadiers, French's Scouts, and Survey Corps set out for Carlton by trail, the 90th going by water.

The reveille sounded at the usual unholy hour and we were told that great time was to be made, in fact that Colonel Otter and his flying column would be looked upon as slow freight compared to us but our deputy, etc. etc., has a touch of his chief's complaint and it was 10:30 before we got off. The infantry were to go in heavy marching order, knapsacks and all the rest of it, and so they did and big time they made, but as they travelled in the wagons the fatigue was not severe and as our speed was not much greater than a nursery-maid with a perambulator makes, we did not exactly devour the way, only reaching a point about a mile south of the forks of the Carlton Trail, and seventeen miles from Prince Albert, by nightfall. Monday was a repetition of the previous day, but toward evening we did make the ruins of Carlton, being a total distance of forty miles in two days; verily our speed was rapid, but I think Colonel Otter beat us. Here we were to cross the river, for our troops and French's Scouts were to convoy 170 wagons to Battleford, while the infantry embarking in the steamers were to proceed by river. The next morning the work of ferrying began early, though we were as usual kept standing saddled until late in the afternoon, there being rather an extra allowance of the bungling that invariably accompanied the transport service in the management of this duty, and it was sunset before we camped on the top of the north bank ready for a move next day.

Parolles informs us he is in command of the outfit and gives us a big dissertation as to how HE (with a capital H) is going to run the affair and make these teamsters move around, but verily he reckons without his host, for Sinclair, the "Boss" teamster, has decided to do his own share of the running and subsequent events proved his success.

Discipline, as far as its real meaning is known to Parolles, might be a hieroglyph and even our bugbear, red tape, is shorn of its dignity. No attempt is made to keep the wagons in control or position. It is a race between them to see which will have the best place, and poor Parolles has to exercise all his horsemanship to save himself from being run down by the unruly wagoners. On one occasion, indeed, with his eyes sticking out like a frog's that you have stepped on, he informs a teamster who drives into our ranks, and scatters us like a bursting shell, that he will shoot him, which childish threat only provokes a hoarse "guffaw" from the brawny puncher of mules. Sinclair, knowing his man, camps where and when he pleases, and Parolles has to pocket his dignity and follow suit for he dare not leave the wagons unprotected (?)—fifty-odd men to protect 170 wagons is rather good, but there is no enemy, so it matters little.

Thursday was a repetition of the previous day, but on Friday we had a lesson in expeditious movement that I hope was not lost on us. Some of the wagons began to move before the troop had mounted, so our brave captain, his eye in the proverbial frenzy, shouts, although many of the horses were still unsaddled: "Prepare to mount—mount—files—left turn—forward—trot!" and there is a delightful helter-skelter. Parolles, with his spurs in his charger's ribs, starts off at a canter. Gore, who is No. 1 rear rank, follows and I, who am No. 5 front rank—remember our peculiar drill—ride up alongside him as the intervening files and nearly all the remainder of the troop are yet wrestling with girths and buckles. The teamsters, imagining there is either a race or a panic, whip up their horses and cheer us as we pass with such remarks as "Bully," "Go it," "We're the stuff," for a couple of miles and when Parolles—his anger jolted out of him—slackens his speed, I look back from the vanguard of the solitary three and see the remainder of the troop scattered over at least a mile of prairie, each man riding up with a broad grin on his face and showing that our leader's efforts to get the corps into a good humor by temporary relaxation of our cast-iron discipline have been, in measure, crowned with success. Whether the laugh is at him or not this witness is silent. We fall into our places again and the monotony of the march is resumed until, later in the morning, riding along the trail led by our Parolles who has fallen into gentle slumber, we miss the rattle of wheels behind us and, looking back, discover that the old Indian who drives the leading team is striking off to the westward followed by the whole wagon train whilst we are pointing our horses' noses to Fort Pitt. So P., pocketing his dignity once more (that poor virtue, how roughly it got handled, it was so constantly shoved out of sight), spreads out scouts for Heaven knows what and the rest of the troop fall in behind their copper-colored guide, proceeding in this order until about 9 A.M. when the welcome "halt" and "come to the cook-house door" are blown and we offsaddle for breakfast or dinner or whatever it may be called, as we have already had one meal today. Saddle again and on westward until far across a valley before us the white houses of Battleford appear and Nitchi drops his reins and tumbles out of his wagon, a movement that, executed under P.'s eye and without his orders, ruffles his plumage and renews his slumbering ire. He can't speak Cree and our friend's English is not intelligible, so, still mounted on his war-horse, he seizes the reins of our guide's team and attempts to urge the animals forward—*he* couldn't get lost *now*. That was an excellent sketch Gore made of the "troubles of a commanding officer in the N.W.T.," representing P. with his long stirrups trying to stick in his saddle, his elbows over the top of his head, making ludicrous and ungainly efforts to drive the very small mules, whose enormous ears are all we can see over the seat of the wagon, but like most of P.'s praiseworthy but misdirected zeal, it proves a failure and progress is delayed until our guide remounts—even his nutmeg-colored phiz wrinkled into a grin at this display of equestrian skill. So onward as before to the Saskatchewan, which we reach at about 2 P.M., and across which we are ferried by steamer next day, camping near the barracks of Battleford.

CHAPTER IX

Everyone knows, at least through the medium of the papers, what Battleford is like, so a description of the place is superfluous. There is a fort there, too, built on the ridge of land between the Battle and Saskatchewan rivers. Who built it, I don't know, or for what purpose, I also plead ignorance, but the strategist who placed it where it stands must have been sadly misled as to the theoretic amount of rainfall if he intended the defenders of the post to obtain all their water supply from that source in event of a siege, as there is no well in the fort and no water. Luckily, the Indians did not press the place too closely. Fancy building a fort on a hill and having to send water carts down some five or six hundred yards to the river under an enemy's fire! Hurrah for military science (?).

Here we found Colonel Otter's brigade and some old chums among them and here we began to think of getting back to earning our bread and butter again, for Poundmaker had been frightened by the general's "bluff" and come in and surrendered. But late on Saturday night we received orders to be in readiness to move to Fort Pitt next day as a courier had arrived from General Strange with the report of his fight with Big Bear and his Crees at Stand Up Coulee, and a request, *ça va sans dire*, for reinforcements, and accordingly early morning saw the Prince Albert Brigade again on the move, leaving Colonel Otter's division at Battleford.

General Middleton's alleged reason for this disposal of his forces is that he knew and could depend upon his own brigade, thereby inferring that he couldn't trust the other. It looks very much as if his real reason was a contemptible wish to snub Colonel Otter and his command, as that officer had forestalled his chief and gained some kudos at Cut Knife Hill, about which fight and the wisdom of Colonel Otter's march, battle, and retreat much has been said and written. Not much value can be placed upon the criticisms or opinions of such red-tape tacticians as the generals in this campaign, for such opinions cannot weight against common sense and emanate probably, in the case of the general commanding, from a feeling of envy toward many of his subordinates. But I believe that Colonel Otter's attack and the pluck and determination of his men at the fight of Cut Knife broke Poundmaker's back and prevented him from joining Riel, and that Cut Knife and one other fight were the pluckiest of the season, as in both of these our men were outnumbered by the enemy. In support of what I have said of General Middleton's wish to tie Colonel Otter's hands and prevent him from taking any more wind out of his sails, I will only say that Colonel Herchmer's Police and Major Short's Gatling, which had formed part of Colonel Otter's division, were now attached to the Prince Albert column, leaving Colonel Otter with scarce one mounted man. Comment is unnecessary.

The greater part of the brigade went up the river by steamer, and Herchmer's Police, Boulton's Mounted

Infantry, French's Scouts, and the Survey Corps by the south trail to Fort Pitt early on Sunday morning. Noon on Tuesday, two days later, found the whole brigade on the north side of the Saskatchewan about five miles below Fort Pitt where once more under the baton of red tape the consequent BUNGLING (with a big B) became prevalent.

General Strange had attacked Big Bear at a small creek near Frenchman Butte and, as the Indian chief had held the position and General Strange had retired, the creek and valley were promptly named Stand Up Coulee. I have seen the report ("Ahem! official," as Sir Joseph Porter would say) of the affair, but as it and all the official accounts of actions in this campaign partake of the nature of that written by the old sea captain in one of Maryatt's novels, it is hardly worth remembering. I daresay General Strange defeated Big Bear—the enemy were always licked—but why did General Strange retire fourteen miles to Fort Pitt? Strategy, I suppose. He leaves the Indians in their position and then sends word to his commander that he has "corralled" the Indians. After a bit he concludes that it would be advisable to find out where the Indians are and discovers that the "degraded and undisciplined savage, you know," has disregarded the courtesy of war, cut a road through the bush east and northeast, eluded the vigilance of the militarist, and may be on his way to the North Pole for all our general knows to the contrary. That whole manoeuvre, like the other scientific tactics of the campaign, is something one needs a rare amount of education to

understand, appreciate, or applaud, so I won't attempt
it but I may say in justice to General S., that I have
been told by certain of his command that he was justified in not feeling confidence in the "Johnny
Canuck" part of the brigade under him, and that he
had reason for distrusting their steadiness in action—
perhaps so!

However, General Strange was camped at the
Coulee, Big Bear *et al*. had vanished, and General
Middleton was at the river near Fort Pitt on Tuesday,
June 3rd,[12] early in the morning, and one would suppose that a march towards General S.'s camp would
be begun at once, but as that would require due consideration and an immediate move would be undignified, none was made.

We were directed to camp and a number of the infantry—who were by trade mechanics—forthwith set
to work to manufacture packsaddles although there is
an excellent wagon trail. About sixty of these so-called
packsaddles were turned out during the day, though
what use they were no one knew, certainly not for
packing, as out of the lot probably not one was fit
for the purpose for which it was intended.

The next morning the mounted men proceeded to
General Strange's camp, reaching it before noon,
and shortly afterward that officer struck his tents
and moved in a northwesterly direction toward
Onion Lake, his campground being occupied by
General Middleton, who, with fifty men of each of
the 90th, 10th, and Midland Battalions, arrived during the afternoon.

About midnight on Wednesday a courier arrived and reported the fight between Major Steele's command and Big Bear's Indians at a lake placed from thirty-five to fifty-five miles distant, and at 4 A.M. on Thursday we were on the move following the trail, mounted men, infantry, Gatlings, and all. The packsaddles? Oh! yes! we did not forget the packsaddles, they were brought also—in the wagons.

I suppose the idea of wagons following an Indian trail through a thickly wooded country is rather startling in civilized people whose acquaintance with the noble red man is derived chiefly from the works of Fenimore Cooper or Parkman, but the Indian has sadly degenerated since the days of Pontiac, and the trail left by Big Bear was no faint and indistinct track made by men with moccasined feet in single file or any such absurdity, it was a broad road cut through the woods, better than many a Canadian bush road, beaten by the feet of some hundreds of men and horses and the wheels of nearly a hundred carts, for General Bear had carried off sundry spoils from the unfortunate settlers at Frog Lake, and over it horsemen could easily travel six miles an hour.

A mile or two out we found a relic of the Coulee fight in the shape of an Indian killed by the fragments of a shell. He was, I believe, coming out with a flag of truce when the brilliant youth in command of the gun made a target of him. I have further heard that he was the only Indian killed by the troops that day, so their shooting did not rise above the average.

About five miles from camp we hit upon an old cart trail from Fort Pitt leading in a northeasterly direction, and a halt was called, for deliberation very likely, as it was evident that the Indians had followed this old road and "such an extraordinary thing, you know, must be considered, by Jove." Saddles were taken off and the boys were rubbing down and looking to their horses, for it was understood that fifty miles were to be covered before camping, in fact, that we were to reach Loon Lake, the scene of Steele's fight, when up go the infantry tents and ours were ordered to follow their example.

The astonishment on every face and the curses "not loud but deep" heaped on the general's head could be understood and appreciated only by those present and, indeed, had I not actually been there I could hardly believe that a man calling himself a soldier and a general could dawdle and delay in such a ridiculous, senseless, and childish manner. When one remembers that he had some two hundred men in his command and that forty miles distant along a cart trail, Major Steele with forty-six men had the previous morning attacked probably thrice that number of Indians, driven them out of their camp, and was at that moment waiting for us; that each horseman could carry from three to five days' provisions and reach the scene that night; that supplies and forage could be rapidly pushed along the trail after us; and that had even half the horses been killed by the journey, their loss would have been as nothing compared with the value of a decisive blow, and the Indians were so demoralized by Steele's attack that we should have been able to demand their surrender and the delivery of the prisoners, some of whom were women and children, or to obliterate the whole tribe.

And what is done? The camp is turned into a factory for travails, as if the idiocy of useless packsaddles were not enough, and from about 10 A.M. on Thursday until Friday night, nearly two days, we are in camp pottering over these primitive conveyances. What is a travail? As many people have never seen a travail or travoie, I will try to describe one. Suppose a couple of long poles between which a horse is harnessed as between the shafts of a cart. The rear ends of the poles trail on the ground and the load is carried on a framework of cross-bars just clear of the horse's hind legs and you have a travail; but do not think you can imagine how small a load can be transported on one or what antics a horse accustomed to the civilized harness of a double team would perform when he found himself saddled with this primitive style of go-cart.

On Friday night the infantry were sent back to Fort Pitt and next morning, after this very necessary halt in our rapid forced march (?), we moved forward again, mounted men, Gatlings, wagons—oh, yes! wagons— and the travails?—packed on top of the wagons.

A few miles on we found Steele and his command— that officer not having been able to follow up his advantage from lack of supplies and ammunition—and at once notice the genius and forethought required to make a forced march with due regard for the proprieties. What a vast advantage education confers on a man; here is Steele, a poor ignorant devil of a Canadian, with his seventy men away up in this blawsted, howling wilderness, you know, and no wagons, no tents, no comforts; positively nothing, you know. We come upon a little open patch and see drawn up and waiting for us Major Steele's troop of mounted men, bronzed by sun and wind and toughened by hardship and exposure. Led by a MAN and unencumbered by red tape, they had pushed rapidly after these Indians, fought and beaten them and, after waiting vainly for support for two days, were now ready to show us the way. Truly they are like the scouts one used to read about, and yet, beyond some few lines barely mentioning the fight, I have seen nothing written of this plucky officer and his command.

We feel a conscious superiority in our great leader's method of procedure when we contrast the victorious march of our host with that of Steele. With us everything has been done with regard for dignity and thought and the eternal fitness of things. Travails, packsaddles, wagons, Gatlings, supplies, surgeons, and hospital comforts, and all that is the correct thing where speed is required. Orders are issued at night with unfailing exactness and the start in the morning is never more than an hour or two behind time. Couriers take dispatches southward and special warcorrespondents chronicle our advance and describe the terrible nature of our many hardships in such glowing terms that all Canada stands amazed at the marvellous determination of our gifted commander, and if the fact of there being prisoners in Big Bear's hands who are every day getting further from us comes to our remembrance at times, we are so satisfied with our own greatness that they trouble us but little. Who dare judge us?

The Survey Corps formed the pioneer troop and, although delayed by "brushing up" some of the mud holes of this impassable (?) trail, we cover nearly twenty miles in a short day. Now and then we crossed soft mud holes and occasionally horses and indifferent riders parted company therein. Once, indeed, his generalship, the commander-in-chief, afforded us some little amusement by sliding over his horse's quarters and coming down in a most undignified sitting posture in the rich black mud. He did not fall with grace either, being somewhat of the build of Falstaff and of a very much brighter complexion — and I regret to say that the respect due his rank did not smother the laughter of the boys as he climbed into the saddle again. How we wished that the mud hole had been bottomless and that he had sunk out of sight but there was no such luck; like the Old Man of the Sea he rides his Canadian Sinbad and we cannot so easily get rid of him.

Next day (Sunday) was a repetition of the former. The dense and impenetrable forest is small poplar averaging the thickness of a man's arm growing over a gently rolling country with occasional small ponds and marshes, and the faint trail is a good bush road. There are very few mud holes of any account and scarce one blackfly or mosquito to worry men or horses. Nature, too, is aiding us as she best can, for

Lewis Redman Ord

brighter or more delightful weather is seldom seen.
We have left our tents at the camp of Sunday morning and so our flying column continues its forced
march into the trackless wilderness. We halt for noon
near One-Horse Lake and the wagons overtake us; his
generalship lunches near us and we remember that
song of the major-general in the "Pirates of Penzance."

"And when I know precisely what is meant by
'Commissariat'" as we look over our hard tack and
corned beef and see him tucking into marmalade,
jam, etc—(oh! we're a hardy lot, we are, we are, we
are!). Then we remount and forward again and the
monotony is broken by the sight of a sorrel horse
across the valley in which lies One-Horse Lake. A
horse does not count for much, particularly as it is
one lately belonging to Steele's command, but of
course some bright youth in his vivid imagination
sees two men and we thirst for gore as we handle our
rifles and send back word to the Great Mogul who
tells us to "keep a couple of men dismounted ahead"
and otherwise provides for our safety.

Here the country becomes a little more uneven and
a mile or so further on we ford a small rapid stream
and shortly afterward strike probably the same
stream, now sluggish and deep. A single-track bridge
crosses it and the axes of the pioneer corps soon
make this large enough for our wagons so that nightfall sees us reach the hill overlooking the scene of
Steele's encounter with the Indians at Loon Lake, the
immense distance of about eighteen miles from the
morning start-point.

That was a plucky fight, and one for which Major Steele and his troop deserve real credit. If one believes General Strange's report of the Stand Up Coulee affair, Steele must have here attacked six hundred Indians, and even putting their numbers at one hundred and fifty (it is probable that these are the six hundred), it was the most dashing skirmish of the whole campaign. Major Steele's available men were forty-six in number[13] making the odds three to one and yet our Great I Am, with over two hundred and fifty men and two Gatlings, seems afraid to overtake these same Indians.

All along the trail, wherever an abandoned Indian camp was passed, there was a rush for loot and trophies, and as the general and his aides could not always be first in, he had issued orders on Sunday that no one was to go ahead of the advance guard or leave camp after halting, for somehow Gatling Howard, who was with the column, always managed to get before the commander. And now when we camped on the hill at Loon Lake his generalship and aide proceed down into the Indian camp on a tour of inspection, the Mogul flattering himself that at last he is successful and the first man in. Visions of furs better than those he got at Batoche fill his mind's eye when he sees a figure moving about among the tepee poles and begins to wish for his bodyguard and Gatlings, for may it not mean Indians and scalping?—and what a prize the chief of the soldiers would make for Big Bear! Why, the army would be lost without all that skill to direct it! But the figure sauntered out into full view, and instead of the dirty blanket of an Indian it wears a neat dark blue jacket with brass buttons, riding breeches into the pockets of which its hands are thrust and immense boots and a forage cap is tipped carelessly on the back of its head. Doubt and dismay fill the general's mind; nearer it comes, whistling a quickstep, unarmed save for a pistol in its right boot, kicking over and examining abandoned stores as though there were not an Indian in the country and the general, his fears replaced by offended dignity as he sees the very man his orders were aimed at, shouts out:

"D---n it! Can't I get anywhere before you?" for the tune is "Yankee Doodle" and the man is the Yankee Captain.

CHAPTER X

This turning in prepared to start with three days' provisions is getting a little tiresome, but the sight of the
battleground has livened us up a bit and we lay our
heads on our saddles on this Sunday night, hoping
that at last our commander is going to show his energy
and that the early move tomorrow really means business. The wagons are to be left behind guarded by
the Gatling batteries and French's Scouts and the rest
of us with three days' provisions are in the saddle at
6 A.M. It is our turn to form the advance guard and
we move forward to take the lead, when Captain
Haig meets us and crushes our hopes with orders to
move back to our ground as new information has arrived, so we mentally swear at the general as we
gloomily obey.

What the information is the Lord only knows, but
we wait until 9:30 and then again, followed by the
wagons, ford the lake and continue on the trail. As we
leave camp, alongside the path we come upon another
and more ghastly sign of the enemy—the first Indian
killed by Steele's band—and I guess that if ever there
was a Nitchie astonished that was the one. Big Bear
had so poor an opinion of white men after his brushes
with General Strange that he scarcely dreamed of being followed and when Steele reached the hill overlooking his camp at Loon Lake on Wednesday morning, he was totally unexpected by the Indians, who in
fancied security were striking their lodges below.

While moving his men forward to the attack on foot through the brush, the Indian picket starts back along the trail to scout for signs of the soldiers. He probably does it only as a matter of form and he feels uncommonly fit after his "tuck in" of pork and etceteras — spoils of his bow and spear at Frog Lake such as he never got from the Indian Department — as he rides up the hill where the scouts lie, for his heels joggle Indian fashion against the horse's ribs and he hums the monotonous "Hi-hi-hay, hay-hi-yah, hi-yah-hi-yah, hay-hi-yah" that is war song and every other song for him. But he is waited for, a scout hears him and with cocked rifle stands ready to help him sound the alarm. The dusky warrior, riding at a trot, appears over the crest of the hill; the low chant rises into an astonished yell cut short by the crack of the repeater, and the riderless horse gallops back to camp whilst the savage lies shot through the heart on the slope, and before the echoes of his voice have died away they are drowned by the rifles of Steele's men as they begin the pluckiest fight of the season.

Steele, as I have said, had forty-six men against probably one hundred and fifty and yet he attacked them, drove them out, and was only prevented from pushing his advantage by the arm of the lake, which he would have been obliged to cross under fire. After the affair, the Indians had come back and picked up their comrade and were probably taking him away when some alarm caused them to drop him and there he lay. The scouts had cut open the bundle to find out who he was and our friend has nothing but the blanket fastened to his neck as we pass him. He is a disgusting object but we think of the Frog Lake settlers and feel rather glad—you see, he is a good Indian now. Our general, reminded by the sight of Steele's success and jealous of it remarks that "some of our men are worse than the savages," but never issues any orders for the funeral of the dear departed. Nor did he at Batoche, I may add, leaving the dead rebels lying about the field. He did not at Fish Creek either, at least not immediately after the affair, but that was for a deuced good reason—he never got near enough to the field to see if there were any of the enemy killed or not.

We have no scruples about the Indian scout and, leaving him by the roadside, we ford the arm of the lake and proceed. Up and down among the hills the trail winds northeastward, past another campground and numbers of abandoned carts about three miles on, turns westward, and comes upon the lake where it discharges its waters, and northward toward the Beaver River. Another stoppage, more orders, more confusion; the river is not forty yards wide and the bottom is hard sand with only a dozen feet where a horse would have to swim, but it is quite enough to stop us. A lot of timber cut by the Indians for houses lies along the shore and after some of the usual delay for consideration, definite orders are issued to Colonel Herchmer's Police to make rafts, ferry the saddles and accoutrements, and swim the horses. Two rafts are in time put together, but the timber is green and heavy and each will hold only one or two saddles and two men, so it is likely to be a tedious process. We find an old canoe, leaky and nearly going to pieces, but a little heat applied to the seams of the birch bark makes it serve and we begin to ferry the Survey Corps' saddles until ordered to desist, as they might get mixed with those of the police. So we ferry policemen instead, nearly getting swamped by some of them and when they and their horses are on the west side we are very close behind them. All the mounted troops are across by nightfall and we camp in the woods close to the ferry, thus concluding another of our big days and forced marches by a distance of about six miles.

The road ends east of the ford, and the wagons can really come no further by this trail, so once more we begin to hope for a push along the well-beaten horse track before us, but our hitherto unshaken faith in the skill (?), energy (?), and untiring determination (?) of our chief is failing a little and the hope is a faint one. A stretch of marshy land lies west of us and close by our camp at the edge of this marsh, we found the body of an Indian woman. The poor creature was in a sort of kneeling position, her body hanging forward so as to throw its weight on the slender cord with which she had strangled herself. A small collie dog with poor Delaney's name on the collar was keeping guard over her and the faithful little brute was at first quite vicious when we came near. From this it was supposed that she had been a servant of Delaney's but some of the halfbreeds said that her husband was the surprised scout, that being a very heavy woman she had been left behind by the tribe and hearing our approach had committed suicide in preference to falling into our hands.

That night there was a grand council-of-war held in the great man-of-war's tent, and again three days' provisions and early start were on the bill of fare, and we roll ourselves up in our blankets by the fire and think this really looks like business; no tents, no wagons, no encumbrances; surely we are off in earnest now. We have had our supper of tea, hard tack, and corned beef, our horses have had a good feed of oats and with revived hopes of a shot at the noble red man, we glide off into dreamland and oblivion, when "crack!" goes a loud report in the middle of the sleeping men and every one is awake in a moment. Startled from the arms of Somnus to the reality, the hardship (?), and the danger (?) of our position, we behold by the flickering light of the fire our Parolles, who had been giving us a lecture about lying still in event of a night attack, tucking his shirt into his trousers with enough martial ardor in his eye to burn a hole through a blanket and then—"crack!" rings out another shot. We reach out for our rifle leaning against a tree at our head and wait for something to turn up. But nothing turns up; there is no such luck as a night attack, if any of us are green enough to expect one, and the shots prove to have been a couple of cartridges falling out of a policeman's belt into the fire over which it was drying; and grumbling and disappointed we go off to sleep again.

Perhaps the sound of a rifle shot, unheard for so long a time, brings back to our noble commander a remembrance of all the lives that are in his charge; perhaps he thinks there is too much risk in pushing forward and leaving his wagons and supplies;

perhaps—the Lord knows what. But after turning out at some unholy hour and making all preparations for an advance, our wretched horses are kept saddled standing in the campground—which by the way is spruce bush and every one knows what an excellent pasture for horses that must be—for about three hours and then we are told that the muskeg before us is quite impassable, etc., etc., and that we cannot go on.

Unfortunately we must obey, so after exploding a certain number of strong expressions, we turn the ponies out to feed in the marsh and set out to examine this terrible and insurmountable obstacle. We find that a stretch of wet land probably a mile across lies between us and the high ground to the west—low and marshy it is true, but covered with a thick growth of willows and, although it is somewhat soft above, the frost is still in the ground a foot below the surface, and horses can cross. There might be some bad spots but it would never stop a Canadian. However our disposer is not a Canadian (thank Heaven) so we walk south along the point on which our camp lies and confirm the opinion formed on the previous day. Big Bear knows that he is pursued by an old woman, and the crossing and recrossing of the lake is just a little dodge of his to throw the avenging angel off the scent, and very effectively he has done it. From the south extremity of the point we get a clearer and better view of the west shores of the lake than when riding up east of it yesterday, and are now certain that the whole column, wagons, Gatlings and all, could be easily moved up the west side through the small scattering timber until we hit the Indians' trail west of and beyond the marsh, thus avoiding lake, ford, and muskeg, and encountering no difficulties whatever, for the timber is small and scattered and the land unbroken by ravine or valley from Steele's battleground to opposite our camp. There is some little satisfaction in knowing this as regards ourselves but it only makes us think less of our commander than ever and we sulkily turn back to camp where we find that with the aid of the old canoe and a trolling spoon, Gatling and one of the troop have secured some fish, so we sit down to supper and drown sorrow and disgust in copious draughts of tea.

Oh! Tea; thou sublime and blessed infusion of sloe leaves, brown paper, bark, old rags, and general refuse! How flat would life be without thee! How often hast thou disguised the nauseous flavor of alkaline water in the summer heat of the plains and revived our shivering bodies when the mercury is shrivelled up until it is solid! What zest dost thou lend to the ubiquitous pork and beans of our native land and now, as we follow our hardy and indefatigable leader far into the impenetrable forests of the frozen north, fighting and bleeding and suffering, and swearing and all the rest of it for our beloved and grateful country. How thankful do we feel that the idiots who manage the transport and commissariat services have not succeeded in robbing us of thee! They may take our beans and our dried apples, our bacon and our sugar, our molasses and our flour, and they have done so; but with thee, as we dissect the dark and bloody mystery that bears the name of Armour[14] and break our last set of teeth on the biscuits of Portage la Prairie;

with thee we can forget even the imbecility of our leaders and suffer and be strong.

Those were pleasant evenings round the campfire; Gatling Howard, full of amusing anecdote and reminiscence, made one of us; we all had roughed it in bush and plain, and again we stalked deer and antelope, brought down the strong winged bird, or hooked our biggest salmon over our game of cribbage as if we were out on a picnic, not a single blackfly or mosquito, and such delicious cool nights. Verily old dame Nature is showing us the pleasant side of her face and were it not for the glint of the firelight on pistol or rifle or the bad language of some hot-tempered comrade impatient at our delay, we could almost forget our errand and the skilful tactician commanding us.

And whilst we chaff and spin yarns and score up the points around our fire, at the general's tent is gathered a solemn conclave considering the weighty responsibility of risking our valuable lives in attempting this bottomless morass over which some hundreds of Indians and ponies have crossed within two days. And a brilliant and most intelligent lot they are: a major-general, a captain of Royal Engineers, an infantry lieutenant, an Indian Department official, and a major of militia, each knowing less than the other, offer suggestions and advice *ad nauseam*. Herchmer and Steele are not asked for opinions for our disposer does not admire the police, and the council, after much deliberation, having little brains to guide them, evolve the following plan:

More early starting, rationed for the usual three days, and tomorrow morning we are to cross the muskeg in the following order: Boulton, Steele, Surveyors, and lastly Herchmer's Police. That looks all right but there is a philosophy in such order of going that may be thus translated: Boulton is Steele's senior and therefore will be in command and Boulton, who is all red tape, will wait until ordered to go on, and keep Steele also. Had Herchmer gone first—well, Herchmer is Boulton's senior, and with him in command their respective guardian angels would need to look sharp after Big Bear's skin and the general's credit for the devil of a rag of either would be left. I may add that Boulton told me afterward that it would have been very risky to leave the guns and wagons. Had Herchmer with the mounted men once got across that muskeg, as he could have crossed, he would have been on top of the Indian camp while his commander was wondering whether there was any jam for dinner or not.

However, we have orders to cross and we turn in for a good night's sleep, confident even to the last that the "big push" is to be made and that before tomorrow's sunset we shall be squaring accounts with Big Bear. But, alas! once more we have built our hopes on too feeble a foundation and with the morrow comes the musical voice of the aide telling our captain that "The general has sent me to tell you he has made up his mind to return to Fort Pitt." We are now getting so accustomed to it that we don't swear very much, too sick of the vacillation of our commander to do much but swear mildly at ourselves for expecting anything else. Last night, mind you, the orders were to cross and pursue, but when the captains have retired, each to his particular spruce tree and the general is left alone in his tent—the only tent in the camp—the frightful risk of going far away from the Gatlings and wagons, of putting long stretches of forest between himself and his preserve and marma-lade jars, of braving the attack of the deadly blackfly and gore-seeking mosquito, of sleeping on the hard ground with his bones cushioned by only his half-dozen blankets and their natural clothing of fat, the awful hazard thus pictured must have been too much for him.

If these are not his reasons we have yet to hear them, as our opinion of his reasoning faculties is thus aptly expressed in the words of Shakespeare:

GENERAL. My honest lads I will tell you what I am about.
CANADIAN. Two yards and more.

Another probable reason may have been that he would have been obliged to leave behind the spring mattress he slept on (a spring mattress sent out for the wounded, but used by the great man while waiting for casualties—just to keep its springs soft, I suppose; so hardy and energetic a soldier would scorn any other pretext).

But the result of his cogitations is that we are ordered to retreat and we recross the river by the flimsy floating bridge that has been built over it, carrying the saddles and swimming the horses, carefully destroy the travails and the old canoe, and burn a lot of carts abandoned by the Indians at their last camp. Destroying of bridges is, of course, one of the rules of etiquette observed by all great militarists, so our Xerxes orders his soldiery to carry out this strategical move—we are not to lose a point of scientific training in the art of war, if he can help it—and we faithfully obey. Many of the carts were owned by settlers at Frog Lake and other places and as they could go no further north would all be taken back southward by the Indians and very likely handed over to the Indian Department when this little storm is over; and for the rest that belonged to the Indians, well in most cases they were supplied by the government and burning them only gives the said government another opportunity of spending money and giving another lot to their grateful red pensioners, so it is as well to burn them all. Leaving behind us such impedimenta as packsaddles and travails, neither of which had been used, and turning our backs upon Big Bear's supposed position, we wind southward among the hills toward the Saskatchewan and our general shows a rapidity of movement and steadfast determination of purpose that would greatly astonish us if displayed in any other strategic evolution than that of retreat. Indeed this expedition is marvellous for him, for we cover in one day the distance it had taken two to compass on the forward march and camp at our old ground on Saturday night. Thursday brings us within a few miles of Fort Pitt and early next morning we rejoin the main body of the brigade on the hill above the ruined post and begin to think of the trip back to civilization. But we are premature. Long before nightfall rumors hum over the camp that General Strange has found a cache of three hundred bags of flour at the Beaver River and that Big Bear is making in that direction. Why the devil Big Bear should be supposed to be such a helpless imbecile as to rush into the seductive embraces of even General Strange this deponent sayeth not, but our "Warrior" evidently thinks him fool enough and fearful that some of his own laurels may fall upon his brother general, resolves upon another of his deeply planned and skilfully executed strategic movements.

Chapter XI

Oh, lucky infantry! blessed by being left alone. Upon us poor devils of mounted men devolves the glory of carrying out this one more hazardous and daring stroke and on Saturday morning after a night's rest in the camp of our comrades of the scarlet and black tunics, Herchmer's, Steele's, and Boulton's troops, the Gatlings and Survey Corps, leave for Frog Lake and covering the intervening thirty-odd miles, camp near the tents of the Midland Battalion close to the ruins of the once thriving little settlement.

I know of no sight more striking in all this campaign than the graves of two of the murdered settlers buried by the Midland Battalion. Lying one on each side of the trail just where the poor fellows made their last stand and were shot down in cold blood, the little mounds over them marked by a simple wooden cross, will for many years be a monument to cowardly treachery and a warning against trusting an Indian unless the scoundrel is dead.

We are off early on Sunday morning and, leaving the Saskatchewan road, take a trail that skirts the west side of Frog Lake and runs in a northeasterly direction to the Beaver River. General Strange's column has already passed along it and it is in excellent condition, and the day's march brings us to the house where this enormous quantity of supplies was discovered. The said cache, however, proved upon inspection to consist of about thirty bags of flour instead of three hundred and they were guarded by a detachment of the 92nd Winnipeg.

Having heard that the general had asked for volunteers to locate Big Bear's camp—(I may say now that I believe this report was a lie pure and simple and write myself down a most egregious ass for giving it a moment's credence)—I went over to copy orders and found Captain Haig divesting himself of his garments and getting ready for bed, in other words, taking off his breeches. I copied the orders and then told the gallant captain that, hearing that the general had asked for volunteers, we begged to offer our services, whereupon a mountain of blankets in the tent became disturbed by a gigantic convulsion and a huge red face surmounted by a woollen nightcap appeared.

"What's that?" said the Mogul.

I repeated my remarks.

"Who are you?"

"Survey Corps, sir."

"You think you can find Big Bear's camp?"

"Sure of it!"

"Well, I've no doubt your services will be of great value and as soon as we reach the Beaver I'll make use of you."

"Thank you, sir," and I retire.

We have talked the matter over and feel confident we can hit Big Bear's trail west of the muskeg (?) that stopped our commander in a day or a little more and thence it will be child's play to locate the camp if we get the chance; but truly there is much virtue in it, for next morning we reach General Strange's camp only a few miles north and, although we tackle the general and his aide again, we get no satisfaction and have to give it up.

We camped on a pretty strip of prairie land near the little mission church at the Beaver and though we growled a good deal at the inactivity and fired curses at the general for this one more fool's errand, our horses enjoy the rest and feed on the succulent grass and vetches that they have not had for many a day, and we ourselves improve the shining hour by taking several baths—true, we have no soap and no change of clothes, having worn our present suit since we left Battleford—but we wash our shirts in the creek and button our jackets over our manly breasts until the shirts are dry enough to put on again. Tuesday, Wednesday, and Thursday were thus spent by us but our gallant leader was so greatly concerned and worried over the fate of the prisoners in Big Bear's hands that he occupied himself by a fishing trip out to Gold Lake a few miles away for the last two days.

On Thursday Steele's command was sent by General Strange back to Frog Lake to investigate more discoveries, and the same evening the Mogul returned without any fish and, in consequence of his ill luck and General Strange daring to take so important a step without consulting him, was as savage as the proverbial bear with the sore head. Further word reaches camp that a brush box with Miss McLean's name on it had been found near Turtle Lake and as I copy orders at the general's tent, Captain Haig, R.E., who gives me this little piece of news, expresses his thankfulness that "There is something reliable at last," which gratitude is no doubt shared by his superior, for the orders are for an early march and return to Fort Pitt tomorrow. The discovery of a brush box, forsooth, is considered reliable information and yet a few days ago we were on the Indian trail and within a short distance of their camp—for I am told they heard the two cartridges accidentally exploded at Loon Lake—and abandoned the pursuit. Comment is scarcely necessary.

However, we need not excite ourselves over this valuable and important discovery of female toilet paraphernalia and we are spared another wild goose chase to Turtle Lake by the return of Indian scouts sent out by General Strange with the report that Big Bear's band had been split up, that the prisoners, including the owner of the brush box, had been kept by the friendly Wood Cree and afterward released by them, and were now on their way to Fort Pitt.

On Friday the reveille sounds at 4 A.M. and at 5:30 General Middleton's division was on its way back along the trail southward. Of course, it was now too late to do any rescuing, but our general was off, before any of us, at high speed in a light wagon to receive the thanks and gratitude of those poor prisoners, the safety of whose lives bear witness to his indomitable perseverance, fertile resources, and untiring energy; for after the account I have given I need not say that Big Bear's experience of this terrible adversary must have taught him that General Middleton was determined to get between him and the North Pole—that being the natural habitat of Ursa Major, where he probably had more flour cached—if it took all summer, and worn out by the bloodhound nature of his pursuer, threw up the game and let the prisoners go.

By sundown we were once more at Frog Lake where many of us were banqueted by the Midland Battalion who had received sundry dainties from Ontario, and after so long a penance on corned beef and hard tack we could thoroughly appreciate the many good things set before us, so many indeed that even our plainsman's appetites succumb and, after super-human efforts and many returns to the attack, we are forced to cry enough. Chief among his officers, in his efforts to make us comfortable as in everything else, pressing good things upon each in turn of the dusty and ragged scouts who are his guests, one pleasant remembrance not easily to be effaced, is that of the gentlemanly, courteous, and cordial hospitality of the Midland commander, in whose death a few days later the country sustained a severe loss and one not soon to be replaced.[15]

A few hours' ride on Saturday brought us to Fort Pitt, where our Alexander, "tired of the long war," is content to let us potter about aimlessly for another week, when at last the fact there is no excuse for detaining us longer pierces even his massive intellect, and orders are given us to return to Moose Jaw and home. On Monday, June 29th, our emancipation day, we find ourselves on the south side of the Saskatchewan eastward bound and as we look back at the white tents of the troops a solemn oath goes up to never volunteer again until major-generals of a different material are forthcoming. And now comparatively free—subject to the petty whims of only our Parolles whose infantile blunders have been clouded by the elephantine stupidity and gigantic bungles of the major-general, as the unpleasant whiff of a bad cigar is obliterated by the overpowering odor of a Chinese stink-pot of the largest size—we are almost happy. In a very few days even his little reign will be over, so with a sigh of heartfelt thankfulness we turn our horses' heads eastward—and—good-bye.

CHAPTER XII

As Canadians, we may learn a valuable lesson from this campaign if we can look at it sensibly and teach our rulers to drop some of their red tape. Educated as we have been under the wing of the Imperial Government—with Great Britain and her great men and great deeds as examples of all that is just, wise, and valiant—descended from Englishmen or United Empire Loyalists, we find it hard to dissent from our fathers in their faith and reverence for everything British. Before this 1885 rebellion, we had been taught to respect and revere British military skill and prowess as equalled by possibly only that of Germany, but this experience of ours causes us to wonder whether this is not all idolatry, and whether our modern representatives of these gods and heroes are not mere creatures of very ordinary clay. The cast-iron conceit of an Englishman stiffens him out with the idea that an Englishman is better at anything than any other man can be, and we have inherited a little of this snobbishness. Even in this little affair in our own country much senseless bosh in the way of heaping credit pell-mell upon everything and everyone in any manner connected with the management has been indulged in. The correspondents of a few of the newspapers placed matters in a truthful light, but as a rule the journalists daubed praise over everything, flinging most of it over the general, it is true, but letting a good many undeserved drops fall upon those under him. No doubt the volunteers deserve credit for their response to the call their country made upon them. It was their duty, and right well did they perform that duty, and better would they have performed it had they been more fortunate in their leaders. But let us give them no more credit than they do deserve. This trash about the fearful hardships they suffered—the cold and wet and misery, the long and arduous forced marches, the exposure to an Arctic climate—looks very well on paper and doubtless gives the boys a rare chance of spreading themselves as heroes and veterans, but did it never strike the paragraphists who indulge in it that it is hardly a good advertisement of our Canadian Northwest. Most of the stories of hardship are lies—in good plain language, lies—and the reality not nearly as bad as about half of countrymen endure year in and year out without a murmur. True, it may be urged that as we travelled to Winnipeg over the U.S. lines we did not suffer the misery of the men who were sent via the then unfinished Canadian Pacific Railway. Possibly there was some little cold weather for men who lived sedentary lives and had only camped out for pleasure, but I have asked many of the engineers and employees on the construction of the railway over which they were carried, and all agree that there were no extremes of cold at the time the troops passed through. So I am inclined to think that accounts of this part of the expedition, as well as all the rest, have been greatly exaggerated.

For privations—well, that it is a privation to have to live on corned beef and hard tack with scarce a change of diet for several months and submit to the vagaries of an old woman for the same length of time I will admit, particularly as both are unnecessary evils and although I have had no small share of hard food and rough work in my life, that submission was the most severe trial I ever experienced.

"Obedience is the first duty of a soldier," says the time-honored saw, and obedience toward the officer directing was always shown. But I maintain that we have the right to criticise his conduct if we can and also that of his brother general. In defence of the latter, I have heard men who served on his division urge that he was hampered by his superior's commands about engaging the enemy and support his conduct of the action at Stand Up Coulee by saying that he really could not depend upon the Johnny Canuck part of his brigade. Possibly so, but these arguments cannot be brought in support of the Great Bungler, and after an impartial review of the management of the campaign I defy anyone of ordinary common sense to endorse any credit given for forethought, energy, military skill, etc. Nothing but contempt can be felt for the vacillating and undecided manner in which this responsible trust was carried out, and the childish and narrow selfishness, and envy of all credit earned by other officers during the campaign, is worthy of scorn. Witness the treatment of Colonel Otter and his movement to Beaver River to forestall General Strange and subsequent return to Fort Pitt to receive the released prisoners.

I have heard it argued that the delay making pack-saddles and travails and tardy pursuit (?) of Big Bear was only prudence, that he must wait for supplies as his command might be cut off and starved and all the rest of it. Utter bosh every word. Major Steele with seventy-two men was far in front of him with but little provisions or ammunition and, had the enemy been in such force as to necessitate the caution (?) observed by General Middleton with his two-hundred-odd, they would have turned upon Steele and swept him and his troop out of existence, while the commander-in-chief was waiting for his (private) supplies (of delicacies) to arrive.

It will be replied also that the many halts were made because the information furnished the general by the scouts was unreliable, that he never knew of the muskeg, etc., etc. Possibly. I knew only two of the halfbreed scouts—two men as honest and trustworthy as any in the Territories—and as for their reports not being accurate—well, they were only accustomed to guiding men, and it is natural that they should omit to talk of little mud puddles; and if the general could not trust them, why did he not make use of his white scouts whom he not only neglected to employ, but who were distinctly ordered not to scout or leave camp?

Of course he pandered to the Canadian public by giving all sorts of praise to his troops—which "taffy" the troops swallowed delightedly—but as he patted their backs he patted his own: "You are a hardy lot of men and good soldiers. Great difficulties you have overcome and severe hardship you have endured and I was your leader and if you deserve honor, much more do I," is in fact all his laudation of the volunteers can mean, for to decry his troops would be to decry himself.

His jealousy of Howard I can well understand when I remember that that officer's name was coupled with his own in Winnipeg and many parts of Canada as one of the chief characters of the campaign. "Canada First" is my motto but everyone must admit that Howard was a hundred times better fitted to command the expedition than any other officer except Colonel Williams, or Herchmer or Steele of the police, and it is quite natural that any of these should incur the major-general's dislike. But his deprecation of the Gatlings since his return is puzzling and rather inconsistent when one remembers that, not content with the machine gun that joined his column after Fish Creek, he took the other from Colonel Otter and that wherever he went the two guns accompanied him. Even up into the bush and brush of Loon Lake and the Beaver, where there was really some doubt as to their utility, they followed the column and the obstacle that stopped them turned him back also. As to their value in action, let us place against his great authority the opinion of two men who have seen perhaps as much service as he has — Lord Wolseley and Lord Charles Beresford — who believe that "the machine gun is the gun of the future."

I cannot overlook the management, or rather the mismanagement of the transport and commissariat services, as I regard both as having been simply disgraceful. Although the Militia Department was most bountiful in its purchase of supplies for the troops, tons of stores never reached the men, notwithstanding the immense number of transport teams employed in addition to the steamers on the Saskatchewan — a number amply sufficient, had they been properly looked after, which they decidedly were not. But we were surveyors, having been accustomed to rough it, though we grumbled a good deal at times. I have not dwelt as much as I might upon the inefficiency of these departments. It is to be hoped that someone made money out of it and I have no doubt someone did, although the carelessness and ignorance of the officials is blamable and I have yet to hear how the commissariat and transport officers can be exonerated.

In excuse of General Middleton, it should be remembered that this was probably the first occasion wherein he had to depend upon his own resources. He had seen service as a young man but had been merely perhaps a brave officer carrying out the instructions of a superior and relying upon that superior's ability and not upon himself.

The office of Major-General Commanding the Militia of Canada had been, previous to 1885, as far as active generalship went, almost a sinecure and was probably filled by the imperial authorities with officers possessing no particular ability or genius, but a good deal of political influence, and it is possible that this latter gained the position for General Middleton. The rebellion took place. He was placed in command of about 5,000 men to attack at most one-fifth of that number. The government was most lavish in everything in the way of supplies. Knowing nothing of the country or method of travel and blinded with a sense of his own importance, he was above advice of any kind and, from the day he left Qu'Appelle until his return to Winnipeg, his course was one continued series of gross blunders, the result of conceit and stupidity. The rebels made no attack upon him and he reached Clarke's Crossing unopposed; the rest of the campaign I have tried to write up; and it is curious to remark that every useful engagement with the rebels was undertaken either without his orders or in direct opposition to them. Well, the troops were in the end successful as they were bound to be. The Northwest Territories may be grateful to the general, for far more money got into the country through him than would have been spent had the control of affairs been in the hands of a more efficient commander, who would have crushed the disturbance in a month, but the rest of Canada who had to pay does not owe him any thanks. It is true that the hasty and too-liberal wiseheads who make our laws voted him $20,000 and no doubt they are sorry for it. But let us thank the moral and mental weakness of the rebel forces rather than the skill of General Middleton for the return of peace and order. Had the rebels, poorly armed and badly organized as they were, been led by a plucky and determined captain, instead of lauding General Middleton, the country would be mourning the loss of hundreds of her young men, sacrificed by his unfitness to command. Such a disturbance may never and it is to be hoped will never occur again; but it is our duty to provide efficient means to quell such an uprising in the event of its taking place and at home we must look for these means. We have the men, as the campaign proved—for our own country and our own defence our rank and file can hold their own—and we have the officers, too.

Is it not quite time that this appointing British officers should be done away with? If we must have a major-general commanding the militia, we can find thoroughly able Canadians to fill the post, far more competent than either of the generals in active command in the Northwest and more worthy than many who have led British troops elsewhere. For no matter what Englishmen may think of the Zulu, Boer, and Sudan campaigns, the rest of the world knows very well that a great deal of the generalship in these, as well as in our own humble little affair, was a most disgraceful bungle.

Notes

1. John Stoughton Dennis, 1856–1938, was the son of J.S. Dennis of Red River fame. Like his father, the younger Dennis was a surveyor with some military pretensions. After the rebellion, he went on to a long and distinguished career in government and business. He was Chief Inspector of Surveys for the Canadian Government, Chief Commissioner of the Department of Public Works for the Northwest Territories, Chief Commissioner of Colonization and Development for the C.P.R., and, in 1917, President of the Engineering Institute of Canada. During the First World War he was Director of Transportation and Intelligence for the Canadian Brigade in Siberia. See *The Canadian Surveyor*. 6, no. 7 (January 1939): 26.

2. The author refers to Dennis as Parolles throughout the rest of the book. The quotation is from Shakespeare's *All's Well That Ends Well*, act IV, scene III: "this is Monsieur Parolles, the gallant militarist—that was his own phrase—that had the whole theorie of war in the knot of his scarf, and the practice in the chape of his dagger."

3. Lieutenant-Colonel George Taylor Denison was a well-known Toronto militia officer who had written a prize-winning history of cavalry. Denison participated in the Rebellion as commander of the Governor-General's Body Guards.

4. The Sioux referred to here were remnants of those who had sought refuge north of the border when pursued by the U.S. Army after the Minnesota massacre of 1862.

5. The phrase "another ten thousand" undoubtedly refers to Sir John A. Macdonald's infamous telegram to Sir Hugh Allan, during the Pacific Scandal election of 1872. Ord's readers in the 1880s would immediately grasp the implied insult.

6. "Shemōgonsūe" would appear to be Ord's transliteration of the Cree word "Simākunisehkaw," which means "he keeps order" and could thus be roughly translated as "soldier." "Okeemagh," usually spelled "Okeemaw" in modern usage, means "leader" or "chief."

7. Hotspur was the nickname of Sir Henry Percy, son of the Duke of Northumberland, who rebelled against Henry IV. The name is a synonym for rashness and impetuosity. See Shakespeare, *Henry IV, Part I*.

8. Ord's estimate of Middleton's version of the numbers on each side is remarkably accurate. Middleton reported to Caron several days after Batoche that the rebels numbered 500 and his own men 480. See Desmond Morton and Reginald H. Roy, eds., *Telegrams of the North-West Campaign 1885* (Toronto: Champlain Society, 1972) p. 298, Middleton to Caron, 18 May 1885.

9. Ernest J. Chambers was a Montreal reporter who accompanied the Batoche column and later became a prolific writer of military and regimental histories.

10. The general and two other officers, Hayter Reed and S.L. Bedson, had appropriated some furs belonging to a Métis named Charles Bremner, who was arrested for having a rifle belonging to a mounted policeman killed in the rebellion. Ironically, in view of later events, the furs were promptly stolen by someone else and Middleton never saw them again. Bremner, a very persistent man, pursued the matter for five years after the rebellion. Finally in 1890 it was investigated by a Select Committee of the House of Commons. The committee found Middleton's actions to be illegal, and the scandal forced him to resign the presidency of an insurance company.

11. Zenophon (usually spelled Xenophon in modern usage) was a Greek historian of the fourth cenutury B.C. His most famous work, *Anabasis*, tells the story of the retreat of ten thousand Greek soldiers from Mesopotamia after an unsuccessful rebellion against Persia.

12. Ord is mistaken about this date. It should be 2 June.

13. Seventy is the correct number of Steele's men at Loon Lake, not forty-six. S.B. Steele, *Forty Years in Canada* (New York, 1915), p. 224.

14. This is a reference to the canned beef obtained by the Canadian government in Chicago. Early in the campaign there were rumors that it had been poisoned by the Fenians.

15. Lieutenant-Colonel Arthur Williams, M.P., died of typhoid fever as the troops were on their way home.

The Diary of Lieutenant R.S. Cassels

■

Northwest Field Force,
March 30th to July 23rd,
1885

Richard Scougall Cassels

MONDAY, MARCH 30TH

Today at 12:15 P.M. we steam slowly away from the Union Station, sadly parting from our many friends but soon regaining cheerfulness at the thought that work lies before us. After the excitement and strain of the past two days, we appreciate the luxury of rest, and we quietly settle down and make ourselves comfortable. That is, as comfortable as we can in our very crowded quarters. Much speculation is indulged in as to the chances of the rebellion collapsing before we reach the Northwest and the general impression seems to be that it will not be necessary for us to pass Winnipeg.

On our train are "C" Company Infantry School Corps —eighty men—under Major Smith, Mr. Wadmore, and Mr. Sears and our own Queen's Own contingent. We have been ordered to bring 250 men only, but inspection by the adjutant discloses the fact that twenty-three extra men have smuggled themselves on board. Our officers are as follows: Colonel Miller; Major Allan; Surgeon Lesslie; Captain and Adjutant Delamere; Quartermaster Heakes; Captains Brown, Kersteman, McGee, and McDonald; Lieutenants Mutton, Hughes, Brock, Cassels, Gunther, Scott, Lee, and George. The 10th Grenadiers contingent are to follow us on another train. Colonel Otter, in command of the Toronto Brigade, comes with us. He appoints Sears his brigade major and Dr. Strange, brigade surgeon. We have also on board reporters of the *Globe* and *Mail* and Mr. Cunningham and Mr. Doucet,[1] the latter a brother-in-law of the general and at present an engineer on the Canadian Pacific Railway.

I almost feel as if the last two days had been a dream. At one o'clock on Saturday morning I am roused by the adjutant, told of the Duck Lake affair, and notified that the regiment is called out. After that one had no time to collect one's thoughts. Scurrying from house to house during the night warning the men, parading in the morning, and remaining in the drill shed till two; then when orders reach us that 250 men only are required, choosing the lucky ones and seeing to their proper equipment; inspection in the evening by Colonel Otter—no time is left on the Saturday, certainly, for one's own affairs. Sunday is somewhat quieter, but much remains to be done. The parade for distribution of toques, mufflers, and underclothing takes much time, and then odd matters remain to be looked after, so that on this day, too, one is allowed no rest and today, of course, until we reach our train, we do not even try to think of anything. Now I can analyze my feelings about this affair and I came to the conclusion that I am very lucky to have the chance to go. Naturally, one feels a little troubled at leaving one's friends in this indefinite way, but change is pleasant and one is sure to see something worth seeing, and then with so many good fellows with one, loneliness is scarcely to be feared.

The first thing that rouses us after we leave Toronto is the sight of the Yorkville station. We rush out here and have a glimpse at several friends. After this we have an uneventful run to Peterborough, reaching that place about four. We find here a Guard of Honor drawn up at the station and as we pass they salute and cheer us. Heavy sleet and rain all day and little to be seen.

About 11 P.M. we reach Carleton Junction and here have supper, much to our gratification. Each man has brought a certain amount of provender with him, but cold snacks do not properly take the place of our accustomed hot meals. The accommodation at Carleton is limited and the men are fed in relays so that much time is consumed in the process of consumption. The officers wait till the last. I am in luck and get on the soft side of a pretty waiting girl who gives me eight cups of very good coffee without a murmur.

At Carleton I have the very great pleasure of a chat with Mrs. Blake.[2] She has come down from Ottawa with Mr. Beatty and Mr. Mulock[3] to say good-bye and presents us with a flag. The Grenadiers catch up to us at Carleton, but we leave before them.

TUESDAY, MARCH 31ST

We leave Carleton Junction about two this morning and turn in at once. "Turn in" means literally "turn in," for unless we do that and curl ourselves up in almost inconceivable attitudes, sleep is an impossibility. We manage to rest, however, to a by no means unsatisfactory extent.

Early in the afternoon we reach Mattawa and are furnished with a very good dinner. Then we are allowed an hour or two to stretch our legs and wander up, to, and through the village—a most beautiful place it is. The stores of the hamlet do a thriving trade—moccasins—"Creefee" and Indian are purchased in quantities and everything in the shape of canned stuff eagerly bought up. As we are about to leave the station, Major Allan[4] discovers that he has lost his purse and a large sum of money and remains behind to look for it, intending to come on with the Grenadiers whose train comes in as we depart.

We see now some very wild but very beautiful scenery—much like that of the lower St. Lawrence. The river—snow-covered now—winds near us on one side and the steep rocky hills rise beside us on the other—every here and there we pass a patch of brûlée, and then the resemblance to the Murray Bay wilderness strikes us more forcibly still. We see no good timber near the railway: it is, we are told at Mattawa, all some distance from the line. Tonight it is very cold, clear, and bright. The moonlit snow and waving pine trees afford us material for poetic fancies. The men who are in too good spirits to be poetically inclined amuse themselves by drafting regulations for their proper government while on board and then systematically break their own regulations in order to have the fun of being tried, condemned, and punished (if possible) in some absurd and ingenious way, the judge being responsible for the procedure and punishment.

Wednesday, April 1st

We reach Biscotasing about two this morning, bitterly cold and very hungry. We are soon warmed and fed however and find that we have fallen among anything but thieves. I and some other officers are looked after by a Mr. Renaud, a Canadian Pacific Railway engineer and a nephew of Mr. A.H. Campbell. He is kindness itself and we thoroughly appreciate his attentions.

Biscotasing—the word means "clear water"—is the last station on the regular line of railway and is the headquarters of the construction department. Here during the winter the Canadian Pacific Railway have had employed some six thousand men: all have lived in tents. This seems almost incredible when one knows that the mercury frequently freezes in this region, but so it is. Even at this date we fell the cold greatly and the thermometer is, we find, well below zero.

We leave Biscotasing about four and make a station called Lake Nemagosenda about 11:30. Here there are only one or two log shanties. We are given by the occupants some hot tea, which is as the poet says, "grateful and comforting."

After this we run slowly all day and about seven reach Dog Lake, where we are given supper in the navvies' shanties. This supper is a delightful experience and, to most of us, the first taste of real bush life. The low-ceilinged rough log cabin looks quaint and comfortable: good things abound, appetites are not wanting, that meal is a thing to read about. Many are anxious to enter the employment of the Canadian Pacific Railway, but we are warned that not always does the "board" groan beneath its load of delicacies as it does today and we refrain. For the present, however, we enjoy ourselves and why should we not when to "occupy" and amuse us we have tea, coffee, milk (condensed), sugar, beef,

109

salmon, lobster, mackerel, beans, peaches and apples, and bread and cakes.

At Dog Lake, Major Allan joins us. He has found his money: we at first congratulate him on his good luck and eagerly ask what means he took to trace that which was lost. Strange to say he does not seem eager to enlighten us. Inquiry from outside sources reveals the fact that after two hours' earnest and enthusiastic search, much forcible language, and many offers of noble rewards, the missing purse was discovered by the gallant Major himself in "the other pocket."

After supper we go by rail four miles to the end of the track. We have before us a break of fifty-one miles and are to drive this distance in sleighs. Fifty-five teams await us, but these are not enough, and much of our luggage has to be left behind in charge of a rear guard of eighteen men under Lieutenant Gunther.' We are much delayed in getting away but at last we are safely stowed and start about 11 P.M. The 10th remain at Dog Lake waiting for teams expected every hour.

THURSDAY, APRIL 2ND

We drove all last night through a very wild and beautiful country. The bright moonlight enabled us to fully appreciate the features of the scene, and very exciting our experience was. Most of the time we drove along the line of railway—the right of way—as it is called, but very often we plunged into gloomy impassable-looking forests. The road in most places very rough, though we meet with no mishaps. The cold is very trying and renders sleep quite impossible;

every now and then one is forced to take a smart run to keep one's very marrow from freezing. At some unearthly hour in the morning we stopped at a small camp and some of the lucky ones secured a cup of tea, but it was not till eight this morning after a drive of thirty-five miles that we had a chance to rest and warm ourselves. Our haven was Magpie Lake, where there is a large camp. Here we had a fairly good breakfast, much the same in style as our supper of the evening before; the accommodation is more limited, however, and we are therefore not so comfortable.

About eleven we leave Magpie Lake and after a most delightful drive of five hours we reach the track again at a place hereafter to be known to fame as Camp Desolation. The day is very bright and fine and we thoroughly enjoy our sixteen miles by daylight. Not to mention the scenery which always charms and pleases, we have the excitement of making our way over a very rough and very much drifted road. Upsets are a thing of constant occurrence but are a source of nothing but amusement and howls of delight rise from the expectant onlookers as some subtle snowbank claims its unwary victims. In our sleigh are Major Allan, Captain Brown,[6] Hughes, and myself, and we are very fortunate. We are driven by the champion zehu of the district—Angus McKinnon by name—a most amusing character. Quite a lad—very Scotch—in fact, almost unable to speak English—and very quaint in his speech and actions. He has, as have all the other teamsters, a thorough command of the intricacies of the English "swear words." These he uses with a startling frequency and forcibleness, but it is but a gentle failing. The teamsters as a rule are a very rough lot, of all nations and kindred: many Swedes, Finlanders, French, in fact, as a foreman told me, there are plenty of every nationality but Christians. The horses are very fine willing beasts, marvellously strong and sure-footed.

We see no game at all during our drive. Deer are plentiful near Mattawa but we run across none. I, dreaming of grizzlies and dear knows whatnot, ask an intelligent native at Magpie Lake this morning if there is any game to be had—"Oh yes, sir" replies the I.N., "we mostly plays poker."

At Camp Desolation no train awaits us as we expected and we stand shivering and hungry for three hours before the cars arrive, and then we find that we have to ride 107 miles in open flatcars. There is no help for it and we pack in as best we may. Each man has but one thin government blanket and prepares for a cold night, but none of us expect what we unfortunately have to go through.

Friday, April 3rd

The horrors of last night are simply indescribable. We leave Camp Desolation about seven, rather cold and hungry, but for some time we enjoy ourselves fairly well. The mode of progression is to say the least of it somewhat novel: the sleepers are merely laid on the snow unballasted and unlevelled; sometimes we seem to be plunging down veritable precipices, so steep are the grades, and at all times oscillation is so violent that one momentarily expects the car to leave the track bodily. Soon, however, we find that it is becoming too cold to allow any interest to be taken in anything but the question of how not to freeze and even that question, in spite of the vigorous efforts of some of the more cheerful and pluckier spirits to keep the men's courage up, ceases ere long to bother our poor despondent fellows. The thermometer by actual observation goes down to five below zero, the wind is biting, our cramped quarters render movement of any kind impossible, and at last we simply make up our minds to freeze. Jock McLennan, who has been the life of No. 4 so far, works hard, but when as a last sally he rings up His Satanic Majesty, informs him that a collection of thirty-one cents has been taken up for His Majesty's exchequer and begs him to turn on the hot tube for fifteen minutes and is then not rewarded with a laugh, he too curls up and prepares to die. All things have an end. About 2:30 A.M. we reach a camp called Heron Bay ninety miles from Camp Desolation and have a meal. I was about to say breakfast but it is really the dinner of the day before yesterday. Many of our poor fellows have to be lifted out of the car, so stiff with cold are they, but warmth and food soon revive them and their troubles are no sooner over than they are forgotten. Only two or three men, wonderful to say, are much the worse for the experience of the night.

We leave Heron Bay about six, refreshed and cheerful, and soon catch our first glimpse of Lake Superior. A run of an hour and a half brings us to Port Munro, seventeen miles from Heron Bay, and here we find the second break in the track, one of eighteen miles and across this we are to march. At Port Munro we have a wonderful view, everything looks bright in the morning sun, and the grand hills and distant lake make for us a scene of great beauty. The work of disembarkation proceeds rapidly. Each company, as it is ready, marches off. "C" School leading, then No. 1, and so on. At the camp on the lake shore we are given some sandwiches, cakes, and coffee and then vigorously begin our tramp. Our company—No. 1—starts at noon exactly and we make the eighteen miles in six hours and a half. Very good time it is, too, over heavy roads and with arms and accoutrements as a load; moreover, we have no stragglers. This performance makes me feel that I have been lucky in being assigned to No. 1, evidently good stuff. Our road skirts along the shore of the lake, and we have grand stretches of scenery. Magnificent rocks rise beside us and every now and then we gaze on fantastic creations in pure clear ice, the result of the spray of the autumn waves.

We reach the track at a place called McKellar's Harbour and, as a train is waiting for us, the staff "C" School and Companies 1 and 2 run down at once to Jack Fish Bay, a large settlement seven miles distant. Companies 3 and 4 are to follow. We have a very good supper at Jack Fish Bay and then are turned in to a large empty warehouse for the night—and it is a night of luxury.

SATURDAY, APRIL 4TH

We rise this morning much the better for our night's rest, the first we have had since we left Toronto, but

114

we scarcely know each other so terribly burned and swollen are our faces: the scorching sun and bitter winds have a very distressing effect.

Our unfortunate comrades of Nos. 3 and 4 do not reach Jack Fish Bay till this morning. The train returning for them runs off the track and they spend a most miserable night in the open.

We prepare for another march today across the third break — twenty-three miles — but fortunately enough sleighs are on hand to furnish accommodation for us all and we drive instead. "C" School and Nos. 1 and 2 start soon after breakfast, the other two companies remain behind to rest awhile.

We reach track at a place called Waiston's Landing. There is no train ready for us and we shiver for four mortal hours, most of the time exposed to a sleety rain. Then the welcome whistle is heard, the train comes in sight, and with little delay we embark and run down to McKay's Harbour, seven miles. It is dark when we reach this place and snowing hard; no arrangements have apparently been made for our food or shelter and, often wandering aimlessly around for what seems an eternity, we are thrust into the damp dirty hold of a propeller for the night, that is, most of the men are. A few of the men and nearly all the officers are put up at the Canadian Pacific Railway hospital. The doctor in charge, Armstrong, is most kind. The meal furnished us tonight is most miserable, but we are too tired and heartsore to grumble.

SUNDAY, APRIL 5TH

I had a most delightful sleep last night, occupying one of the hospital cots and am myself again today. Nos. 3 and 4 join us this morning early and all are ready to leave McKay's Harbour, the most wretched hole we have been in yet. We miss Doucet today and find he has remained at Jack Fish Bay where he is stationed.

We leave McKay's Harbour about ten, two men short. Beaumont of "H" Co. with congestion of the lungs and another man with something of the same sort remain in hospital.

The day is bright and warm and the open cars enable us to see properly the very beautiful country we are passing through, for by far the finest scenery on the North Shore meets us here. On the railway itself are many points of interest—deep cuttings—overhanging rocks—long tunnels—one appreciates the difficulties of construction of a line in such a country.

This is our first Sunday out and we observe the day by singing vigorously and with fine effect many of our good old hymns. More than one heart feels sore and sad at the thought of the dear friends and the peaceful at home.

A very enjoyable run of forty-seven miles brings us to the Nipigon and to our fourth and last break. We leave the cars at two and make Red Rock on the west side of the Nipigon, nine miles distant, at half past five. Bad roads and heavy loads account for the slow time. We get a telegram here telling us that all is well at home and that things are still looking bad in the Northwest. That satisfies us—we shall be wanted after all.

116

A train awaits us at Red Rock but the quarters are altogether too cramped—in many cases six men being crowded in one double seat. More cars are promised at Port Arthur and we are content to wait. Our baggage is some hours behind owing to lack of transport, and we lie quietly at Red Rock all evening.

The men are able to compare notes about the marches and the question of the most suitable footgear for this kind of peculiar state of affairs is vehemently discussed. Nearly all agree, however, that the ordinary lace boot with two pair of socks is the best for the walk: the eagerly sought-for beefees, moccasins, and rubber boots have proved of little use. The slush in the day time wets one's feet in boots, to be sure, but the cold at night does not, when in them, affect one so much. Luxury, however, consists in Indian moccasins with india rubber over them.

We enjoy a magnificent sunset this evening and see the famous bay of the Nipigon in all its glory—very, very beautiful it is; one can scarcely imagine how lovely it must be in summer.

MONDAY, APRIL 6TH

We leave Red Rock sometime this morning early and reach Port Arthur, sixty-six miles distant, about six. The citizens wish to give us a breakfast here, but the colonel is anxious to push on and declines the invitation. We stop only a few minutes while some more cars are put on. We are actually treated to the luxury of a Pullman—most unheard of, nay, unthought of, comfort.

At Port Arthur we get papers—Winnipeg papers—as late as 4th inst. No news in them of importance, but things look serious, and we see there is no chance of being turned back at Winnipeg.

Shortly after leaving Port Arthur we see running near the track, or rather we see a white line which we are told is the far-famed Kaministiquia, a very beautiful stream, they say, in summer and we can well believe it.

At a small station called Savanne seventy-five miles from Port Arthur a short stoppage is made and we officers manage to secure some cake and coffee — cake and coffee of a very superior order, too. The conductor tells us that this is considered the best eating house on the Canadian Pacific Railway between Port Arthur and the Rockies and, judging by what we obtained, taking the proprietor as we did by surprise, the reputation is not undeserved.

All day we run through a desolate and dreary country, and about half past seven reach Rat Portage the notorious. The officers drive up to the Rideout Hotel and have supper — bottled ale at fifty cents per bottle the chief luxury. The men are not allowed to leave the cars, much to the disgust, no doubt, of mine host of the Rideout and to their own, but they perforce content themselves with such scraps of grog as they still have on hand. It is too late to see anything of the place; the mud is tested, however, in a brave attempt to struggle from the hotel to the station, the bus having departed before some parting ceremonies could be satisfactorily attended to by some energetic young officers. Soon after leaving Rat Portage, Gus Nanton[7] makes his appearance, having run down from Winnipeg on a special. He brings with

him a few letters and certain welcome creature comforts. Song and mirth are indulged in for some hours;
musical talent is unearthed (Mr. Cunningham sings
for us most sweetly dear old "Annie Laure"), and
after a pleasant evening we turn in for a comfortable
night's rest.

TUESDAY, APRIL 7TH

We wake about 6 A.M. after a delightful night's rest
in the Pullman and find ourselves in Winnipeg. A
miserable cold raw windy morning it is and everything looks desolate. The men are marched off to various hotels for breakfast and then dismissed for the day
with instructions to be at the station at 4 P.M.; evidently we are not to delay here. The officers go in a
body to Leland's and the way the viands are finished
is a caution; the waiters stand aghast. We have not
had a civilized meal, however, for eight days — indeed,
have had only eleven meals of any kind in that time —
and our good appetites are not to be wondered at.

After breakfast Harry Brock and I are taken in
charge by J.D. Cameron[8] and Robinson.[9] They gently
remark that we might be the better of a bath: I in
theory quite agree with them — water has not touched
me since I left Toronto, but feel a natural reluctance
to removing the covering of grime that has stood by
me so faithfully. However, persuaded by them I indulge in soap and hot water and have to confess that
a certain accession of comfort has been derived from
the cleansing process. My personal appearance is certainly, however, not improved, the unaccustomed
luxury of a wash is too much for my sunburnt

complexion and I emerge with my face scarcely recognizable—hardly enough skin left in fact to keep the patches together.

The first person I run across is my worthy Aunt Soph and under her able guidance I do Winnipeg thoroughly, inspect every shop in the place, handle and price (but fail to buy) every article in each, am introduced to every man, woman, and child in the borough, the living creature my estimable aunt does not know I have yet to discover. I am very much surprised and very much pleased to meet Miss Evelyn Galt. She has just come up from Montreal and gives me late news of my people. Call on Mrs. Mulock— find her in the midst of moving and she advises me to lunch with Willie[10] at the club and this I have the pleasure of doing. After lunch have an hour or two to myself and answer one or two letters that have reached me here, then go quietly down to the station. See any number of fellows I know and everyone is only too kind. The men all turn up in good time charmed with Winnipeg and its inhabitants. Here they laugh at the idea of our having to do anything and say the people of Ontario are much more excited about this farcical rebellion than they are. The station is crowded with people anxious to see us off, and we depart about five amid the hearty cheers of the assembled crowd. Willie Mulock and Mrs. Mulock with great kindness send for Harry Mickle,[11] Hume, and myself two large baskets of provisions—a very welcome supply—and Cameron, Bowen, and Robinson give us quantities of fruit and reading material.

Very soon we see before us the often heard of
prairie, and peculiar is the effect the first sight of it
has: miles and miles as far as eye can reach of dreary
yellow flatness—no bush—no tree—no house to break
the monotonous dead level. We are told that this is
prairie at its worst and we are only too willing to
believe it.

About seven we stop at Portage la Prairie, only for
a few minutes, however, to take in water. A miser-
able-looking place it is and I pity Harry and Adele as
I think of the years spent by them in it. After leaving
Portage we have a very good concert in No. 4 Company's car. The brigadier and all the officers put in an
appearance and we have some capital choruses,
speeches, and solos. We are told that we are to have
something to eat when we reach Brandon and anx-
iously wait for the happy moment of arrival. It
comes at last but not till half past ten. It is too late of
course to see anything of this, as we are told, very
pretty place. We do have something to eat, however;
the cars are invaded by the sprightly damsels of the
hamlet armed with steaming jugs of coffee and bags
of tempting cakes and the delicacies, aided by the
charms of the fair donors, quite soften the hearts of
our wax-warm warriors. Much necessarily rapid flir-
tation is indulged in, the gay young major as usual
distinguishing himself, the false and malicious designa-
tion of him as a married man by an envious rival
having no effect in the way of stopping his victorious
career. A tour of the cars after Brandon is left behind
shows that the boys have done fair execution. Rib-
bons that have doubtless figured in many a previous

bun fight, handkerchiefs that have certainly seen better days, wave now triumphantly on many an unaccustomed manly bosom. The order is to turn in as hard work may lie before us on the morrow, and quiet soon settles on the scene of the erstwhile revelry.

WEDNESDAY, APRIL 8TH

Qu'Appelle station—Troy as it is properly called—we make early in the morning and after a short delay we disembark in heavy marching order, march to a convenient piece of prairie, and pitch our tents. This, of course, for the first time and the work, so novel, is slowly done. However, at last no further dressing and shouting remain to be indulged in, the canvas is hoisted, pegs driven, guy ropes tightened, and our abodes are ready. The next thing to be looked after is grog. We have no means of cooking anything, our camp equipage being with the rear guard, and we perforce content ourselves with the simple government ration of hard biscuit and corned beef—the first introduction to the former luxury for most of us. I recognize at once an old Quebec friend.

At Qu'Appelle we find "B" Battery—Major Short[12] in command—waiting for us. "A" Battery and the 90th are with the general at Touchwood Hills. We, it seems, are to go west and work up to Battleford, probably. "C" School leaves us today. The Right Half Company under Major Smith with Scott of "Ours" attached are to join the general, the Left Half Company under Mr. Wadmore, Harry Brock with him, leave by rail for a place called Swift Current some distance west, where there is a large quantity of supplies.

I am on duty and am up all night. It is quite impossible to keep warm and even in the tents the men seem to suffer severely; a chorus of coughing most distressing to hear is kept up with monotonous persistence.

THURSDAY, APRIL 9TH

The morning dawns bright and clear and soon genial warmth dispels the gloom and stiffness of the night. A hasty breakfast is indulged in and then all hands are ordered out for drill, skirmishing the chief attraction. The Grenadiers arrive in the morning but are pushed on at once to join the general, leaving Qu'Appelle in wagons. Our long-lost rear guard rejoins us and is warmly welcomed, as is also our baggage. Cooking can now be indulged in. The Company of Guards from Ottawa came up with the 10th and camp beside us; a tidy-looking lot of fellows they are under the command of Captain Todd[13] and Gray, my old-time friend, the first lieutenant. A new brigade is formed today — "B" Battery, Guards, "C" School, and ourselves, and a very handy little force it will make. Mutton is today appointed brigade quartermaster and leaves us for the staff, so that we are becoming very short of officers.

A mail reaches us today but I sad to say am not remembered.

We see Boulton's Scouts — the "Cowboy Brigade" — today. They dress in white helmets, brown duck-shooting jackets, corduroys, and tops, and a very serviceable-looking set they are; most of them we find are young Englishmen and the majority are gentlemen.

FRIDAY, APRIL 10TH

Last night was again bitterly cold; it seems impossible to keep warm and sleep is a mere farce. We now each have a double and single blanket but this seems to be quite insufficient to engender any warmth in our miserable shivering carcasses. The morning is bright and warm and a brisk bout of skirmishing pulls us together.

We get orders to leave this afternoon for Swift Current and after dinner strike out tents and prepare to embark. Our train is ready about five and we get off without delay, not sorry to see the last of Qu'Appelle at any rate for the present. It is a beautiful place, lying quietly in the valley surrounded by rolling prairie, but we have been anything but comfortable during our stay here, half-frozen and ill-fed. Most of the officers and many of the men have been taking their meals at one of the three hotels (so called) the settlement boasts of, but three times fifty cents each day makes a great inroad into our scanty means.

About dusk we approach Regina, the capital of the great Northwest, and a sweet-looking capital it is; lying low in a miserable half-swamp, half-prairie, the scattered wooden shanties look most forlorn in the gathering gloam and falling snow and we pass on with no reluctance. At the station I see for a minute White[14] and Roderick McLean.

Supper is promised at a place called Moose Jaw — and "someone" is deputed to telegraph to have preparations duly made. A rush into the Moose Jaw station dining hall on our arrival makes us at once realize that "someone" the indefinite has as usual blundered; no sizzling sausages or savory steak await the ardent attack of the hungry horde and we return sad and supperless to the friendly shelter of our car. Here we content ourselves as best we may with the faithful corned beef and hard tack, some unwary spirits washing down this dry provender with libations of a concoction hitherto, thank God, unknown to us, called "Moose Jaw Hop Beer." The unfortunate partakers of this vile beverage pass a night of uneasiness—nay, even agony.

SATURDAY, APRIL 11TH

We enjoy a night of warmth and comfort in the cars and pitch camp in the early morning close to the railway. "C" School have taken up their quarters in the station. Swift Current is a very small place, merely a railway depot in fact with a few stores and houses. A few days ago the place was raided by Indians who helped themselves to anything and everything that pleased them. The country is very wretched near here, no wood or water. Water for drinking purposes is brought in tanks by rail from Calgary three hundred miles to the west. Camped here waiting for us are about one hundred Mounted Police under Colonel Herchmer,[15] and we now learn definitely that our destination is Battleford. That place is almost due north and about two hundred miles distant; the trip there is not likely to be pleasant. We bring with us from Qu'Appelle some fifty wagons and the necessary number of horses. These teams will carry our supplies.

After dinner we have battalion drill and when this is over Harry and I have a grand run of some six or seven miles over the prairie. We see numbers of buffalo skulls and try our revolvers at these very enticing targets but see none of the living animals: the last buffalo in the country was killed, we are told, last summer. We find great numbers of most beautiful purple crocus; it seems almost impossible that flowers should bloom in weather such as we are having. On our way back to camp we run across a small turf-built stockade and the ingenious and romantic Harry at once weaves a blood-curdling tale in connection therewith.

The 65th of Montreal pass in the afternoon en route to Calgary.

SUNDAY, APRIL 12TH

We have last night another cold experience but we are now beginning to be accustomed to the slight inconvenience of frozen toes and do not allow trifles of this kind to interfere with our night's rest.

Early this morning Colonel Otter[16] comes up from Qu'Appelle and with him came "B" Battery and the Guards; also Captain Howard[17] of the United States Militia and in his charge two Gatling guns. These curious implements of destruction we inspect with interest, and their trial is watched eagerly. A few rounds are fired at some duck on a distant pond—no execution is done apparently, but the rapidity of fire shows us how very deadly a weapon of this kind might be on proper occasions. We want now to see one tried on the Indians; from what we hear they seem to have definitely risen and we shall probably have some hard work before they are quieted again.

126

We have service this morning and very pleasant and much appreciated it is. Acheson officiates and cuts the service rather short, giving us, however, numerous hymns.

We get orders today to be ready to start in the morning, and three or four of us determine to make an effort to have one civilized meal before we start. We accordingly visit the station dining hall, and loudly call for the best the house affords. The board is coldly furnished forth with fat pork and "apple sass," but thanks to the gentle divinity who presides over the genial tea tray we enjoy ourselves, getting, however, as a baser nature cynically remarks, forty cents' worth of smile and only ten cents' worth of supper.

Monday, April 13th

I was on duty and up all night. The weather was much milder thanks to a welcome southerly wind and I was comparatively comfortable. One has lots of time for meditation during these lonely midnight watches and one's thoughts are apt to take on a rather sad thing; induced thereto not alone by the natural gloominess of the large dark night but also to no slight extent by the musically melancholy circumambient "All's well" of the mournful voiced chain of sentries.

The "Rouse" sounds at 4 a.m. and we make an early start, "C" School in advance, next the artillery, and then ourselves. We have an easy march of twelve miles and pitch camp near a small slough, that is, pond. The weather is milder and the men are happy. One or two rather footsore, however, already.

TUESDAY, APRIL 14TH

Last night we slept without disturbance and today start at 6:30 in the cold gray dawn and make a fairly good stretch of eighteen miles. The Queen's Own are first today and No. 1 forms the advance guard. For the present owing to want of officers I have been transferred from No. 1 to No. 4. As soon as the sun rises, the men find marching hard work and weary, warm, and way-worn we gladly reach the welcome banks of the Saskatchewan. Near the river we pass through a wonderful defile, winding in a most extraordinary way through steep sandy hills; trouble was feared here but fortunately we get through without molestation. We also pass today a deserted Indian encampment and here we see "buried," so to speak, but really fastened to the branch of a small tree, a little Indian baby.

We can find nothing to break the monotony of the march today but a not over-exciting observation of the antics of the ambulance mule. This is a purchase of the surgeon's and very proud he is of the turnout. To the heretical mind the resemblance to a costermonger's equipage is very marked; the mongrel pie-bald pony, the little red-wheeled green cart, and—well, the natty (?) corporal to whose care was consigned this precious pill-purveying "nocturne in all colors" might feel hurt if the comparison were pushed any further.

At the river we meet the police once more: they came here ahead of us a day or two ago to see if the coast was clear and are to act as scouts in the future. They have with them one of the famous mountain howitzers. A very handy-looking little gun it is, a brass seven-pounder and weighing only, carriage and all, some four hundred pounds.

Toward dusk much excitement is caused by the announcement that some figures can be seen on one of the distant hills. We at once conclude that our Indian friends are taking observations as there are no settlers in this part of the country. The gallant captain and senior subaltern of No. 1 form themselves into a reconnoitering party, make a bold sally, and approach the disturbers. It is found that they are nothing more than certain teamsters who have wandered somewhat too far from camp. Teamsters are very objectionable and under certain circumstances, especially if taken internally, are absolutely fatal, but when kept at a reasonable distance are not immediately dangerous, therefore we camp feeling comparatively secure.

This evening we have some very good songs: the new selections of the Guards being particularly acceptable. The Bugle Band, too, inflict what they are pleased to term music upon us. Now the Bugle Band know about as much about time and tune as a cat does of phrenology, and the result of their wrestlings with any unfortunate inoffending air is better imagined than described. We can only devoutly pray that the infernal "rheumatic" (chromatic) attachments may, by some kind dispensation of Providence, disappear, and that freed from the burdens and responsibilities of a career that is too much for it, the band may dissolve into a useful individuality of blowful buglers.

From Swift Current to the river we pass through a miserable dry sandy, literally, desert country, not a tree or bush to be seen: here there are a few withered poplar trees, but nothing to justify the oft-heard appellation of "well wooded" applied to the banks enclosing the "fertile" valley of the Saskatchewan.

WEDNESDAY, APRIL 15TH

Last night passes without any alarm. This morning it is cold, raw, and foggy and we are, for a time, miserable. Soon the sun makes his presence felt however and everything is lovely. After breakfast Harry and I take advantage of the genial warmth and wash ourselves and some of our immediate belongings, earning in that interesting process at Northwest prices, one dollar and twenty cents. Then we walk down to the river and watch with interest the process of transporting supplies to the north bank. Slow is the progress made. The river—the south branch of the Saskatchewan—is here some three hundred yards wide and, as its name ("Swift Current") denotes, extremely rapid. A steamer has been brought to the crossing and is actively engaged in making passages across, but each trip consumes much time. The steamer itself, the *Northcote*, a most peculiar craft, is in fact merely an immense flat-bottomed scow (she draws only two feet of water) with a little machinery and some cabins; a large wheel at the stern is the propelling instrument. The current and wind render steering a very difficult task and we are told that if the wind rises much more, as it threatens to do, operations will have to be suspended. The police and a large portion of the supplies are taken across, but in the afternoon the wind comes, and nothing further can be done. We grumble much at the delay and to put us in better humor we have to endure a pelting storm of rain for at least two hours. This afternoon we search for specimens of petrified wood and many very good pieces are found, the colonel being especially fortunate. All along the river there are, we are told, quantities of petrifactions.

In the evening the men have an elaborate concert and interspersed with the songs are several capital speeches, the burden of which is complaint against the grub. Pork, beans, and hard tack are very delightful, and certainly, whatever may be the case now when we are in the wilds, we might have had something better when we were on a line of railway and in a well-settled district. The articles forming the mainstay of our daily diet are so far appreciated at any rate as to be called upon to lend their names to various portions of our encampment, and we rejoice in the possession of a "Pork Alley," "Hard Tack Terrace," "Bean Lane," and other equally euphonious localities.

THURSDAY, APRIL 16TH

We have a most miserably cold night and I wake in the morning, or rather rise, for sleep has been an impossibility, to find fully an inch of ice on the water pail in our tent. This is rather too much.

It is still blowing a gale and nothing can be done till evening. A lull comes then and the artillery manage to cross.

In the evening we have a little social reunion in the colonel's tent. Colonel Otter comes in and several of the staff. Songs are indulged in but tonight we miss the sweet voice of Mr. Cunningham, whom we left at Swift Current on his way to the Rockies. I meet tonight Captain Howard and have a long chat with him; he seems a decent fellow but a typical Yank. He tells me he is not coming any further with us but is to wait here for the Midland Battalion and go with them by river to join the general. We are all amazed at Colonel Herchmer's conduct tonight. He, probably with the best intentions in the world, undertakes to read us a lecture on the proper exercise of discipline in a volunteer regiment, hinting very plainly that our men are allowed too much liberty. We do not appreciate his entirely uncalled for and, to say the least of it, not over-polite criticism of his hosts. Our men are a fine willing lot of fellows, and friends that one knows intimately are not to be ordered about like a parcel of slaves.

FRIDAY, APRIL 17TH

Another wretched night, but today the wind has fallen and the prospect of an advance restores our cheerfulness. We cross the river early in the morning and pitch our tents on the north shore about five hundred yards from the river.

A large supply train came in yesterday and brought us a mail. I got nothing and was disconsolate. This is our first mail since leaving Qu'Appelle.

We have now a large number of teamsters with us—some two hundred in all. They look upon the rebellion as a godsend, for it means hard cash to them. They get from $5.00 to $6.00 a day and fair as this price is, the unfortunate government has to pay $8.00 and $10.00, the difference being pocketed by the contractors.

Two companies of the 35th (York and Simcoe Provisional Battalion) march in today and take possession of the ferry. They are to stay here as a guard.

We send back to Swift Current four men sick, all with cold or rheumatism. They hope to rejoin soon.

SATURDAY, APRIL 18TH

Cold, of course, last night and when we poke our heads out in the morning we find two inches of snow on the ground and a sleety rain falling. Not too pleasant, indeed.

We start shortly after twelve on our long march to Battleford, having between 160 and 170 miles (the latter apparently the more correct estimate) to cover. We have enough teams to carry all our provisions and a great portion of our men; half at least will be able to drive at a time and we ought to make good progress. Today we do about twelve miles and a disagreeable march it is: a damp, dull, miserable day and the prairie a sea of mud. We see no vegetation at all and the country seems very wretched.

Tonight we begin to realize that we are in an enemy's country, as we, for the first time, form a "laager." The wagons are placed in an open square, each face about two hundred paces long. The horses are tethered in the inside and the tents pitched on the outside, doors opening toward the wagons. The men are ordered to sleep with their arms beside them, and at the first alarm to make for the wagons. Then their position would be a happy one, a fierce enemy in front and frantic struggling mules and horses, more dangerous still, behind. We also have tonight a countersign, our first experience. "Gopher" is the word chosen and very suitable the choice is. The gopher seems to be the sole representative of four-footed life in this country. A pretty little fellow he is, much like a squirrel but with the peculiar spring and upright posture of the kangaroo. The prairie is honeycombed with their holes.

SUNDAY, APRIL 19TH

I am on duty last night and have a long dreary cold night. Reveille sounds about 4 A.M., when it is still quite dark, and we start shortly before seven. It soon becomes bright and warm and the mud appears again under the influence of the rays of the hot sun.

Marching becomes rather tiring and I am not sorry when we halt for dinner, after five hours and a half of hard work, beside a small pool of melted snow. This the only good (?) water we had so far seen. One or two pools we had passed, but the water was too alkaline for me. God knows how this country can ever amount to anything without wood or water. We march after dinner for three hours and a half and halt beside a small slough. We calculate that we have made twenty-eight miles and I feel satisfied as I have walked all the way.

Owing to some mismanagement, no proper supply of wood has been brought with us, and there is none to be had tonight. Nothing in the shape of fuel is to be had for miles and miles and our poor fellows are obliged to content themselves after a hard day's work with beef, biscuit, and cold water. We came to the conclusion that the biscuit at present being served out to us are some left behind by Sir Garnet after the Red River Expedition.

Tonight pickets are thrown out and cold work it is for the unfortunates who have to do duty.

It is hard to realize that this is Sunday: rather unlike a peaceful day of rest in dear old Toronto.

MONDAY, APRIL 20TH

I have a pleasant night's rest, thanks to extra blankets I am able to avail myself of owing to the absence on picket duty of my estimable tentmate Harry Brock. He, poor fellow, comes in about 5 A.M. chilled to the marrow.

We start in good time after a miserable cold breakfast and put in over five hours of good hard work. Then we dine, but what a dinner—hard tack and oatmeal and water. No wood to be had yet. We push on for another four hours in the afternoon, and make altogether today about thirty-two miles. The pace is very quick but I manage to walk all the way.

Great profanity is indulged in when it is found that again we have no means of doing any cooking. The men are rapidly becoming mutinous. Fortunately, though too late to be of use tonight, some teams laden with wood catch up to us and great preparations are made for a good meal in the morning.

TUESDAY, APRIL 21ST

Last night we have a little spice of excitement. A shot from one of the picket sentries alarms the camp.

Inquiry elicits the fact, however, that the unfortunate sentry loses himself and his head and fires the shot to attract attention. He does attract attention but not altogether of the nature he is likely to appreciate.

We start in capital time this morning and travel for six hours, the day bright, warm, and pleasant. We then halt for our noonday rest of two hours. On again then for nearly four hours. We make again fully thirty-two miles and I walk all day. The pace is quicker even than it was yesterday but we are somewhat delayed in crossing a creek called Eagle Creek. But for this, distance covered would have been somewhat greater. As we advance more wagons become available for the men and now few have to walk at all. Tomorrow all who wish, nearly, will be able to drive.

We have to supply all the pickets tonight and send out four officers and ninety-two N.C.O.s and men, a pretty large draft.

A courier catches us tonight and brings us news of the Fort Pitt disaster[18] and gives a bad account of the state of affairs at Battleford. We become more anxious than ever, if that were possible, to press on.

WEDNESDAY, APRIL 22ND

On duty last night and of course no sleep. Another sentry distinguished himself and fires at what he stoutly asserts to be a man on horseback. Nothing comes of it.

We start about half past five and hurry on at a tremendous pace. The country is very hilly and broken and about eight miles out we come to a belt of thick scrub. Trouble is feared here and two companies are ordered out as skirmishers. I go with one, but the scouts come back and report all clear and we drop back quietly into place. We have a very short halt and then press on again. About five shots are suddenly heard toward the head of the column and all is excitement. Our skirmishers are ordered to the front and after a tremendous double we reach a piece of rising ground and see in the distance a number of Indians making north as fast as their ponies can carry them. Our scouts have had quite a little skirmish, wounded one Indian, and captured a wagon, some ponies, and blankets. We camp soon after this occurrence and prepare to keep a sharp lookout. Fortunately we are in a very favorable position, no hills or woods near us.

A trader who has come up with us from Swift Current finds, untouched in the scrub we passed through this morning, a cache of groceries he had made when the trouble first began. He does a roaring trade in tobacco, figs, candies, etc.

Today we make fully thirty-five miles and I am reasonably tired. I go on my own feet all day but very often have to run to keep up and the work is rather trying. However, we have only about thirty miles more to do.

THURSDAY, APRIL 23RD

Last night was quiet but very cold and today it is bitter. Snow flurries every little while and ice on all the sloughs. We have an early start and make good progress: all the men ride. In the afternoon I am obliged at last to ride, too. We are going downhill

and through Indian reserves, and it would never do
to be left behind. We make only thirty miles,
however, halting quite early in the afternoon about
two miles from Battleford.

This afternoon we see houses again and find that
we have reached the reserve of the Stonies. We see
among others the houses of Payne and Tremont, two
of the Indian instructors, both of whom have been
murdered. Payne married a squaw and was a good
friend to the people he taught, but they took his life
at the first opportunity. So much for Indian gratitude.
In one of the Indian houses our scouts find a squaw –
dead – with a bullet through her head. She is painted
in full war paint and may have been killed in some of
the skirmishes near Battleford. No one is to be seen
on the reserve. Men, women, and children are all off
on the warpath. The Stonies are Sioux Indians and
bear a very unenviable reputation.

We can see Battleford when about eight miles
away from a height of land and are disgusted to
notice clouds of smoke rising from the settlement.
We are ordered to camp, however, much as we
should like to press on and render help if help be
needed. It is not considered advisable to advance
when night is approaching. The scouts, however, go
on to make investigations. In the evening shots are
heard from the direction of the town and twenty-five
of the Mounted Police start off to see what the trouble is; Lesslie[19] goes with them. They came back all
right and report that the scouts exchanged a few
shots with some odd Indians but that the main body
who have been besieging the town have departed.

Before leaving they set fire to Judge Rouleau's house as a last mark of defiance and this was the building we saw burning. It was a house on the south side of the Battle River—the main settlement is on the north side and is still, and the people have been made aware of our approach. One of the garrison was, we hear, killed last night while on picket duty.

I am congratulated tonight on having walked virtually the whole way from Swift Current to Battleford and am informed by my men that I have been christened the "Demon Walker."

Bowman of No. 4 (University at Large) is run over today and is badly bruised and shaken but not, we hope, dangerously hurt.

FRIDAY, APRIL 24TH

We have a quiet but as usual cold night. We do not turn out early in the morning as there is now no more necessity for hurry, but march off quietly about nine and soon reach our long looked-for goal.

We halt on the high ground overlooking the Battle River while the brigadier and staff cross the river and enter the fort. They return ere long and give a graphic account of the welcome they have received from the poor people who have been besieged here and in terror of their lives for the last six weeks. We are told that we are to stay where we are for the present and camp is pitched on an open space near a large building now or rather lately used as an Industrial School. It was formerly, we hear, Government House and is quite a palace in a country like this. After the tents are pitched we are able to go about and take observations, and then the extent of the ravages committed becomes apparent. On this side of the river there were originally some dozen houses and two or three stores forming what is called the Old Town. Four or five of these houses have been burned, the others dismantled and pillaged, and the stores completely gutted. Scarcely anything has escaped: what could not be taken has been destroyed. About us we see scattered in dismal confusion feathers, photos, books, tins, furniture, and desolation reigns supreme. The Indians have, we hear, been holding high carnival here for some weeks: they were out of rifle-shot from the fort and shells were too precious to be often sent at them. Each night an attack was expected but, beyond firing at the men drawing water from the Battle River (the source of the supply), they molested the garrison but little.

Battleford is very beautifully situated. The Old Town as before stated is on the south bank of the Battle River; the New Town and fort lie on a grassy plain sloping south, and between the Saskatchewan and Battle rivers, about a mile and half from the junction of the two. The ground rises sharply from each river and numerous groves of trees lend to the scene a beauty to which we have for some time been unaccustomed.

As soon as the men are dismissed they begin to forage (of course not openly as all foraging is forbidden) and one or two "finds" are the result. One lucky individual is seen depositing quietly in his tent a very fine-looking turkey. He relates with much glee the story of its capture. A sergeant of a sister corps who has managed to make himself peculiarly obnoxious to our fellows by his overbearing manner, was observed by him to deposit the turkey among some brush outside the lines, fearing probably to be seen if he attempted to bring it in daylight. Our man walked boldly off with the bird. The worthy sergeant had to look on in grim silence, for betrayal of himself would have been the only result of any outcry. Another case of the biter bit was that of our worthy orderly, and in this case I indirectly suffered. Our good lad heard the joyful clucking of a hen some distance from camp and on proceeding to investigate found the noise proceeded from a little shed in rear of the school. There he found and immediately caught a fine fat fowl and then looked about for the confidently expected eggs. He crawled through a small opening and got into a little hay bin, carrying the unfortunate hen with him. Here he was overjoyed to find some eight or ten beautiful eggs and immediately put them carefully one by one through the opening and on a shelf nearby, and then prepared to crawl out again. Just as he was about to do this our gallant major entered accompanied by a parson (the owner of the establishment as we afterward found). The major saw the eggs at once, backed toward them, kept the attention of the parson carefully engaged, and pocketed the hen-warts. The original finder's rage may be imagined but not described. Great was his difficulty to prevent discovery of his whereabouts by noise occasioned by the struggles of the half-strangled hen, and trembling with anger and fear he had to watch the disappearance of his treasures.

This afternoon we sent a party back to the Stonies' reserve. They found and brought back some pigs, oats, etc., but nothing of much use. They also found and buried the body of Payne. He had been shot and then terribly hacked and mutilated.

Saw Captain Nash[20] when we came in this morning, he having crossed over to welcome us. Looks much the same as when he left Toronto, but grayer and thinner.

We this evening have tea in a house and, battered and wrecked though the house is, we feel as if the luxury were almost too great. We manage to light a fire, too, and are warm and comfortable for the first time for many, many days. I, alas, have to go out tonight on picket duty.

SATURDAY, APRIL 25TH

Last night I had the pleasure of being out on picket duty and cold and anxious work it is. The prospect of being potted any minute from one of the numerous clumps of bushes that one's duty obliges one to pass is not pleasant but that is comparatively nothing to the misery one suffers from the cold. I could not keep even reasonably warm and yet I was clad fairly well, one would think. My garments were: two thick woolen undershirts, one flannel shirt, two suits of woolen drawers, waistcoat, chamois jacket tunic, trousers, greatcoat, two pair of socks, boots, gloves, cap, toque, and muffler.

The night was beautifully clear and we saw a magnificent lunar rainbow during the progress of a slight shower.

On coming back to camp this morning we hear the news of the fight yesterday with the breeds. The reports are very vague and unsatisfactory, but what little we do hear is not very cheering. As soon as I am off duty I cross to the fort and endeavor to gain further information, but nothing is known.

I was quite overcome when I visited the fort and saw the miseries the poor people there have been enduring. A small enclosure two hundred yards square with one or two log houses or barracks and store houses, and inside this enclosure were pent up for more than a month 530 people, of whom over three hundred were women and children. Dozens and dozens had to huddle together in one tent. In the commandant's house, a two-storey frame cottage, seventy-two persons were quartered. Food was scarce and water to be produced only at the risk of death. No wonder these poor creatures were glad to see us. The fort is about half a mile from the town and the inhabitants were not allowed to remain there, it being too far away to be under protection, though strange to say the Indians did not make any attempt to pillage or burn it. In the town are some forty houses and stores; some of the buildings comfortable-looking enough, too, though none of them elaborate. I did the town thoroughly, no very difficult task, and then ran across and had a look at the Saskatchewan. This is the north branch of the river, and a very fine stream it is—here about half a mile wide and in places fairly deep; the current tremendous and the water in consequence very muddy. The town is about three-quarters of a mile from the Saskatchewan and about the same distance from the Battle River. The latter river we cross by means of a very ingenious ferry. A wire cable is stretched across the stream and a scow is marked along this, the current's power being utilized by means of a system of pulleys. On the cable are two freely moving pulleys; a rope is attached to each of these, passing from one to another, and in doing so running through two other pulleys, one at each end of the scow; when one wished to cross, the scow is turned partially upstream, the current endeavors, of course, to push it downward, but the angular pressure makes the pulleys move along the cable. The Battle River is not very wide, about seventy or eighty yards, but at this time of year is deep and very rapid. It flows, we are told, all the way from the Rockies. Later in the season when the water falls a bridge is built across it.

I saw at the fort today a number of the police who escaped from Fort Pitt. They had a wonderful escape and behaved very pluckily; came down nearly one hundred miles in an open scow and in very cold wet weather. They speak most warmly of the bravery of the McLean girls, who insisted upon taking their turn of duty with the men, and handled their rifles during the attack on the fort with the greatest coolness. The girls wanted to come down with the police but the father insisted upon their giving themselves up to Big Bear—a fatal mistake, the police think.

We hear this afternoon that Hughes and Mutton[21] have been given their step and the colonel, in honor of the event, produces a bottle this evening from the carefully guarded hoard and the health of the new captains is enthusiastically drunk.

Sunday, April 26th

A beautiful bright clear morning and all the troops are assembled for service. The Reverend Thomas Clarke, Principal of the Indian School officiates, assisted by Acheson. We all appreciate the service, but do not appreciate the efforts of the Bugle Band, who are supposed to play the hymns but who produce only some incoherent babblings, so to speak, of stray notes.

We hear today that it is intended to throw up an earthwork round the school building and use it as a storehouse and headquarters, and that the work will commence tomorrow. The school is quite a large building and before the seat of government was changed to Regina, was the Government House of the Northwest Territories. In the school there were, all last winter, about forty Indian boys, fed, clothed, and taught for nothing. At the first word of any rising all but one made off. One remained faithful and did what he could to warn and save his teachers. Captain Nash was one of the instructors at the school and used to live in the building.

Monday, April 27th

Yesterday toward evening we had a heavy shower, today it is again bright and clear.

All day long all available men are kept at work at the Government House fortifications and matters are fairly advanced. We throw up an embankment to the north and east and make a rampart of cord wood to the west and south.

I hear today that an expedition of some kind is going out to see what the Indians are doing and apply to the brigadier for leave to go. He agrees to take me, if possible, but thinks there will probably be nothing to do. Most of the men are to cross the river as soon as possible and only a small garrison will be left on this side.

A mail goes out today, the carrier being a teamster and not one of the regular couriers. He returns a few hours after his start in a state of wild excitement and states that he was seen and chased by Indians and had to drop the mail bags and run for it. Unfortunately for him some teams come in the evening and bring the bags with them and give us the true version of the morning's occurrence. He had seen the teams approaching him and had at once made off in terror. The regular mail couriers, of whom we have two, are very plucky fellows and think nothing, apparently, of their lonely ride through the country of a treacherous enemy. We feel much surprised to see valuable supplies sent up here without an escort. I do not know whose business it is to see that the trains are properly protected, but it certainly does seem a very rash proceeding to allow them to make the trip in an entirely defenceless condition.

A mail comes in this evening and I get no less than seven letters. No papers reach us, the government evidently thinking that it is not worthwhile spending a hundred dollars or so in forwarding reading matter to us, though there seems to be lots of money thrown about for anything that we do not want.

TUESDAY, APRIL 28TH

I was on picket again last night and did not suffer very much, the weather being reasonably mild. Saw magnificent northern lights all night, their brilliancy very wonderful.

Another fine bright day. All hands again at work at Government House and the defences are completed. The citadel is then dignified with the appellation "Fort Otter" and that name is hammered in letters of brass (nails) on the planks of the portcullis.

I am today told that I am to go with the column. Only one company of our fellows will be taken and Brown, Hughes, and Brock, the senior captain and two senior subalterns, have first chance. To get over the difficulty I am to be attached to "C" School. In consequence of the notification I have to write a good many letters and spend most of the day in this occupation.

A supply of boots and a few trousers reach us today. The boots are useful and there is a pair for each man but we prize the trousers most highly. They do not come before they are needed. Many of the men, if living in a civilized community, would now be under the painful necessity of wearing an ulster or of remaining in some quiet secluded corner. One gallant private was observed the other day to have on a greatcoat, the right sleeve of which was extraordinarily short and not at all of equal length to the left. The reason of this phenomenon was inquired and the G.P. replied that, "he had been obliged to withdraw a portion of the right subdivision of his greatcoat to reinforce the rear guard of his pants."

WEDNESDAY, APRIL 29TH

Very cold miserable night and a dreary morning. Nos. 2 and 3 Companies cross the Battle River this morning and pitch camp about midway between the town and the fort. Colonel Miller[22] is in command and is appointed commandant of Battleford. No. 1 Company is to go to the Front and No. 4 is to remain here under Major Allan. The Flying Column is, we hear tonight, to consist of the artillery, "C" School, Captain Nash's Company of Rifles, some of the Guards, and our own company and, of course, some police. Tonight I am in orders attached to "C" School. We are warned to be ready to leave in the morning and in the evening Brock and I cross to the camp and bring back three or four men who are to go on the expedition in the place of men of No. 1 who are not considered to be quite up to the mark. We say good-bye to all the fellows.

THURSDAY, APRIL 30TH

Another cold night and another most dreary day. We have no orders yet about leaving and wander about all morning in a state of dismal uncertainty. In the afternoon we hear pretty definitely that we shall at all events not leave today and Brock and I run over to the fort. Things are looking much better there. Many of the townspeople have gone back to their houses; some of the settlers have been given tents and made to camp outside the fort, and those remaining there are consequently much more comfortable.

A mail arrives this afternoon and we get newspapers up to the 14th inst. I this time get only one, but that a very welcome, letter.

In the evening all sorts of rumors are afloat about the proposed expedition and at last we begin to think that it is to be abandoned. Apparently the general will not sanction it. A man comes in today stating that he has escaped from Poundmaker. He is, however, known to the police and does not bear a good reputation, so off he is marched.

As things are so uncertain we have, since our comrades left us, been living in a most unsystematic and hand-to-mouth manner. Have no regular meals of our own but take potluck when we can with the men, and on the whole have been most thoroughly uncomfortable. Today the brigadier gives us leave to use two rooms in Fort Otter and we hope to have a mess of our own in working order ere long.

We are joined today by two surgeons and four students sent up by the government. They tell us that a Red Cross Corps has been equipped in Toronto and that Dr. Nattress[23] is coming in charge. They passed Nattress and his staff at the Saskatchewan where they are waiting for an escort, being afraid to come on without one. These surgeons can tell us nothing about the engagement.

FRIDAY, MAY IST

Last night extremely cold and raw; this morning bright and warm. We are ordered to be ready to leave this afternoon for the Front and spend the morning getting things in shape.

The object of the expedition is, we hear, to make a reconnaissance. It is not thought that there will be any fighting to do and if there is, Poundmaker has, we hear, only two hundred men and ought not to be able to do very much. The brigadier and staff evidently think that Poundmaker will surrender if we get near him at all.

About 4 P.M. the column starts. Our force is eight
scouts; sixty Mounted Police under Captain Neale;[24]
"B" Battery, eighty men under Major Short; "C"
School, forty-five men under Lieutenant Wadmore;[25]
No. 1 Company, Queen's Own Rifles, under Captain
Brown, fifty-five men; Battleford Rifles under Cap-
tain Nash, forty men; twenty men of the Guards
under Lieutenant Gray and Queen's Own Rifles Am-
bulance Corps; Surgeon Lesslie; Sergeant Fere and
eight men; Colonel Otter in command; and Colonel
Herchmer, Surgeon Strange,[26] Captain Mutton and
Lieutenant Sears[27] on the staff.

Hume Cronyn, E.C. Acheson,[28] and Blakeley of
"K," McLennan and Prior of "T," Farin Wallace and
Grierson of "H," Fraser and A.J. Boyd of "F" are at-
tached to No. 1.

We have some fifty wagons and push on rapidly
till nightfall then make a laager and prepare to rest
quietly till the moon rises. In the meantime we have
something to eat and sit down quietly and discuss the
prospects of the morrow. Poundmaker is supposed to
be some thirty-five miles off and we hope to reach his
camp by dawn. There is, of course, no chance of surprising him. His scouts have probably long ere this
noticed our advance, for signal fires have been burning all afternoon on the distant hills, but we want to
reach him before he has time to move off.

SATURDAY, MAY 2ND

I have today for the first time seen fighting and
been under fire and as yet it is rather difficult to
quietly think out the details of the affair.

Last night we rested for some four hours while it was too dark to travel and then about 11:30 P.M., when the moon had risen, pressed on again. The night was not very bright and the road ran through a wild and rolling country, so that we did not move quickly. I was too excited to feel sleepy and had lots of time to indulge in meditation; sometimes I would wonder whether anything was likely to happen and whether some of us would not come back again, but as a rule I, and, I think, most of the other fellows, had very little thought of danger. We certainly felt serious, but why no one could tell.

In the early dawn we reached Poundmaker's reservation. Here there are a few houses but no one was visible and we hurried on. About half past four we came to a wide open plain and found that here there had evidently been a very large camp. The marks of numerous tepees and fires could be plainly seen and it was evident that the camp had been but lately vacated. We halted at this camp for some time while the scouts searched some clumps of bush that were near by. In front of the camp and quite close to it was a large creek and rising from this on the far side were high hills intersected with numerous ravines. After a short delay the scouts returned and by this time, it being quite light, we could see far away on the distant hills a herd of cattle grazing and one or two mounted men riding about. Here, evidently, were our friends. As they were at least two miles away it was decided to cross the creek, climb the hill, and have breakfast and rest the horses before pushing on. The stream proved to be rather hard to cross.

After crossing it we had some five hundred yards of scrubby marshy lands to go through and then we began to climb the hill. The scouts were riding quietly near the guns, the men had dismounted, and were walking by twos and threes along the trail when suddenly, just as the scouts reached the top of the first steep ascent, I heard a rattle of rifles ahead and then in a minute or two saw the police and some artillery lying down firing briskly over the crest of the hill and the guns and Gatling also working for all they were worth. At the same time bullets began to fly round us and puffs of smoke floated from the bushes on the right and left, showing us where they came from. Evidently we were in a trap. The men fortunately had their rifles in their hands and it was the work of a very few moments to form up and take the positions assigned to us. And this was the situation. Roughly speaking we occupied a triangular inclined plane—the apex resting on the creek and the base running along the crest of the hill. In front of the hill and parallel to the crest was a ravine, about two hundred yards distant, and running down from this ravine on each side of us and in a direction pretty nearly parallel to the sides of triangle was another ravine. On the far side of the ravine on the right there was open ground, but on the left for a long distance the whole country was rolling and bushy, and it was from this side that the heaviest firing seemed to come. "C" School was ordered to protect the right flank and clear the ravine on that side, while to the Queen's Own and Guards were assigned a similar duty on the left. The Battleford men were to look after the rear. The police and artillery were busily engaged in front.

This was at 5:15 A.M.; as to what happened after that, except in my own immediate vicinity, I know nothing but by hearsay. I saw no more of the Guards, Battleford Rifles, and our fellows till we were on our way home.

For half an hour we had quite hot enough work and the bullets came flying about us in a not over-pleasant manner. We were exposed to fire from three sides and had to grin and bear it. After half an hour or so we had quite silenced any fire on the right, that is, our own immediate front and could easily keep the ravine clear as the Indians could not reach it without exposing themselves and this they never dared to do. Colonel Otter, asking how things were and being told this, ordered Mr. Wadmore to take the men up to the Front and reinforce the line there and at the same time he asked me to take a couple of men and carry some ammunition to the fighting line. While doing this I had a chance of seeing how things were going on. The wagons I found were formed in a square in a dip in the ground, the horses fastened to them and the Mounted Police horses formed in a corral a short distance from the wagons. So far no men near me had been hit, but I heard the cry of "Ambulance" several times, though too busy to notice particularly where or why the cry was raised. Now sad to say I saw only too well why the bearers were needed. A small square was formed with wagons and here Strange and Lesslie were busily engaged. Several poor fellows were lying there that needed no further looking after, but others were having wounds bound up and being made as comfortable as was possible.

We get the ammunition and, carrying it across the exposed space as quickly as possible, reach the guns and the front of the line. Here the fighting is still hot and several men are hit, but gradually the fire in our front slackens and bullets come in any quantity only from the left. There the Queen's Own are evidently having plenty of work: the rattle of rifles is unceasing, where I am the Gatling is worked whenever there appears to be a chance, and every now and then the guns throw a shell or two at the enemy. Unfortunately we have with us the Mounted Police guns – the small howitzers – and they prove to be utter failures. In the first place they are not heavy enough and in the second place they are not even in working order. After the first few shots the trails went to pieces and, before any further shots could be fired, the gun had to be fastened as best it could with ropes. Very little could be done with guns in this condition but all that could be done was done by Major Short and Captain Rutherford.[29] Their pluck and coolness was in striking contrast to the miserable skulking spirit shown by the French-Canadian gunners who "funked" decidedly and were of no use whatever. Major Short and one or two men worked one gun by themselves and made some beautiful long shots at the tepees, which could be seen about a thousand yards away, and at groups of horsemen who supposed they were out of all danger. I stayed near the guns for a considerable time till Colonel Otter and Colonel Herchmer decided that we could not advance and must retire. This was about eleven. The fire of the enemy seemed to be almost completely silenced but it was thought that we could not advance without great loss through the broken country in front of us, in the face of an evidently numerous foe. The wagons and guns were to be taken across the creek and the Gatling, artillery, and "C" School were to stay on the hill to cover the retreat. I ran across to rejoin "C" School, who were now on the right front, and gave Mr. Wadmore the order. I found that while I was away one poor fellow had been shot dead, having been hit in three places as he raised himself to fire.

Between half past eleven and twelve we got the order to retire, and then came the most trying part of the day. We had got about three hundred yards from the crest of the hill before the Indians knew what was up and appeared on it, but then a heavy fire opened on us and mighty hard work it was to walk quietly down with the bullets whistling by. The men behaved however with great coolness and steadiness and the artillery and ourselves retired alternately fifty yards or so at a time, then halted and kept up a steady fire. The Gatling was now near the creek and opened on the Indians and Captain Rutherford sent some shells among them from the far side and they evidently felt they had had enough. They did not attempt to follow us past the creek and this we crossed quietly, the men, with admirable coolness, each waiting his turn to cross the stream by a log that lay across it and refusing to gain time by wading through the water.

Across the creek we found everything prepared for a start and we got in our wagons without delay and made off.

I was very much rejoiced to find Hume and my other particular friends safe. All agreed that No. 1 had behaved magnificently, Colonel Otter saying they fought like tigers; but, strange to say, they had not lost a man, though six had been wounded.

Our total loss was six killed outright and eighteen wounded and, of these, two cannot possibly live, while two or three others are in a very dangerous condition.

We drive for about an hour and then stop and water the horses and have something to eat and not before we need it. We have had nothing since last night and are almost exhausted now that the excitement is over. After a short rest we press on and reach Battleford about 11 P.M. The journey is very trying to the poor fellows who have been hit; they are made as comfortable as possible with blankets, but the jolting over the rough road causes them agony. At Fort Otter they receive some much needed attention.

I do not quite understand as yet what my sensations really were when I first came under fire. I did not feel afraid exactly but I certainly did feel that it would be much nicer to be somewhere else. After a time when other fellows were struck and I continued to escape I felt as if I should get through all right and did not think about the danger.

Our Ambulance Corps came in for great praise for their conduct; they seemed to be always on hand when needed and exposed themselves with the greatest pluck. None of them were hit, though narrow escapes were frequent. One man shows his cap with two bullet holes through it; another has a button cut from his tunic; the coat of a third is ripped across his back by a ball, and so on.

Other marvellous escapes are heard of. Major Short has lost the gold braid from one side of his forage cap. Fraser (of "F" Company) has his hair ruffled and his scalp grazed. McKell is just touched on the temple, and so on. I was not touched and had no such decidedly near shave as these, but one bullet struck the earth a few inches from my head and was quite as close as was pleasant. Another ball came whistling by me and buried itself with a sickening thud in, as I thought, the man next me about a foot away. I turned expecting to see him knocked over, but his helmet only had suffered. At one time I was lying down with my sword resting on my hip and shining brightly in the sun; some fellow evidently saw this and fired three shots at me. The last time he very nearly had me and I quietly adjourned.

The fellows say Acheson and Lloyd[30] behaved very well, carrying in a wounded man under a heavy fire, Lloyd himself being wounded while doing this. Hume Cronyn and Blakeley too carried off some of the men.

Early in the day the Indians made a rush for the guns and nearly had them. The artillery fell back at first but were rallied by Short and drove the redskins back.

Horrible-looking fellows these Indians are and they fought in a way that surprised the police, who have been accustomed to look upon them as arrant cowards. They are the *beau ideal* of skirmishers, expose themselves but little, and move with marvellous quickness. Frequently they would show a blanket or some article of attire to draw our fire and then pot at the unfortunate individual who had exposed himself. One or two of the dead I examined. They had nothing on but a shirt and leggings and a blanket over the shoulder. The hair long and plaited and the faces and bodies painted—most ferocious-looking wretches.

The place where the fight took place is known as Cut Knife Hill and is an ancient battleground of the Cree. Here they fought a desperate battle with the Blackfeet and drove them from the country. The second victory on this ground will cause them to regard themselves as here invincible.

It is too bad to think that we have had to retire, but though we have retreated I think we have given a good deal more than we got. The Indians have evidently been pretty well punished or they would certainly not have allowed us to return undisturbed. The men were full of fight but terribly tired and, with an exhausted force and disabled guns, it was considered too risky to press on. A great mistake it was not to take our field guns; in this as in other matters we have been deceived. We were told that the country was quite impassable for heavy guns and we found that, though not without difficulty, we could have brought them. Then we have been altogether deceived as to the strength and intentions of the Indians. However, it cannot be helped and we must only hope for better luck next time.

Sunday, May 3rd

We sleep this morning till a late hour and are glad enough to rest quietly all day. Heavy pickets were out last night but no alarm occurs. Today we are all anxious to hear news of the fight.

Two poor fellows die this morning, they have been quite unconscious since they were struck, both shot through the head. I was very sorry to see poor little Winder among the dead. He is a young English fellow—a gentleman—very bright and good-looking—who has been working as a teamster, and has a farm near Brandon. He was the last man struck and had just taken rifle to "have a shot at the beggars" before driving his horses off. Most of the teamsters behaved very badly; they were not expected to fight but they would not even drive their teams where they were told. The war correspondents who were to do great things also behaved disgracefully and they had to keep them in countenance. One who ought to have known better, the quartermaster sergeant of "C" School, kept himself carefully under cover. He has been hated by the men all along and now they cheerfully exchange hatred for contempt.

The Toronto Red Cross Corps join us this afternoon, just in the nick of time. They are very indignant when they hear the stories that have been circulated about them by the members of the rival organization and promise to make it hot for those gentlemen. The delay in their advance has been caused by want of transport. Nattress had to go back from the Saskatchewan to Swift Current to get teams and then could only obtain from General Laurie,[31] who is in charge, enough teams to carry the staff and their absolute necessaries. The hospital supplies had to remain behind, the old fool saying that these were "luxuries" and not "necessaries." Consequently the poor fellows hit yesterday have to get on as best they may with fat pork and biscuits, and nice food it is for a sick man.

A large marquee, brought up by us for a mess tent, is put up across the river as a hospital and the wounded are taken across.

MONDAY, MAY 4TH

Everything quiet last night. Today beautifully bright and warm.

We this morning bury our dead. The graves are dug in a quiet spot on the banks of the Saskatchewan and we lay our comrades there side by side. One of the killed was a Roman Catholic and a separate service is held over him then we have the English service, fire the three volleys, and sadly depart. It certainly was a most solemn burial. One realizes what a serious and sudden thing such a death is and we wonder when and where the next man's turn may come.

Our wounded are doing well today and are brightening up after the first shock. The doctors speak hopefully of them all. Poor food is the great drawback, but the climate and air are magnificent.

TUESDAY, MAY 5TH

I was on picket duty last night and had no excitement. Very cold toward morning, though, and we wonder when spring comes in this desolate country. The days are bright and warm at last, but the nights — one shivers when one thinks of them.

Today I return to duty with the Queen's Own and rejoin No. 1 Company. Spend the day writing letters. In the afternoon I make a most joyful discovery. In Fort Otter I find a harmonium, much battered and knocked about, but still able to send forth recognizable sounds. One of our men, an organ-builder, gets to work at it and soon has a very fair instrument at my service. There is now something to live for.

This afternoon Captain Todd sees a suspicious-looking character on some distant hills. He takes twenty men and gives chase. The supposed Indian turns out to be a Queen's Own man who is out foraging and he is consigned ignominiously to the guard tent. Our fellows are always up to some mischief; the brigadier says he never knows where he will find them next.

WEDNESDAY, MAY 6TH

The cold last night was something unbearable; some peculiarity about it left us powerless to protect ourselves. We nearly froze in our tents and the men on picket suffered severely.

The day is cold and dreary and we have nothing particular to do. Orders are given today that No. 1 Company is to remain here in charge of Fort Otter and all the other troops to cross. The staff and the police cross this afternoon.

We get a mail today and are able to enjoy our letters.

THURSDAY, MAY 7TH

Last night much pleasanter, comparatively warm, in fact.

This morning I cross the river and do Battleford. Business is evidently reviving. I find in one place Moose Jaw beer exposed for sale. Undeterred by previous sad experience I experiment once more and with difficulty survive. I stay to dinner at the mess

161

and am in luck. Actually have some fresh fish. These were presented to the colonel by a grateful native. The treat is almost too much; the first fresh food of any kind I have had since leaving Swift Current.

"C" School and No. 4 Company cross this afternoon, and No. 1 Company move into the enclosure at Fort Otter and pitch their tents. The artillery refuse to remain outside by themselves and crowd into the house for the night, leaving their tents standing.

About 8 P.M. the guards alarm us and state that mounted men are approaching. We prepare for emergencies but soon find the alarming horsemen are Major Short and some other officers who have been out for a canter.

We get a mail this evening—papers down to April 20th and letters down to the 27th. No one gives us any particulars about the general's fight, apparently taking for granted that we know all about it. We hear of the supplies that the good people at home are sending us and feel grateful accordingly. We also hear that General Laurie has stated that he would not forward such trash to us and we curse him freely.

One of our scouts was, we hear, killed this morning while out near Cut Knife; we have however, no particulars.

FRIDAY, MAY 8TH

We have a quiet night and this morning the artillery depart, much to our delight. They are a dirty, noisy, unsoldierly lot and quite unworthy of their officers, who are as decent fellows as one would care to meet. Two of them, Captain Rutherford and Lieutenant Prower (the latter attached merely), dine with us today.

As soon as the artillery go we get things in something like order. We manage to fit up one nice bright room for a dining room and sitting room and make ourselves comfortable there with a stove. Another room we make our sleeping apartment. No beds, of course, but we shall be comparatively clean and cozy on the floor. The men are to keep to the tents. We shall have to keep up a pretty large guard and one officer will be up each night.

In the afternoon I pay the camp a short visit — nothing going on. Men are working at a bridge across the Battle River and expect to have it finished in a few days. Merely posts sunk in the mud and cross-pieces run across.

We hear that the scout was not killed yesterday, but was captured. He is a halfbreed and it is thought he allowed himself to be taken.

Major Allan and Harry Mickle, who is now doing duty as a lieutenant, visit us this evening and bring us papers down to April 25th. In them we find accounts of the fight at Fish Creek. Papers brought in by a supply train.

SATURDAY, MAY 9TH

A beautiful warm day. I am on duty and spend the day with a fatigue party cleaning our domain and getting things into order. Soon we expect to have everything shipshape. Fill a number of sandbags, too, and place them in position on the walls.

The brigadier and Dr. Strange pay us a visit in the afternoon and seem to be pleased with our efforts to improve the fort. Tell us a cricket match is in progress on the other side and all the youth and beauty of Battleford present. They also tell us that a dispatch has come from Clarke's Crossing stating that heavy firing is going on at the Front. Another engagement, of course, but no particulars.

I kill today no less than three mosquitoes. We think of the marvels we have heard of the size and ferocity of the Northwest mosquito and tremble at the thought of his approach.

SUNDAY, MAY 10TH

On duty last night. About 11:30 P.M. the sergeant of the guard reports that he heard three shots from the direction of the ferry where a picket is stationed. I see the signal light at the camp working and waken Captain Brown and our signal men. Then I take a file of men and go down to the ferry to see what the trouble is. We have a mighty unpleasant walk of five hundred yards in the dark. I find that a sentry at the ferry has been fired upon and returned the fire, and the men are evidently very much excited. Stay a short time obtaining full particulars and then make our way back to the fort and very glad we are to get there. We find that the guard at the camp thought they saw lights at the fort and heard shots and so began to signal to us. We explain what has happened and keep a sharp lookout for the night but nothing further alarms us.

We have a fine warm day and Acheson comes over and has service for us, speaking very feelingly of our merciful escape on the 2nd. I run the musical portion of the service and we have some very fine hymns. Have a choir of eight men, all members of choirs in Toronto and nearly all with more than ordinarily fine voices.

We do not try any chants today; my Presbyterian fingers require more practice before they can grind these out with the requisite neatness and dispatch.

Captains Mutton and Mickle come to church and they and the parson stay to dinner. We astonish and gratify them by the elaborate spread. We have no better rations than our comrades across the river, but we have magnificent facilities for cooking and our men surprise us every now and then with some indescribable but very palatable concoctions. The complaints are bitter about the food over the way. The pork is not very good and the corned beef is shunned; consequently hard tack and tea form the staple articles of diet. We have today corned beef pie, pork pancakes and syrup, apple tarts, rolls, and tea. The rolls we very aptly call "nine-pounders."

In the afternoon I run over the camp but hear no further news about the fighting. Brock[32] and Baird[33] (who has been promoted to a lieutenant) come back with me and we sing hymns vigorously for a couple of hours with much enthusiasm and enjoyment, if not with very much sweetness.

Monday, May 11th

Captain Brown, who was on duty last night, tells us this morning that some five or six shots were fired last night near the ferry. He did not call us. On inquiry this morning we find that the Battleford Home Guard were on guard last night at the river and, mistaking some stray cattle for Indians, opened fire and then ran. Unfortunately no cows were killed or we might have forgiven the alarm.

We have at breakfast another novelty—what our cook calls "dough-boys." Captain Brown thinks "sudden death" would be a more suitable name. Captain Hughes (who is R.C.) proposes that they be called "dogans" because they are "toughs." To compensate us for our struggle with this delicacy we are favored with a delightful stew of corned beef, potatoes, and turnips. Astonished inquiry elicits the fact that the vegetables have been "yaffled." Yaffle means "to appropriate without the consent of the owner" and in this country when anything is concerned, the consent of the owner can very often be conveniently dispensed with.

The bridge is today completed and the glory of the ferry departs.

TUESDAY, MAY 12TH

Another bright warm day. I have all hands at work all day and a marked improvement in the appearance of the place is the result. It really looks very well indeed now. No good grass about it unfortunately but all stray paper and sticks have been carefully put out of sight and the sand neatly raked. Our chief trouble here is caused by the high winds that seem to prevail here all day. The sand is blown about in a very unpleasant manner and gives us much work to keep tents and houses neat and clean.

I am today invited to try a Northwest drink: ingredients—axle grease, red ink, and pain killer. I decline. Another of Radway's Ready Relief and Cazenna Pepper fails to tempt me. I am told that *the* beverage is a concoction of spirits of wine—coal-oil and extract of tobacco; this is to be prepared and offered me at a future date. All these are really imbibed in this country.

The "oldest inhabitant" speaking to me about the uncertainty of the climate said to me "I came here five years ago a have never taken off my underclothing since."

WEDNESDAY, MAY 13TH

Up all last night on duty but no alarm occurs. Today is beautifully bright and warm and I go over to the camp for a short time. Captains Delamere[34] and Macdonald[35] and Lieutenant Lee[36] come back with me to dinner and exclaim at our luxurious establishment. Newby of the guards and Mickle come over in the afternoon and bring us the good news from the general. We are all delighted at the prospect of getting home and this news we all feel means home. Newby and Mickle stay to tea but leave early. The Battleford Home Guard are in charge of the bridge and that means death to the benighted traveller.

We have now been at Fort Otter a week. The original intention was to relieve us at the expiration of this time and send another company over. We are altogether too comfortable, however, and want to stay. Captain Brown sees Colonel Otter, who very kindly says that he could not possibly be better satisfied than to leave a responsible charge in such good hands, and as the general idea at the camp and in the town is that we are in a position of deadly danger, we quietly encourage this view and soon find that we shall not be disturbed.

THURSDAY, MAY 14TH

Cloudy and threatening in the morning and heavy showers and high winds in the afternoon.

We have an exciting day. One of the mail carriers comes in this morning and tells us that some fifteen miles away he met a number of teamsters riding south as fast as their horses could carry them. Some twenty teams on their way here had been attacked by Indians and only five or six of the men escaped. The courier very pluckily came on and got in safely, though he was seen and pursued.

Shortly after this some five or six Mounted Police ride in hurriedly and tell us that they were fired upon some six miles away when out on patrol duty and have, sad to say, lost one man killed and one wounded. This comes of our enforced inaction. The general has persistently refused to allow us to move against Poundmaker again and he, being undisturbed, has become bold once more.

FRIDAY, MAY 15TH

We increased our guard last night but have no trouble. Today is bright and clear and we work at our defences all day.

Baird and Harry come over in the afternoon and give us particulars of the great news from the general.

A party of scouts and police go out today to the scene of yesterday's disaster. They find the body of the policeman killed yesterday wrapped carefully in canvas and decently buried. Most unusual respect to the dead to be shown by Indians. We learn from the scouts that the Indians camped about six miles away last night and are now apparently working east. The supply train captured yesterday was a small and not important one but the next time we may not be so lucky. Perhaps now an escort will be sent with the supply trains and a proper guard kept at the halting places. We hear of one station where one solitary man is in charge and there are stored thousands boxes of beef and biscuit and, more valuable still, a great many rifles and much ammunition. This is a station only some forty miles away and easily within reach of the Nitchies.

SATURDAY, MAY 16TH

I was on duty all night and have no trouble. About 1 A.M. a sentry and I have a consultation as to the advisability of shooting what afterward we discover to be a pig. There is now very little difficulty in keeping a good lookout, the nights are so wonderfully bright; we have only three or four hours of what can be called darkness. So much ineffective firing took place on the part of sentries that now they are supplied with buckshot cartridge, and if they do try to hit anyone they ought to kill something, though probably not what they aim at. We are very proud of the fact that none of our sentries have yet been foolish enough to alarm us unnecessarily.

The colonel honors us by dining with us today. We give him an "elegant spread"—baked pike (captured by the winning smile of our orderly, who has made a conquest of a too-susceptible dusky maiden), rabbit pie (rabbits swarm near here and our men are beginning to catch numbers of them), plum pudding (without the plums and etceteras), apple tart, and a few precious potatoes. Then we have tea, cocoa prepared in what the colonel is pleased to call my "inimitable style," and, last but not least, whisky and water. We supply the water, no slight thing in this country, but we have a beautiful well and the colonel brings over the bottle. He asks us to fill our glasses and we drink "The Queen" with great enthusiasm when he announces the delightful news of Riel's capture.

Captain Hughes goes out today with a squad of men and captures a cow and pig. The cow is a great find and the thought of milk affords us much gratification. The pig, strange to say, comes to an untimely end. It apparently becomes enraged at some thoughtless taunt flung at it by one of the guards and commits suicide by rushing on an unsheathed bayonet. It is a sad fate but we dry our tears and consign the body to our ice-house. This is another grand standby at Fort Otter; we really can be quite comfortable now here.

We have a choir practice this evening and the singing promises to be very good tomorrow. Major Allan, Macdonald, and Brock look in for a short time.

SUNDAY, MAY 17TH

A very fine beautiful day. Last night our sentries saw two mounted men ride along the trail but had no chance for a shot.

Today we have a delightful service, the music being really very fine; we indulge in Jackson's "Te Deum" and in very pretty chants for the benite and benedictors. We have also four hymns and wind up with "God Save the Queen." The fame of our services has gone abroad and a number of officers come over today. Only Baird and the parson (Acheson) stay to dinner, however.

In the afternoon I go over to the town and stay for the Presbyterian service. Reverend Cameron preaches and the sermon is very interesting and enjoyable.

Afterward we go the hospital and have a chat with the fellows—all doing well and now, we hope, out of danger.

Stay to tea at the camp and then McGee,[37] Brock, and Harry come over for some music. Men engaged in the rendition of pleasing sacred melodies. We learn by signal that Riel has been court-martialed and shot. Joy sits on every countenance and we sing our glorious old anthem with great enthusiasm and effect.

At the town today many fears are expressed for our safety here. Poundmaker is supposed to be still quite close to us and the townspeople expect us to be wiped out. We do not worry, however.

Monday, May 18th

Last night Captain Hughes was on duty and rushes in about midnight and alarms us. Shots have been fired near us, he says, and Captain Brown and I grasp our swords and revolvers and make for the walls. No further shots are heard and we retire again. In the morning we find that the Battleford men have again been distinguishing themselves.

We today place more sandbags on our walls and get several windows in good condition for sharpshooters. Then we stretch wires in front of our ramparts and feel that we have considerably improved our powers of defence. Five of our pioneers are sent over this morning to make some loopholes for us and to build a lookout for us on the roof.

The unfortunate policeman Elliot,[38] the last victim, was buried yesterday with military honors, the tenth man who has fallen.

We are disgusted to find that the report of Riel's execution is untrue; really too bad not to have put an end to the brute.

Busy reading the Honorable Alex Morris's *Indian Treaties*[39] today. Find that our friend Poundmaker's proper name in Cree is "Oopeetookerahanafreeweezin." No wonder he was too much for us.

TUESDAY, MAY 19TH

Up all night, no alarm. Weather now mild and pleasant and last night we see a great deal of lightning. The sunrise is very fine but stormy-looking and, sure enough, in the afternoon we have heavy squalls of rain and hail. Colonel Otter and Colonel Herchmer visit us in the afternoon and are much pleased at the appearance of everything. Mutton and Wadmore also look in and take what they are pleased to call "sketches" of the fort. Then Lesslie and Major Allan come to tea so that we are kept busy entertaining our guests. We find that during the squall this afternoon the hospital tent was blown down and the unfortunate patients thoroughly drenched. They were carried into the police barracks as soon as possible and made comfortable once more.

We have a great treat today. Hughes brings over to dinner the Roman Catholic priest the Reverend A.H. Biganesse, a remarkably clever, entertaining man. He has spent six years among the Indians and is thoroughly acquainted with their ways and character.

For several hours he delights us by story after story of the red man. He sympathizes very much with them in this trouble. They are, he says, just like children, know when they do wrong, but never think of consequences, and the young braves are almost beyond any control, though the chiefs and councillors have lots of common sense. Many of the chiefs are very fine men. Poundmaker is a handsome, shrewd Indian and much respected by the Cree. His name should literally be interpreted "the man who sits near the pound," and is derived from the old custom of driving buffalo into an enclosure, when one man remained hidden near the entrance and closed the gate on the captives. This was the post of honor, and a position that required a man of skill and nerve. Poundmaker cannot speak English or French. A son of his at the Mission School at Edmonton is quite well educated and will be a "great chief."

The Indians often ill-treated by the whites — cheated, cursed, and oppressed. The settlers often take advantage of them, make a bargain with them to work for a certain reward and, when the work is finished, send them off without any recompense. From the whites the Indians have learned to lie and steal. Naturally most honest and truthful and, even now, if an Indian says you can depend on what he says, you are quit safe in doing so. One intelligent Stoney's sole knowledge of English consisted in his ability to repeat the well-known phrase "Get out, damn you," with which he was greeted as he approached any white man's dwelling.

The Father speaks Cree fluently and told us many curious things about the language. It is easy to learn to a certain extent but there are many very fine distinctions that are picked up only with great difficulty. There are no tenses or declensions, but each state of facts is expressed by a different word and they are very fond of compounds. A very strange thing is that the children, when they are able to speak, always speak just as their elders; never have any difficulty about grammatical contractions or what corresponds thereto. This certainly is a great advance on our much vaunted system of education.

There are a number of halfbreeds at present with Poundmaker. They did not wish to join in the rising, but Riel sent word to Poundmaker to compel them to go with him, and off they had to march. The halfbreed settlement was some distance from Battleford and all the inhabitants are now with the Indians. With them is also their priest, a very fine man Father Biganesse says.

The Indians here are pagans. They will not become Christians because they know they must change their manner of life. Most of the men have two or three wives and these women do all the work. The men are very lazy, though now they are becoming better in this respect and are willing to do what they can to earn a living. They are not able to stand continuous labor. The disappearance of the buffalo was a terrible loss to them. From that animal they supplied all their wants. Now very often they are reduced to dreadful straits. The government allowance goes a very little way and is in fact often gobbled up by voracious and not over-honest storekeepers without reaching poor (?) at all. They are tremendous eaters when they have a chance, disposing of five or six meals a day, but on the other hand when nothing is to be had, going calmly for days unfed without trouble. They will eat what no dog would touch. Then he gives us a couple of instances. In one tepee in the spring when things are at the worst as a rule, he found the family dining off soup made by boiling some sacking in which bacon had been wrapped, and which had been used as bedding all winter, the water being obtained by melting snow that was taken from the floor of the mansion.

Another case was that of a chief who had a number of very good dogs. One spring things went very hard with the old gentleman and one dog after another had to be killed and eaten to keep him from starving. At last only one, the favorite companion, was left. The pangs of hunger became too fierce to be borne and at last the old man decided that this dog, too, must go. He went out much troubled and very loath to put an end to his friend when a brilliant idea struck him. He cut off his dear dog's tail, picked the bones clean, and was revived, handed the remnants to the faithful animal himself, and both were preserved.

Indians are very fond of talking. When they know they are to make a speech, they stay apart several days to prepare themselves, and then very often speak very forcibly and beautifully. If they want anything they never come and ask for it directly but enter into a long conversation on all sorts of irrelevant subjects and then gradually explain the object of the visit. The Indian etiquette is on coming into a house or lodge to sit smoking for a considerable time without uttering a word, then they begin their talk.

They are very much ashamed of themselves if they are betrayed into speaking angrily or excitedly and think it a terrible reproach to be sneered at for loud talking. They never quarrel with one another directly but make accusations against or complaints of one another to a third party, who is the recipient of the mutual recriminations and acts as conductor of the flame. Of course when they get liquor they lose all control of themselves and are then terrible fiends. They are very superstitious and will not touch a dead body, have a great dread of ghosts, and always move camp if a member of the tribe dies. They are very vindictive, never forgetting or forgiving an insult, and an angry word they consider a very grave insult, indeed, so that one has to be very careful in dealing with them.

Father Biganesse does not think the Indians would kill a prisoner; they know it is to their interest to take as many alive as possible. They would kill wounded men, however, because they think that the best thing to do. The Indians, he thinks, are poor shots. They are in the habit of creeping up to their game and never fire till they get close. They are not much accustomed to rifles and cannot judge range well.

WEDNESDAY, MAY 20TH

All quiet last night. This morning we go on with our defensive preparations and Captain Hughes constructs an elaborate abatis—the men say to give the Indians cover.

In the afternoon I go over to the camp and stay to tea. Our supplies are, we hear, well on their way now and it is decided to send a party of one hundred men down to meet the train. One company of our men is to go and No. 4 is chosen (Captain Kersteman[40] being the next senior captain to Captain Brown).

I get back to the fort about eight and a very few minutes afterward we are astonished to see a priest and a breed ride rapidly up to the gate. In a moment we are all out and find that the priest is none other than the one spoken of by Father Biganesse yesterday and that he has come in from Poundmaker with an offer of surrender. The Indians are some fifty miles away or more this morning and are making their way back slowly. We at once send the priest to the brigadier under a proper escort. Behind the priest a short distance come some twenty-five prisoners sent in by Poundmaker. They are the teamsters and some breeds, and are overjoyed to get back safely. They have been fairly well treated but once or twice a discussion has taken place as to the advisability of shooting them, and their position has not been altogether a happy one. It seems that their capture was after all quite accidental. Poundmaker and his band were making off as fast as they could to the east and unfortunately just as they crossed the trail met our wagons.

There is great rejoicing tonight at the thought that we may soon be home. With Riel and Poundmaker disposed of, we may reasonably hope to be free ere long. Big Bear should not be able to give much trouble.

THURSDAY, MAY 21ST

I was on duty last night and was particularly careful for fear of treachery.

We have showers all morning, the rainy season is evidently at hand and with it will come the dreaded mosquito.

The Pioneers complete their work today and return to camp. We have a most magnificent outlook on the roof and have a sentry posted there during daylight, that is, at present from 3 A.M. to 9 P.M.

Dr. Strange, Major Allan, Sears, Mutton, Kersteman, and Harry come over this evening and we have some music.

The priest, the Reverend Father Cochin,[41] returns to Poundmaker this evening with Colonel Otter's answer. The colonel tells Poundmaker the general will be here in a day or two and that he must come in and give himself up.

FRIDAY, MAY 22ND

All quiet again last night. A magnificent bright day. I go over to the camp but there is nothing going on there. The men grumble very much at the heavy duty they have to perform; fatigues nearly every day and guards and pickets each night, every man on duty as a rule every alternate night. I return very well satisfied to our own snug, happy quarters.

Private Watts rejoins today from hospital. He is not yet discharged but is now able to be about.

We are told that a courier is going down in the morning and we write letters this evening – getting very much disgusted at the long delay in receiving any mails.

For some time we have had drill or bayonet exercise every afternoon, and our men are beginning to work splendidly together, a fine-looking and very fine-hearted lot of fellows they are.

SATURDAY, MAY 23RD

Another fine warm day. Father Cochin returns from Poundmaker and says he is coming in to surrender. Two more prisoners come in, halfbreed women—the whole of the halfbreeds are to be here on Monday.

The priest gives us some information about the fight at Cut Knife. He was present for a time and thinks we had a marvellous escape. The Indians had surrounded us entirely and thought they would kill us all; we were in full view but our fire was so hot they never had a chance to aim at us properly and thus we were saved. The priest does not know how many Indians were killed; he buried five of his own people and there were others besides these. The body of Osgoode of the Guards, whom we were unable to carry off, was buried by him. Poundmaker had with him in the fight 380 braves and about forty halfbreeds and besides these there were some two hundred old men and boys who remained in the camp. Riel had told the Indians that the Yankees were coming to help him and when they saw the dark tunics of the Queen's Own they thought they were friendly and would turn on the redcoats as soon as firing began. The Indians were pretty well finished and Poundmaker wanted to surrender, saying that other troops were coming up and if they fought like the ones at Cut Knife, they could do nothing. The Stonies persuaded him to hold out, however, and as day after day passed without molestation, they decided to move and try and join Riel. Every day they expected to be attacked and advanced in fear and trembling. They would march a few miles each morning and then spend the rest of the day in making rifle-pits and preparing to resist us. At last came the news of Riel's defeat and they saw the game was up.

The priest does not think we could have advanced at Cut Knife. A deep ravine was before us and we should have been terribly cut up in crossing that.

SUNDAY, MAY 24TH

Raining hard this morning but about nine it cleared and became beautifully fine and bright.

At Reveille we hoisted a minature Royal Standard and a Canadian Ensign (the latter yaffled by our gallant commandant from the brigade officer) and our bugler sounded a flourish.

We have service this morning—Broughall officiating—and go in for specially fine hymns and chants. The effect of the "Te Deum" is somewhat marred however by the inattention of the "soprano," who turns over a page five bars too soon, the unfortunate organist failing lamentably in his attempt to overcome the difficulty caused by this "previousness." Have a number of officers at the service, there being no church parade today across the river.

After church the garrison fall in, present arms, give three cheers, and dip the Colors. Then the men are dismissed and supplied by us with some extras for dinner and show their loyalty by readily disposing of the good things. We have quite a party ourselves—the parson (Broughall), Lieutenants Gray and Todd of the Guards, and Major Allan, Captain Macdonald, and Lieutenants George[42] and Mickle of "Ours," and astonish our guests by our bill of fare: snowbird soup, rabbit pie, canned corned beef, brawn, beans, rhubarb pudding, apple tart, rolls, tea, and coffee.

The rhubarb, by the way, has a history. I discovered some plants ten days ago and have carefully watched and tended them since. Yesterday the owner of the garden in which the plants had been found by me came in to see us and casually remarked that he had come over to see his garden and to pick a little rhubarb for his Sunday dinner; said, moreover, that his rhubarb was a rule very fine and that he would bring us some on the way back. At that very time all the tender shoots that had flourished in the favoured spot were quietly simmering in our pots. Our friend did not return.

The general comes in tonight about eight by steamer. Captain Hughes goes over to hear the news. He tells us on his return that the general has brought up six companies of the Midland, "A" Battery, and some scouts; the other troops are expected in a day or two. We now hear full accounts of Batoche.

MONDAY, MAY 25TH

I was on duty all night and have the men up at a very early hour and see that everything is in thoroughly good order.

About half past eight we receive orders to parade at the camp at ten and shortly after nine Captain

Brown and thirty-five men march off, leaving me in charge of the fort with some ten files. The company no sooner cross the river and reach the brigade office than they are ordered back, the scouts having reported that the Indians are coming in and it being deemed advisable to keep all our force in the fort. The general is to come over and inspect us in the afternoon.

We watch with great enjoyment the review of the troops on the Battleford Common. A beautiful sight it is in the bright sunlight. We ourselves are not to be outdone and go through the official program, forming a Battalion with our guard and company (Captain Hughes taking command) and marching past Captain Brown, our reviewing officer, in column, quarter-column, and at the double; having first, of course, given the "Royal Salute" and three hearty cheers.

About 4 P.M. we are warned that the general and his staff are crossing the bridge. We are just nicely prepared for him when he rides up and, after acknowledging our salute, inspects us, and is highly complimentary. He goes over the building and spends some time in the lookout nest and departs evidently under the impression that we are a deal too comfortable. We hear that he does not approve of comfort and expect to get "notice to quit."

This afternoon we can see some three miles away a number of horsemen and wagons and the smoke of campfires. Colonel Herchmer rides out to inspect them and finds that they are the halfbreeds who have been with Poundmaker and tells us they are coming in the morning. Poundmaker himself is expected tomorrow.

TUESDAY, MAY 26TH

A very beautiful day. Early in the morning the half-breeds come in—some thirty families—and a dirty-looking lot they are.

Just after breakfast the lookout sentry reports that two horsemen are coming in and these turn out to be an Indian and halfbreed who report that Poundmaker is just behind. Colonel Williams, who just at this time rides up, takes charge of the Indian and gallops off with him to report to the general. Soon we see a band of horsemen approaching rapidly and ere long the renowned Cree chief appears before us. Captain Brown is unfortunately at the brigade office but Captain Hughes and myself receive the braves at the gate of our fortress with becoming dignity. Poundmaker is accompanied by some fifteen subchiefs and councillors and the appearance of the band is very picturesque and striking. The Great Chief himself is a very remarkable looking man: tall, very handsome, and intelligent-looking and dignified to a degree. He wears a handsome war cap made of the head of a cinnamon bear, with a long tuft of feathers floating from it, a leather jacket studded with brass nails and worked with beads, long beaded leggings coming up to his hips, and brightly colored moccasins, while over his shoulders hangs a very gaily colored blanket. The others are dressed in much the same manner and all are elaborately painted. Poundmaker shakes hands

183

with us without dismounting or uncovering but all the others get off their horses and take off their caps before they approach us. After a short talk we send the party on to the general and when Captain Brown comes back hear from him an account of the pow-wow between the chiefs and our commander; the scene must have been a very curious one and the whole affair not a little interesting. Poundmaker and some of his chief men are put under arrest, the others are sent off to their reserve and all stolen property is ordered to be given up. All day long the Indians continue to come in bringing with them many rifles, ponies, wagons, and other spoils: they look most unlovingly at us as they pass and evidently are not at all pleased at the present phase of affairs.

The 90th come in this afternoon and most of the officers spend the evening at our camp. Captain Brown and I go over and have a very jolly time. The 90th officers are a most decent lot and we get on swimmingly together. They are all terribly down on the general: say he has lots of pluck but no head and threw away chance after chance. We also hear a good deal about the Midlanders. They have managed to make themselves pretty universally disliked – had a company and a half at Batoche but talk as if they had done everything there. Two of their officers yesterday had the bad taste to visit the Mounted Police camp and accuse the Prince Albert Police of cowardice. Very soon they found it too hot and had to depart; today they have been ordered to make a public apology.

A mail is to leave tomorrow and today many letters are written. We are quite in despair now and never expect to hear from our friends again.

WEDNESDAY, MAY 27TH

We have rain this morning for a short time and a few showers through the day. A large number of Indians come in bringing with them some eighty wagons and carts and over one hundred horses; these are all seized and the Indians sent away.

Have a very jolly and very good dinner today — Captain Howard of Gatling fame, Major Buchan[43] and Lieutenant Campbell[44] of the 90th, and Captain Macdonald our guests. We have a neat repast — rabbit pie, brawn, mushrooms, currant pudding, apple tart, rolls, doughnuts, and tea and coffee. I am much complimented on my housekeeping.

Howard gives us a very quaint and entertaining account of the campaign. He is tremendously down on the general and as he is not in our service is able to express his opinions with charming frankness.

This morning Lesslie comes over with a large fatigue party and works for some time at one of the large rooms, putting it in order. He tells us a concert is to be given by the regiment. We feel that we might, without being considered as putting on too much side, have been consulted about the affair.

Today pickets are done away with across the river and we reduce our guard here. After this we decide that it will not be necessary to sit up all night but that a visit every two or three hours to the sentries will be sufficient.

Thursday, May 28th

A very fine warm day. The Grenadiers and "C" School march into camp this morning having arrived by steamer late last night.

The chief Moosemin [*sic*] comes in today. He has been loyal during the trouble and is well received.

The regimental concert in the evening is a very great success, the songs and speeches being capital. The only drawback is the want of space; crowding spoils all comfort. The general and most of the officers are present. There are many rumors afloat about the general's treatment of Colonel Otter. No one knows exactly what has occurred but he has certainly given the brigadier a wigging; probably because the old man thinks he has been done out of some chance of glory.

Scouts from General Strange reach us today. Big Bear has escaped him, apparently, and gone off to the north but we get no definite informaiton.

Today volunteers are asked for, for service here. Not an officer or man in our company is willing to remain. The fact that volunteers are needed shows pretty plainly that it is the intention to send most of the troops home. We rejoice.

Friday, May 29th

A fine warm day. Very quiet. Many officers visit us and talk "Batoche" till we are ill. It is really amusing, the calm way in which these fellows talk to us about the heavy fighting they have done. Heaven knows none of the fights have amounted to much, but as they go Cut Knife is not to be despised. There we lost in one morning as many men as were killed at Batoche in four days out of a force three times as numerous as ours. There they fought nearly three to one; at Cut Knife we had more than our own number of men opposed to us. But then they had a real live general to command them and booming the fight means something very tangible in the future for him. He certainly seems to be a poor specimen; hear some very queer things about his deals in horseflesh and furs and as far as his treatment of some of his officers, that is quite too disgraceful.

Indians continue to flock in today.

SATURDAY, MAY 30TH

Fine and warm. I am on duty and stay in the fort. In the afternoon Moosemin passes with his tribe—a dirty-looking lot of wretches.

Much to our joy a mail at last arrives, our first for sixteen days and our letters are indeed appreciated. The mails of a fortnight we miss, however, and find they are somewhere on the way but exactly where is not known.

Captain Hughes comes over late at night and tells us about General Strange and the general's intention to take only his own brigade to assist him. We feel terribly indignant, for whatever the rules of the service may be about a commander keeping particular troops with him, here at least we are entitled to a show. The other column has done its work and the Indians are our legitimate prey. Jealousy of the too great success of Colonel Otter is at the root of the whole matter.

SUNDAY, MAY 31ST

A cloudy showery day. This morning the troops leave by boat for Fort Pitt.

Acheson holds service for us and Lloyd, Cooper, Morey, and Watts are able to join us. They and Captain Todd and Harry Mickle dine with us.

Macdonald, George, and Baird look in in the evening and our grievances are discussed at length and various modes of showing our resentment proposed. It is felt, however, that nothing can be done, though the affair is an infernal shame. Even the officers in the general's column think this.

MONDAY, JUNE 1ST

Fine and warm. The great excitement of the day is the arrival of Hume Blake.[45] He has left the supplies some sixty miles away, the teamsters wishing to look for some horses that have strayed away and has driven on in a buck-board. The luxuries sent up fill nine wagons and fifteen carts, he tells us, and ought to be in later tomorrow or early on Wednesday. The thought of the approaching feast almost reconciles us to the idea of being kept here while Big Bear is disposed of. A large supply train comes in in the evening, bringing mails with it. We get papers for three weeks down to the 9th of May and sit up till all hours trying to catch up with the times. We are much disgusted at the accounts of the Cut Knife affair but we could expect nothing better from correspondents who keep themselves carefully out of the way behind oat bags and under wagons.

TUESDAY, JUNE 2ND

Fine and clear. There is a brigade parade this morning and most of our company go over; I am left in charge. The brigadier gives the men a talking to about their confounded letter writing and complainings. Speaks very well I am told. The company stay at the camp for dinner.

The brigadier pays me a visit in my loneliness, and has a long chat. Tells me he is going to put the political prisoners in our charge as the accommodation at the fort is too cramped. Some of the artillery came over and put a room in order for the prisoners reception.

Captain and Mrs. Nash also honor me with a visit and stay to dinner. It is quite a novel sensation to take a meal with a lady. The captain has come over to look after some of his belongings and identifies and carries off a number of articles.

WEDNESDAY, JUNE 3RD

A party of officers go off today to see what is detaining the supply train. A short way down the trail they meet a trader coming up who passed the team some thirty-five miles away. They should therefore reach us tomorrow.

Hughes and I go over to the camp in the afternoon and inspect the halfbreeds. See some of the boys practising with bows; they are very skilful with the weapon and take great delight in sending an arrow through a small ring as it rolls rapidly along the ground.

We stay at the camp for tea and when we get back to the fort find that ten prisoners have been sent over to be under our charge. Among them is Pound-maker. He sometime ago prophesied that he would yet occupy the Government House at Battleford and now he does but perhaps not quite in the manner he hoped or expected. Captain Brown is very proud of the formal warrant of commitment and intends to frame the document. Here is a copy.

Battleford, June 3rd, 1885

Brigade Memo

Captain Brown will take charge of and be re-sponsible for the under-named prisoners charged with treason—felony—viz:
Poundmaker
Yellow Mud Blanket
Breaking the Ice
Lean Man
Crooked Leg
Charles Bremner
William Frank
Baptiste Sayers
Harry Sayers
He will see that they are properly fed, and suf-ficient exercise for the preservation of health allowed them.

"W.D. Otter" Lt.-Col.
Comg. Battle'd Coln.

Capt. Brown,
Comg. Detacht. Q.O.R.
Govt. House.

Thirty men of No. 4 under Captain Kersteman go to Fort Pitt this morning as escort to steamer carrying supplies.

Thursday, June 4th

Fine and clear but very windy. Our prisoner, Crooked Leg, is today taken back to the fort: he is accused of murder and we are to have charge of political prisoners only. When the Indian is informed that he is to be moved again he piteously entreats that he may be shot at once and not troubled any more.

Harry Brock and Hume Blake drop in this morning impelled by the wasted visages and mournful entreaties of their comrades to make one more attempt to reach and hasten on the long-delayed supply train. We persuade them to stay to dinner. They depart looking less hungry, indeed, but still, we hope, impressed with the necessity of bringing on the much needed succor. They do not fail us and return about five with the joyful intelligence that the luxuries are close at hand. Sure enough, ere long our eyes rejoice at the vision of white covered wagons coming slowly down the trail and the hard tack siege is it an end. Hurrah for the good ladies of Toronto. Captain Brown and I go over to the camp in the evening; there a scene of wild confusion greets us. Boxes and parcels are everywhere and half a dozen officers are slowly identifying and numbering the various packages and evolving order out of chaos. A hungry crowd of eager-looking privates at first wait in mournful patience for the hoped-for distribution of good things, but it is soon seen that nothing in that way can be accomplished tonight and they are packed off to their tents. With great difficulty we manage to find a package forwarded by "mine host" of the "Hub" to certain officers, and from it take a suspicious-looking oblong parcel addressed to Captain Hughes. This has been eagerly expected by him. He opens it on our return to the fort and finds therein a two-pound can of corned beef. He seems disappointed.

Our Company Sergeant Major Kennedy departs this life today deeply regretted by us all. Business of importance required his presence in Toronto.

FRIDAY, JUNE 5TH

A dull gloomy morning and rain in the afternoon.

No. 1 Company's share of good things reaches Fort Otter this afternoon and we enjoy ourselves amazingly in investigating the contents of the various consignments. We seem to have everything from a plum pudding to a pair of scissors and the "boys" revel in unaccustomed luxuries thoughtless of the morrow. Some kind friend has forwarded a box of Rodmay's Ready Relief; from present appearances this will be very useful in a day or two. Captain Brown is fortunate enough to receive a bottle or two of "7 year-old." We sit up till an advanced hour indulging in cheese, conversation, and cordial and about 1 A.M. are joined by Grand Round in the person of Major Allan. He appreciates the situation and remains till 2:30 A.M. and then departs in a cheerful frame of mind making strenuous efforts to ride through the unopened gate of our fortress.

SATURDAY, JUNE 6TH

Very fine and bright but windy.

A steamer comes down from Fort Pitt last night and brought down four wounded and six sick men. The hospital tent is very much crowded and Cooper, Varey, and Lloyd are sent over to us. They rejoice in the change.

We are very much pleased to hear that Big Bear has departed; it would have been too much if the general had got him.

I see today at the town Mrs. Quinney, who was one of Big Bear's prisoners, and from her learn many interesting particulars about the chief and his band. The prisoners have been fairly well treated, though at first it was touch-and-go with them. Big Bear is very much frightened and much disgusted that promised Fenian aid has failed him.

The Guards went out last night to Cut Knife and return today with the body of Osgoode. They tell us that the position taken by the Indians was immensely strong, coulee behind coulee, and all fortified by rifle-pits: a charge could have led to nothing but disaster. They found six dead Indians in one tepee and saw a number of graves, so that a loss of five only is certainly much below the mark.

Odd parcels make their appearance all through the day and we are astonished when we count up our spoils. Captain Brown has, among other trifles, seventy-five cans of fruit and dry goods enough to furnish a first-class ready-made clothing emporium. I get a large number of useful articles; in many cases nothing indicates the kind donors. A gift of tobacco from the Accountant's Office—Osgoode Hall—much delights me and I rejoice exceedingly in the discovery of an air pillow, a most valuable adjunct to one's comfort in camp life.

Lieutenant Mickle bursts upon us this evening in the radiance of a new beauty. His tailor has "trusted" him for his serge.

SUNDAY, JUNE 7TH

Beautiful bright clear day.

We have a very delightful service this morning, Acheson in charge—a large congregation and very good singing. Colonel Miller, Captain and Mrs. Nash, Dr. Nattress, Dr. Brown, and Acheson dine with us. The repast beggars description: the list of luxuries is too long to be here transcribed; suffice it to say that the meal did no discredit to the snowy cloth and napkins that today astonished our delighted guests.

Poor Osgoode is buried this afternoon, he is laid in the quiet sloping corner where now rest so many of his comrades.

This evening we receive orders to be prepared to move tomorrow to cut off Big Bear's retreat. We rejoice at the prospect of having something to do, but deeply lament at the thought of the many good things that must be left behind. Once more will pork and hard tack become our trusty friends.

Kersteman and his men get back from Fort Pitt tonight just in time. They report everything quiet there.

A mail comes in this evening. No less than twelve letters gladden me and I sit up till 3 A.M. enjoying and answering them.

Monday, June 8th

Another beautiful day.

As we are so soon perforce to forsake the flesh pots of Egypt we determine to make the most of our time and today at breakfast sample every conceivable article. Captain B. and Peel come badly to grief over some compound rejoicing in the taking title of canned clams.

The prisoners are taken to Fort Battleford this morning and we get our traps in order. About 3 p.m. we sadly and reluctantly leave Fort Otter giving three hearty cheers for our old home before filing out of the gate. So ends a very happy chapter in our Northwest life and we turn the page on five weeks of pleasant and profitable existence.

We find the column not quite ready to march but after a short half-hour's delay we start and make our way down to the steamboat landing and proceed to cross to the north bank of the Saskatchewan by the steamer *Baroness*. Crossing is a slow and tedious process. We are obliged to go in detachments and the peculiar character of the river necessitates the taking on each trip of a very roundabout or rather crooked about course—shoals being plentiful, there being, in fact, scarcely water enough to keep the shoals together. It is after nine before we are all on the north shore and then we have to "wood up" the old tub so that it is quite ten before we march up the steep bank and reach our camping ground. We are to start very early in the morning and the night is fine so that we do not pitch tents but bivouac in the open, turning in in our blankets after disposing of a cup of coffee and a morsel of bread and sleeping the sleep of the just.

TUESDAY, JUNE 9TH

Reveille sounds at 3:30 A.M., an unearthly hour to our unaccustomed ears. A hasty breakfast and at 5:15 we start. The new "Otter's Column" is composed of some twenty scouts, thirty men and two guns, "A" Battery under Colonel Montizambert,[46] forty-five "C" School, forty-five Foot Guards, and 250 Queen's Own. We leave most of our buglers and a number of sick and wounded behind. We have with us provisions for ten days and are told that we are to wander with systematic aimlessness for that period over a part of the country to the North known as the Squirrel Plains.

We have a terribly trying march of twelve miles in the morning, the heat being almost overpowering to the men in their present poor condition. A paddle in a friendly slough and a rest of some four hours restore us to something like old-time energy. We start at 3 P.M. and soon reach a stream called Jack Fish Creek fourteen miles from Battleford. This is a stream of clear sparkling water, and so unlike anything we have as yet seen in this country that we imagine there must be some mistake. The water is considerably more than three deep. The command "Prepare to wade" is given and soon a Highland Brigade (only more so) makes a bold dash through the rushing waters and clambers eagerly up the steep bank of the little river. Then we follow its winding course for many miles and about eight reach its source, Jack Fish Lake, twenty-miles out. Not bad for the first day. Here the country is very beautiful—park-like prairie with clumps of trees and pretty little lakes.

We bivouac again curling ourselves in our blankets and dropping off quietly about eleven.

WEDNESDAY, JUNE 10TH

We are roused at three o'clock sharp and off we start shortly after half past four. Another very hot march tires us, but about ten we halt near a small clear lake and are able to indulge in delightful swimming. Our siesta is disturbed by the report of a rifle and a bullet whistles through the branches close to the heads of Harry and myself who are indulging in a snooze somewhat apart from the common herd. We are anxious for a moment or two but no further shots are fired and we find that the one report has been caused by a careless teamster who allowed a rifle to go off during some clumsy handling.

We have to cross several bad muskegs in the afternoon and our progress is considerably interfered with. We do not cover much more than eighteen miles. All day we pass through beautiful country and tonight, as before, find no difficulty in reaching pleasant waters to bathe in. A great boon it is. Then, too, we are gladdened by finding everywhere quantities of sweet-smelling flowers and we feel very hopeful about enjoying the expedition if these good things are to last. We think with some degree of dread of the genial mosquito, but so far we have escaped, and we have veils with us if the charming insect does make his appearance.

This evening some excitement is caused by the sudden appearance of a Nitchie in our midst, one at once imagining that he is a messenger from Big Bear.

It turns out, however, that he is, as far as he will confess and as far as we can know, an innocent and
harmless wanderer whom Sears and the scouts have
run across and sent in and, after careful questioning,
he is allowed to depart.

Another very warm bright day. A pleasant breeze
makes the marching less trying and we get over a
good deal of very lovely country. We reach a point
about four miles from a lake called Turtle Lake and
the scouts reporting that it will be difficult if not impossible to reach that body of water, we retrace our
steps a mile or so in order to stop at a good camping
ground. We go in swimming as usual in the friendly
slough but this time we come badly to grief and
emerge from a refreshing plunge literally covered
with too attentive horse leeches.

This afternoon we pass an Indian grave — a trench
that is about three feet deep with a body lying at the
bottom and sticks laid across the top. An unprincipled
medical student makes off in triumph with the skull
of the poor occupant.

FRIDAY, JUNE 12TH

Rouse as usual about three and make an early start.
The heat is very trying again and we do not at all appreciate an aimless wandering of some ten miles or
so, which the scouts cause us to indulge in. They are
trying to move off in a new direction but come badly
to grief among the numerous muskegs and we halt
disgusted and dispirited after some five hours' hard

work not much more than a mile from our starting point. We are consoled, however, when we find that we are near a stream of clear cold water and have as a camping ground one of the most beautiful spots a man could wish to rest in. We are on the brow of a grassy hill, a green valley running at our feet and groves and lakes innumerable around us and then we look toward the Turtle Hills for a background and feel that even in the Northwest there is something to be thankful for.

A thunder shower somewhat disturbs us in the afternoon but fortunately does not amount to much, and the impromptu shelters hastily prepared by the men are not very severely tried.

We take advantage of our rest and have a pleasant concert in the evening, a luxury we appreciate after prolonged abstinence.

The nights are now very short, in fact, there is virtually no night at all. In this northern country one can read print with ease between half past ten and eleven.

Saturday, June 13th

Had a clear frosty night and the weather this morning has completely changed; we go about in overcoats and even then shiver. We start about our usual time and after a short march reach our old trail of Thursday and make our way once more toward Turtle Lake, stopping some three miles from it at a large creek called Stoney Creek. Here we have lots of time to ourselves and indulge in fishing, capturing several good pike. We have drizzling rain at intervals all day and toward night a steady downpour comes on but we do not pitch tents, the men making shelters with bushes and rubber sheets and being comparatively comfortable.

Enjoy today a very good thing, that is, soup made from compressed vegetables—a very good idea for camp life. Also see today a useful idea for horse dealers—a new mode of keeping horses in hand. One docile animal is led and the others are strung out behind, the head rope of one fastened to the tail of the unfortunate animal that preceded it.

A courier goes back to Battleford today to see if any orders have come for us and takes a mail with him.

SUNDAY, JUNE 14TH

A cold damp miserable night and we are all glad to take advantage of the cook fires at an early hour. After breakfast Nos. 2, 3, and 4 Companies and the Guards march to Turtle Lake, No. 1 Company and "C" School remaining in camp. I go with No. 2, however, and see the lake. A very fine large sheet of water it is and on the southern shore is a Hudson's Bay post, now deserted. We stay at the lake for a few minutes only and then return to camp. Colonel Otter tells us that he wished the men to see the lake and that except with the view of gratifying them he had no object in going there.

The day becomes warm and bright and we pass a pleasant lazy Sunday; have no service but sing hymns for a long time in the evening.

MONDAY, JUNE 15TH

Last night was bitterly cold, thick ice forming and this morning as soon as the sun rises we are enveloped in heavy mist.

Our scouts come in this morning and report that a large band of Indians has lately passed eastward following a trail slightly to the north of our present position. Evidently this must be Big Bear and it is decided to retrace our steps toward Battleford as we cannot go further north, and perhaps we shall obtain some information as to what it is possible for us to do.

At roll call it is found that one of our men, O'Brien, is missing. He went toward the lake this morning and has evidently lost himself. Our company is left behind to look for the poor fellow and the column takes its departure about 4 P.M. We send out several scouting parties and shout and fire rifles at regular intervals but our scouts return without the wanderer and no shouts answer ours and we begin to despair. About ten o'clock, however, we hear a faint cry in the distant marshes, dash in the direction it comes from, and soon bring back our overjoyed comrade. He tells a pitiful tale of his long lonely wanderings through the gloomy swamps but has evidently kept up with great pluck in spite of the trying circumstances and was determined to struggle on to the end. Fortunately he had with him two dogs, and the presence of these animals must have been a great comfort to him. He comes in wet, tired, and dilapidated but soon revives.

Mosquitoes bother us a good deal tonight, the first time that they have really been troublesome, and now we begin to feel that it is possible to believe the hideous tales we have so often listened to of the size and ferocity of the Northwest species of this genial animal.

TUESDAY, JUNE 16TH

We rise this morning at the awful hour of two, having had little more than a couple of hours rest and reach the column at its camp about six miles away shortly after six.

We are disgusted to find that orders have reached us and that we are to be kept out here for some indefinite time longer and are now to make for a lake called Stoney Lake. Brock goes down to Battleford with a guide and some teamsters to bring up supplies. Our stores are nearly exhausted and some articles — sugar and tea — have quite run out.

The column starts soon after we rejoin and we have a long, hot, dusty march of twelve miles — particularly trying naturally to our company — but they all hold out till the welcome camp is reached. The ground chosen is not very good but we are close to good water and cannot complain. The lake is not very large but the water is very clear and the place very charming. Unfortunately rushes grow near the shore and the swimming is not good. We are to camp here several days, we hear, and so tents are pitched for the first time since we left Battleford.

We see quantities of ducks here as well as all through this northern country. We have, however, only one or two guns in the column and can do very little in the way of shooting.

This evening we have a good deal of fun getting up a pool on Brock's return: a very successful auction is held and large prices are realized for the favorite chances.

Wednesday, June 17th

We have a quiet uneventful day. Captain Mutton goes down to Battleford to hurry on supplies as our condition is fast becoming desperate; we have little left now but hard tack and dried apples.

Colonel Otter and a number of officers and some scouts go off today to visit Yellow Sky, a supposedly friendly chief, who is camping some twenty miles away. Lesslie and Hume Blake are of the party.

Harry and I spend the afternoon skylarking on an old raft. It will accommodate one man only and each of us makes desperate efforts to be that one. In the progress of the struggle Harry goes overboard and as he falls flings his pole from him; this striking me, very nearly puts an end to my earthly career and we soberly return to shore.

Men find the black forage caps very warm and trying, and are now manufacturing very natty-looking substitutes out of old flour bags. One good friend cuts my hair and then presents me with a dainty specimen of the new regulation.

Thursday, June 18th

Another uneventful day, but the rest is grateful and comforting. Colonel Otter returns today and the party report that they have had lots of fun and brings back a good many furs. There are about two hundred Indians in the band and most of them have been with Big Bear. We shall probably take some of them to Battleford but do not burden ourselves with them now as provisions are too scarce.

Have an elaborate supper tonight in Sergeant Cranya's tepee. Lieutenant Mickle and myself are the only guests. Our worthy host produces from a hidden store a tin of tongue and we revel in the unaccustomed luxury.

A scout comes in from Fort Pitt today, has no dispatches, and can give us very little news.

FRIDAY, JUNE 19TH

We had a very heavy thunderstorm last night and in the morning everything is damp and muggy. The warm sun soon puts things to right.

Yellow Sky comes in this morning to collect some debts. He is a good-looking Indian, not unlike Poundmaker, but not as fine a looking fellow. He tells us he is moving camp and that his people will pass close to us in the afternoon. A number of men obtain leave and go out in the hope of seeing the Nitchies. Disappointment, however, results as the band has taken a trail that leads them from us. Colonel Miller takes Harry and myself in the ambulance wagon with him and we make a search for the red men but fail to find them. Harry and I decide to walk back when we are some four miles from camp and have a pleasant ramble. We gather quantities of beautiful flowers; the country is positively like a garden, so many and so varied are the plants that bloom everywhere around us.

By some strange mischance, the ammunition wagon today catches fire and we narrowly escape destruction: an explosion would have finished most of us as the store of shell and cartridge is large. Fortunately the smoke was seen before the fire gained much headway and we were saved.

Saturday, June 20th

Very cold in the early morning and blowing a gale, but fine during the day.

We have a route march this morning going out some four miles. The rest of the day passes in the usual lazy manner.

Brock rejoins us this evening and brings a few supplies, one or two letters, and a few odd newspapers. The main supplies will, he says, soon be here. We have today some fresh meat, the product of some of the cattle retaken from the Indians, but the meat is very unpalatable without salt, and practically we live on hard tack and have none too much of that. The colonel, much to our gratification, wins the pool.

Sunday, June 21st

A very fine warm day. Mutton comes in this morning having driven straight through from Battleford, sixty miles in eleven hours.

We have a church parade and a short service: the heat is too great to allow very much to be done.

Have a quiet afternoon and after tea Harry and I take a long walk going through some beautiful country.

The scouts report that they have come on Big Bear's trail and we are told that we are to strike camp tomorrow and attempt to follow him: a pretty indefinite sort of chase, I fear, but it is some comfort to be on the move at all events.

Monday, June 22nd

Very fine and warm.

About 4 p.m. we leave camp and march quietly for three hours, making eight miles, and camp on the banks of a clear running stream. Our route all after-noon lies through a beautiful rolling country and everywhere we see quantities of flowers and fresh-looking grass.

We wear for the first time the blouses and have-locks sent us from Toronto: the latter are neat, cool, and serviceable and the former, made of gray flannel, are most serviceable also and remarkably comfortable though too loose to be very natty. However, the regiment looks much better in the "uniform" such as it is than in the mixture of costumes that hitherto has been visible around us.

We bivouac as early as possible, having been warned that an early start is to be made.

TUESDAY, JUNE 23RD

Reveille this morning at two and a start is effected a few minutes after three, and after four hours and a half of marching we halt on the shore of a beautiful lake called Birch Lake. The scouts who have gone ahead are to meet us here if they gain any informa-tion, and we are ordered to be ready to move at any minute. The day passes quietly and pleasantly, all en-joying glorious bathing and we are by no means dis-pleased when toward evening we are told that we are likely to be here for a day or two.

The camping ground is delightful; a grassy meadow gently sloping down to the shore, pure water at our very feet, and magnificent lake studded with well-wooded islands stretching before us. Quite the most beautiful spot we have as yet seen in the Northwest. We do, after some search, find that a birch tree or two is to be seen in this vicinity and as that species of tree, or in fact of any kind of hard wood, is extremely rare here, the name of the lake is not altogether inappropriate.

Yesterday some Montana cattle in charge of a real live cowboy came up from Battleford and are, we learn, sent for consumptive purposes. The cattle are very wild and a general order warns the men not to approach them. We presume the orders refers to the cattle in their raw state but the warning is equally applicable to any one desiring their acquaintance in any state: a steak manufactured from a fatling of the herd is presented to us today for our midday meal but all attempts to dispatch it are fated.

Wednesday, June 24th

We had, strange to say, much difficulty in obtaining any sleep last night. At first we suffer from heat, our sleeping arrangements having been made with the view of resisting the ordinary Northwestern coolness and a threatening thunderstorm rendering the air unexpectedly close. Wraps are scarcely thrown off when down comes the rain, fortunately only a shower, but quite enough to cause us much inconvenience and after the rain – not the Deluge, but mosquitoes. With the mosquitoes we have an enemy to them and to us (especially to us), a new and improved variety of nighthawk, quite unlike the ordinary nighthawk of commerce, which indulges at most irregularly distracting intervals and from regions wholly unexpected, in cries as of the foul fiend himself in torture. We are allowed a long rest in the morning, however, and are able to make up for lost time.

Scouts came in late last night from Fort Pitt. The general has given up the chase of Big Bear and we are to leave for home, we understand, when we please. Colonel Otter and Captain Mutton drive to Pelican Lake today to see our scouts and return late at night without any definite information, but what he hears induces the brigadier to decide to remain here a few days in the hope of in some way getting on Big Bear's trail.

Some tents are pitched today as several thunder showers appear to be working down upon us, but none come. Most of us sleep out as usual and are rewarded tonight by seeing a most wonderful aurora: the sky at times a deep crimson with bright gleams of golden light flashing across it, something wonderful even for this country of extraordinary celestial phenomena.

The varsity men are delighted to learn today from an old paper that has come in the success of Miss Brown. We have a meeting and enthusiastically cheer her.

Nelson, the spokesman hitherto of the privates, today sells himself to the governing party and becomes what he has been pleased to call a "two striped nuisance"—Private McSand feelingly voices the congratulations of the disconsolate deserted ones.

THURSDAY, JUNE 25TH
Amuse ourselves as usual by swimming, having all day to ourselves.

Sears and the scouts came in. They have communicated with Irvine but have not managed to locate Big Bear. It is almost hopeless to think of finding him for his band has broken up, and innumerable trails traverse the whole country. We do not intend to give up just yet, however, and some of the scouts go off again to see if some of Yellow Sky's band can give us assistance.

A small supply train comes in bringing hard tack, which is very acceptable, we having for some time been reduced to an allowance of three per day. Orders are brought for the immediate return of Dr. Nattress and his staff.

Harry and I attempt to take a stroll this evening, but are ignominiously driven back to camp by mosquitoes. These insects do not trouble us, strange to say, in camp, but as soon as one puts one's nose outside the circle of campfires down the pests swarm in myriads.

FRIDAY, JUNE 26TH

Another blazing hot day and needless to say another disgracefully lazy one, though Harry and I do manage to take a reasonable constitutional in the afternoon.

Dr. Nattress and Brown and Mustard leave for Battleford today, Lee going with them. He is to bring up some supplies if the column does not follow in a day or two.

Indulged in hideous dissipation this evening in shape of whist party, Lieutenant George and Chippy Smith playing Hume Cronyn and me. "Last Post" puts an end to an exciting contest when the score is two rubbers all.

SATURDAY, JUNE 27TH

Damp in morning but soon hot and fine.

Sears and the scouts start off again and take with them four or five Indians (some of Yellow Sky's band).

The colonel and his orderly (Grand) soon afterward leave for Pelican Lake, chiefly to see the country, though perhaps partly in search of loot. Colonel Montizambert and his men start for home in the afternoon, and we find that we are pretty sure to be off in a couple of days.

Small supply train comes in and we get some letters and a few papers, the latest being of date of 11th inst.

Harry and I have a delightful ramble this afternoon, exploring a large portion of the lake, and discovering some wonderfully beautiful spots. We see in the course of our wandering any number of ducks, but have nothing in the shape of firearms and are unable to bag any of the game.

This evening we have some very good music in Hume's tepee. A French teamster charms us with his sweet voice and makes us long for home and Murray Bay as we listen to the familiar habitant folksongs.

SUNDAY, JUNE 28TH

We have a very short service today, the sun being too strong to be borne for any long period and no shade being available.

In the afternoon I take Harry out for a long paddle, a birchbark canoe having been discovered here, and we have a most delightful trip. The lake seems to be about four miles wide by perhaps six long and the water is very clear and pure.

We decide this evening to hold a swimming tournament tomorrow and an elaborate program is drawn up, and an influential committee appointed.

Colonel Miller and Grand came back in good time. Have been through a very rough country but have enjoyed themselves greatly. Have not got much spoil apparently.

Monday, June 29th

Sears and the scouts return early in the morning, having been again unsuccessful. Big Bear, as far as can be learned, has pushed on toward Carlton and we can do nothing more. He is, however, certainly powerless now. We get orders for home this morning and start about three in the afternoon, the heat being even then very trying. We march till 7:45 p.m. through a rather uninteresting country and then halt, hot, dusty and tired, near a dismal-looking slough, having made about twelve miles. Our swimming tournament has, of course, come to nought and so we rush into the uninviting slough and come out covered with weeds and leeches, regretting our temerity.

One or two of the scouts leave again this evening to make a final effort to trace our wandering friend B.B. Not much chance for them, I fear, though no doubt they will do their best as we offer a very substantial reward for the capture of the chief.

Tuesday, June 30th

Last night we were once more astonished to find it rather warm for comfort, for rarely indeed is it anything but very cool here after sundown.

Reveille at 4 a.m. and we start at 5 a.m. making a very hot, fast march of five hours and reaching Jack

211

Fish Lake. This time we pass along the north shore and halt almost opposite the camping ground occupied by us on our first night out from Battleford. The lake is about eight miles wide and eighteen to twenty long, and most beautifully situated. High rolling country on the north and east and well-wooded plains on the south. The water is very clear and extraordinarily soft and, needless to say, we thoroughly enjoy the glorious bathing, especially as the heat all day is tremendous. The lake is a famous fishing ground, Indians coming here from all the northern country. We catch quite a number of very fine pike.

The scouts came back disconsolate and our last hope is abandoned.

We make only a short march of about two miles this afternoon, but wade about one hundred yards waist-deep in water, and save a round of several miles which would necessarily be covered if we marched by the borders of the lake.

WEDNESDAY, JULY 1st

Last night we had a tremendous thunderstorm: the rain came down in torrents and the lightning was appalling. This is the outcome of the hot, muggy weather of the last few days. We rise at three, limp and nerveless.

We start at four and march along the east side of the lake and about five miles out reach Yellow Sky's camp at the southeast corner of the lake. We do not stop here but the scouts bring on some twenty-five prisoners, Indians who are supposed to have been with Big Bear. Shortly after this we meet a number of wagons with supplies on the way to join us. Very soon after leaving Yellow Sky's camp we reached Jack Fish Creek, the discharge of the lake, and follow it till we arrive at the place where we forded it on the first day. It is then about eight o'clock and we have made ten miles. We have still fourteen miles to make to reach Battleford, but there is no good water between the creek and that place, and we decide to have dinner where we are.

While resting, a terrible thunderstorm breaks upon us, and we become soaked. With the rain come hailstones of inconceivable size, many of them being fully three-quarters of an inch in diameter and we have hard work to escape injury. We start as soon as the worst of the storm passes over and march all afternoon at a fast rate, reaching Battleford or rather a point on the north bank of the Saskatchewan opposite that place about 7:20 P.M., having covered today twenty-four miles and not being sorry to turn in. We find that no steamers are here so we pitch tents and prepare to make ourselves comfortable for a day or two.

THURSDAY, JULY 2ND

Had a most delightful night and are not roused till the, for us, absurdly late hour of eight.

At breakfast I hear that Captain Macdonald is going off with twenty men to hunt up some stray Indians who are supposed to be some little way up the river. After much persuasion the colonel gives me leave to go. We all go in wagons and make pretty fair time to Jack Fish Creek following our old trail to that point.

There we dine and then strike off across country to the Saskatchewan, rain pouring down all the time, and follow the banks of the river for some six miles. We see no sign of any Indians on this side and at last halt opposite a large Indian camp, which we take to be that of a chief called Sweet Grass. The river is half a mile wide and we have no means of crossing. We see on the other bank a small punt and there are lots of Indians about but, in spite of the earnest and vociferous invitations of our interpreter, not one for a long time makes any movement. At last after much vigorous shouting and the adoption of the happy expedient of hoisting a not over-clean towel on a ramrod as a token of amity, three of the natives enter the punt and paddle across. One proves to be the Chief Thunder Child who has been neutral during the troubles. He tells us the Indians we are in search of, three men and seven women and children of Big Bear's band, are with his people, having crossed that morning. It is too late to cross tonight and we therefore have to trust to our chances for the morning.

FRIDAY, JULY 3RD

Had very little rest last night. The night cold and rainy, our blankets wet, and the boards of the wagon, in which Macdonald and I stowed ourselves, uncommonly hard. Then some horses seemed to think that we were endeavoring to conceal oats or some other equine delicacy about our lower extremities, and insisted upon rooting vigorously from time to time at that particular portion of our respective persons. Lots of fun for the horses, but rather disturbing to us.

Early in the morning Macdonald and I and Private Spence and the interpreter McKenna cross the river, having hard work to make way in the very strong current, and make our way into the camp. I must confess we all felt slightly nervous when we found ourselves among a large number of braves all looking ready and only too willing to cut our throats and we realized that we were completely cut off from all assistance. However, the chief was fairly civil and we got the men we wanted. How to get them back was the trouble. Fortunately, just then some fifteen police came up having heard of the crossing of the Indians and they took our prisoners off our hands (metaphorically). Only one man was "wanted." He was identified as one of the murderers of the priests at Frog Lake. We soon recross and push on at once to the camp, arriving there about two.

We find that no steamers have as yet come down, but that they are expected every day and that we go on at once by river to Winnipeg. All hands are busily engaged in bringing our belongings across the river as we are to remain on this side till we start. Crossing stores is a work of much difficulty: we have no means of transport but two or three leaky punts and it is no joke to make a passage across the swift river and safely avoid the numerous shoals that beset the track.

SATURDAY, JULY 4TH

I cross the river this morning, the operation occupying one hour and a quarter and necessitating the employment of much muscle and bad language. It is impossible to avoid swearing in this country; the nature of the climate seems to require exercise in this form. They tell rather a good story of a gallant captain who, shocked at the blasphemy prevalent in this company, warned his men that it must be stopped, and gently proceeded to remark, "Damn it men, this damned swearing really must be put an end to." I revisit all the old haunts, but the glory has departed, and I am sad to say cheated out of my moccasins, the faithless halfbreed having disposed of the looked for spoil to "some other man." Most of our stores are now packed and many things we give away. I recross the river comparatively easily, the punt having a light load and the course being somewhat downstream, and then get all my things in order for the start, which is to be tomorrow.

SUNDAY, JULY 5TH

The steamers come down from Fort Pitt early this morning and one crosses to the landing for us. We strike camp about nine and march down to the head of the hill, but then find it is blowing so hard that all movement by river is impossible, so we have to wait as patiently as we may for a lull. It is not till sunset that the captain thinks it safe to move, then we run across to Battleford and take on our stores and the Midland Battalion. We are disgusted that we are not going down with the 90th; the Midlanders are, from all accounts, anything but desirable companions.

We are much grieved to hear of Colonel William's death—hard luck for him just now. One of the 65th has also died and, to add to the general feeling of gloom, the terrible accident to the poor artillery man comes to wind up the day.

Our steamer is the *North-West*, Captain Sheets, and we expect to be fairly comfortable. Crowded, of course, but still we can now put up with a good deal. We are very sorry to be separated from the Guards. They go with the 10th and 90th in the *Marquis* and the 65th have the *Baroness* to themselves.

MONDAY, JULY 6TH

We wake and find ourselves still in sight of Battleford, though we are some distance down the river. We left early this morning but heavy wind soon made it impossible to proceed and we "tie up" quietly at the first convenient corner.

We spend the day "shaking down" in our new quarters and make ourselves fairly comfortable. There is no room to spare and the cooking facilities amount to nothing, but in spite of all drawbacks we manage to do fairly well. Colonel Straubenzie is in command and we have on board General Strange and several of his staff. There are so many officers that there is no room to mess together and each regiment has therefore to keep apart. We fare very well today, our new cook, a Frenchman and formerly of "B" Battery mess, proving an acquisition. This promises well for the trip. We have at dinner grace and bread, two luxuries unknown for months and either a great advance toward civilization. Toward the evening the wind falls and we make a few hours running, passing at one place the *Baroness* on a sandbar, making vigorous efforts to climb over and at another, "B" Battery en route to Prince Albert by land. We tie up for the night about 9:30 P.M.

TUESDAY, JULY 7TH

It blows hard all day but we manage to make some
way, and about 10 A.M. catch up to the *Marquis*.
Soon afterward we reach a place called Telegraph
Coulee and run in to the bank. This place is a provisions depot and we find two companies of the 7th in
camp here in charge. The *Marquis* joins us here and
while stores are being taken on we are able to have a
chat with our friends of other camps and start on our
way refreshed and in great spirits.

We are so far enjoying our sail immensely; the
scenery is not wonderful but there is always something pleasant to look at and the process of navigating
the vessel affords ground for much amusement. The
river itself is a most extraordinary one—a broad,
shallow, muddy stream with tremendous currents
and crosscurrents and full of innumerable shoals,
islands, and sandbars and with low-lying, thickly
wooded banks of clay. The steamers are no less extraordinary than the river, and consist merely of a
large flat-bottomed scowlike frame with gimrack upper works and an immense stern wheel; our boat,
with six hundred men and heavy stores on board,
draws little more than two feet of water. She is two
hundred feet by thirty-six. Apparently there is nothing in the river that can hurt these boats; we run into
the bank when and where we feel inclined and dash
along in the most erratic manner. Shoals are avoided
if convenient but the old boat does not seem to put
herself out on their account if they came in the way.
Sometimes we get over them by sheer force, sometimes climb over them with our poles, and sometimes,

but rarely, back off and try elsewhere. The system of sounding, too, is highly entertaining. An unfortunate hand plants himself in the bow armed with a long pole, which he monotonously and incessantly keeps poking into the unoffending waters, at each dig vociferating vigorously the depth of water that he finds. The changes are oftentimes most startling. "Eight feet," "six feet" "five feet scout," "three feet and a half," "three feet"—is it to be crash? The poleman almost tumbles overboard as the pole fails to meet any resisting substance and all hands join vigorously in the welcome cry of "Noovvo bottom."

About half past seven we reach Fort Carlton, or rather the remains of it, for nothing is not to be seen but some charred timbers. The place is beautifully situated but not where it could hope to be successfully defended, for on three sides it is commanded by closely bordering hills and retreat is cut off by the river in front. A few police are camped here and they proudly tell us of the capture of Big Bear. Soon after leaving Carlton we tie up for the night and ere long the *Marquis* comes down tolerably close to us and follows our example.

WEDNESDAY, JULY 8TH

We reach Prince Albert at 7:30 A.M. and stay there five hours. Unfortunately we are warned that our stay is to be very short and we are, therefore, as we momentarily expect to be ordered to start, unable to wander far from the ship and do the settlement thoroughly. From what we do see, we come to the conclusion that Prince Albert is a very taking place. All the youth, beauty, and fashion of the community assemble to greet us and the "boys" have lots of fun. We call on Big Bear en masse. He is confined in the police barracks and is a most wretched looking specimen. When captured he was literally dying of starvation and even now his bones are almost starting through his skin. I am introduced to the Miss McLeans of Fort Pitt fame and find them good-looking (very good-looking for the Northwest), rather taking, and full of interesting anecdote. I also meet George Moffatt and Drayner, see Colonel Irvine and Major Crozier[47] and wind up by receiving the episcopal benediction from "Saskatchewan Jack"[48] as His Lordship the Bishop of this diocese is here familiarly called. Prince Albert is quite a large place about 1,500 inhabitants, but built in a very straggling manner along the banks of the river and the place suffers from the rivalry between the inhabitants of the old Hudson's Bay portion of it, formerly known as Goschen, and those of the New Town.

We stole a march on the general this morning and got to Prince Albert first. This annoys the old gentleman and he now orders us, although our boat is faster than his, to stay behind.

After leaving Prince Albert we find that the character of the river alters—now a narrow, very rapid stream turning and twisting in a marvellous manner and in one place, about fifteen miles from the settlement, developing into quite a respectable rush of waters, known as "Cool" or Cole's Rapids. Tradition has it that the name is derived, according to the orthography that one may be pleased to prefer, either from the fact that the valuable mineral that spells its name with an "a" was once found near here, or from the fact that a distinguished gentleman bearing a name *idem sonans* with that of this material but with a more aristocratic turn in the spelling once resided in the neighborhood.

About 5 P.M. we reach the Grand Forks of the Saskatchewan, the junction of the north and south branches, and here await us the *Alberta* with a number of wounded men from Saskatoon and a company of the Midland their escort. The general is to take them with him, changes his mind once more (no unusual proceeding for him if all we hear be true), and orders us to go on at full speed to Grand Rapids (at the mouth of the river).

After leaving the Forks, we run rapidly down the main stream, navigation being simple and our progress tremendous. About 8 P.M. we stop and "wood up" at Fort à la Corne, a small Hudson's Bay post, which is not used except in winter, and no one is even in charge now, and then push on and are running when I, nothing loath, turn in.

THURSDAY, JULY 9TH

We had to "tie up" for a short time last night on account of fog but are running at hours quite unheard of by the ordinary sober navigators of the river. Our skipper is determined to make a fast trip. He overdoes it somewhat this morning, however. We leave the main stream and enter a "cut off" known as Big Stone River. The passage is difficult but the captain expects to be able to get through, and success means a gain of sixteen miles. We do get through but lose two hours and half

221

climbing over a sandbar and repairing the damages sustained in the operation. Sadly we acknowledge the truth of the familiar adage, "The longest way round is. . . ."

We see no longer this afternoon the steep sandy banks of the upper river but pass instead between low-lying forests of poplar and spruce, the trees in some cases being very fine indeed. Toward evening the wooded region gives place to one of swamp and weed; the stream broadens perceptibly and becomes comparatively sluggish and we know that the end of our river journey draws nigh.

We have this evening a very pleasant impromptu reunion, entertaining all our brother officers. Saskatchewan water, flavored with burnt brown sugar, or something that tastes like that, discussed amid the cheerful concomitants of song and speech, has the effect of suddenly developing between ourselves and our gallant comrades from the east the friendship that has been latent for the past three days. In the course of the proceedings, General Strange makes a speech that takes us all by storm, and amid vociferous cheering, his toast of "The United Militia of Canada" is enthusiastically done justice to.

Some of the gayer spirits are still up when we touch at The Pas Mission: the hour is too early to enable us to see much, but we gaze reverently at the dim outline of an old wooden church erected here by some of Sir John Franklin's men and by his order.

FRIDAY, JULY 10TH

Another beautiful bright sunny day. We early reach the head of Cedar Lake (into which the river

widens) a large sheet of water, forty-five miles long
and from fifteen to twenty across, and as the glass is
"set fair," cheerfully begin our perilous journey across.
Perilous we very easily see that it is. Very little wind
would raise a sea here that would send our flimsy
craft to pieces and, to avoid danger from delay, we
have to run the risk of danger from fire. For our fur-
naces are fed to their full capacity and quantities of
sparks from the smokestack fall everywhere on our
wooden decks, necessitating much careful watching
to avoid a conflagration. The lake is, however, safely
and speedily crossed, the captain's injunction to the
engineer "make her bump for all she is worth but
don't break anything" being successfully attended to.
After passing the lake we run for a few miles through
a very beautiful stretch of river. The water is quite
clear, the sediment being left behind at the bottom of
the lake, and the shores are rocky and prettily wooded.
Then every now and then we come to what may
almost be termed "rapids," and we all therefore enjoy
our sail immensely. About 5 P.M. we reach the dock at
Grand Rapids, eight hundred miles from Battleford,
and the end of river navigation. The mouth of the river
is some ten miles farther but before it is reached come
the famous Grand Rapids, and these are quite impassable for steamers. Everything has to be portaged across
to the mouth, and a tramway about four miles long has
lately been built to avoid delay in this process. After
dinner (we now have late dinner), Macdonald, Harry,
and I walk down to the mouth of the river and inspect the lower settlement. There is here a Hudson's
Bay store, a house or two, and some good freight
sheds and wharves, and across the river we see a large

Indian village. The Hudson's Bay agent lives here by himself and he tells us from the 16th of last September to the 7th of June he saw no living creatures but Indians and had no communication with the outside world. He did not know till the latter date, when a steamer arrived from Winnipeg, that a rebellion was in progress.

We are staying on the steamer tonight but most of our stores and luggage are taken across to the lower settlement. Here two tugs and some barges are waiting to take us across the lake to Winnipeg.

SATURDAY, JULY 11TH

Several of the officers arrange to run the rapids this morning and I arrange to be one of the party. We go in a York boat, a finely built, serviceable craft much like a whale boat, manned by three Indians. The rapids are nine miles long, most beautiful, and apparently not very dangerous, though four bumps on the rocks in the course of our descent enable us to work up some not unjustifiable excitement and the occupants of the bow seats came in for a partial wetting.

The regiments march across early in the morning and pass the day in a miserable state of uncertainty. We are not yet told off to our respective barges and have to await the general's arrival before settling down.

Rain comes on in the afternoon and makes things look dismal. Most of the men turn in for the night in the warehouses and the Queen's Own Rifles officers manage to stow themselves away in the engine room of one of the tugs.

Numbers of fish are caught here today and the men enjoy the unwonted treat. The officers are able to get meals on the tugs and do full justice to the fare.

Sunday, July 12th

Raining in the morning and blowing a gale. The general comes down about ten, the *Marquis* and *Baroness* having reached Grand Rapids about six, and our order of route is made known. The steamer *Princess* is taken possession of by the general and his staff, Field Officers of 19th, 90th, and Midland and sick, wounded, and nurses. The tug *Colvile*, where there is but little accommodation, is assigned to the Field Officers of the Queen's Own Rifles and 65th. The *Red River*, the smallest barge of our fleet, is given to the 65th, Guards, and 92nd, in all, 350 men; the *Nelson River* carries the 90th and Midland, 520 men; and the *Saskatchewan*, the 10th and ourselves, 570 men. We are not, however, to leave today as the *Alberta* has not made her appearance. We shall, of course, be dreadfully crowded, and in the meantime stay on shore as much as possible. In the afternoon the day clears and Harry and I have a delightful walk, going up by the tramway track to Grand Rapids and coming back by the river, about twelve miles in all. The scenery is most beautiful, everything reminds us of Murray Bay, the trees, rocks, and flowers of the North Shore varieties. At one place close to the river in the midst of a thick wood we come upon a little cemetery; some ten or dozen graves surrounded by a dilapidated palisade and at the head of each grave a wooden cross bearing the

name of the occupant. No dates are to be seen but
the graveyard is evidently an old one.

Some of the officers cross today to the Indian Village and bring back a number of the native dogs—
huskies—dirty, noisy brutes they are, anything but
pleasant neighbors in our cramped quarters.

We are this evening ignominiously kicked out of
the comfortable dining room of the steamer and
return once more to the faithful Jules. He has been
consoling himself during his enforced leisure by culti-
vating the poetic faculty and has burst into quite
vigorous song.

Monday, July 13th

Still dull and showery this morning. The *Alberta*
comes in betimes and everything is prepared for a
start when the Hudson's Bay agent comes down and
complains that the flag of the post, a very elaborate
affair, has been stolen. An order is issued to the effect
that we do not start till the flag is restored, and soon
the missing article mysteriously is found near the pole
from which it lately waved.

Beardy, the chief of the Indians about here, comes
down to pay his respects this morning. He is attired
in his scarlet treaty coat and wears his huge silver
treaty medal. Many offers are made for this but the
old man cannot be induced to part with it. The Indians about here are Swampy Cree—fine-looking
fellows and much more intelligent, apparently, than
their brethren of the Upper Saskatchewan. In former
days the fish diet of the inhabitants of this region
would be held sufficient explanation of this difference

in intellect; now the virtues of this food are more lightly thought of.

We start on our journey across the lake about eleven with three hundred miles to make before we reach the mouth of the Red River. The *Princess* leads, after her the barge *Nelson River*, the *Colvile* next, and following her the barges *Red River* and *Saskatchewan*, the towing rope forming a bond of union between us all. Colonel Miller, Major Allan, and Dr. Lesslie do not take advantage of the opportunity given them of obtaining comfortable quarters on the tug, and decide to stick to the regiment. Their places are taken by Captain Brown, who is suffering from rheumatism, and McGee and Blake, who are suffering probably from some other malady.

We have a run all day. Our only occupation, but that a sufficiently engrossing one, desperate attempts to shake ourselves down in a space which might, with comfortable crowding, accommodate half the numbers now jammed into it. Soon after nightfall a heavy storm strikes us and our barge pitches and rolls frightfully for some time. Very few succumb, fortunately, and about midnight a welcome lull allows us to drop off in gentle slumber.

Tuesday, July 14th

The morning dawns cool and fair after last night's storm. We have made very fair progress and now are merely out of sight of land, a faint blue line to be seen on one side only. In a few hours, however, we work down to the narrows and after a delightful run through this beautiful portion of the lake, press on once more over the broad surface of the southern half. Before entering the narrows, the steamer *Princess* leaves us, taking one barge with her, the former arrangement having been found fatal to all chances of good steering. We follow her gallantly all afternoon, slowly losing ground, and she quietly fades from our visions in the glories of a magnificent sunset.

WEDNESDAY, JULY 15TH

We wake this morning and find ourselves approaching the mouth of the Red River and soon begin to slowly creep up the marsh bordered channel of the famous stream. About eleven we reach Selkirk some twenty-five miles from the mouth, and find waiting here the 90th and Midlanders. We are here given some lunch by the inhabitants of the settlement, a fair-sized place, and then the general and troops are presented with an address. The congratulatory paragraphs of this concoction allude only to the heroes of Fish Creek and Batoche, though all the troops are asked to take advantage of certain material advantages guilelessly advertised in the closing sentences.

The 65th and Midlanders do not go to Winnipeg and we leave them at Selkirk, the Midlanders at any rate being in state of general noisy and disgraceful drunkenness. We do not leave for Winnipeg till after five, much delay having been caused by the amount of stores we have to transport, and have an hour's run by train to that place. The enthusiasm of the Winnipeggers is unbounded and, though their own gallant 90th come in naturally for the lion's share of greeting, we are by no means forgotten. All the regiments march up Main Street to the City Hall and here some addresses, fortunately neither many nor long, are indulged in and then we are told to march off to our quarters. We find it is intended that we should pitch camp on the common near the emigrant sheds, a long distance away and on the outskirts of the city. Tired and hungry, the men wish to go no further and we accordingly pile arms and take off our accoutrements in a vacant lot on Park Avenue, intending to disperse for a meal and then return to bivouac. Heavy rain interferes with this plan and the men are allowed to go for the night, shelter being provided for any who wish it in an as yet unoccupied hotel kindly placed at our disposal. We are told that we are to have a review in the morning and to leave in the afternoon so that we shall have little time to see anything of Winnipeg. We go in for a very elaborate and highly civilized repast and then Harry and I call on Mulock before beating up quarters for the night, not feeling justified in availing ourselves of his kind invitation to take up our abode with him.

THURSDAY, JULY 16th

It rains all night and is still raining when Harry and I rise from our luxurious couch on the floor of Potter House drawing room. A review is evidently an impossibility. We rush down to the Mulocks' for breakfast and then reach our regimental headquarters, find that our arms and traps, though wet, are now safely under cover and that nothing has yet been heard of our departure. We therefore lunch at the club, turn up at another muster parade in the afternoon, and then, the rain having ceased, do the city under Robinson's kind guidance winding up by dinner at Clougher's, the swell Winnipeg restaurant, and putting in the evening at the club. Here we meet the officers of most of the regiments in town. No orders for us yet, though all the troops are to be shipped off as soon as possible and the Halifax men leave tonight.

FRIDAY, JULY 17TH

A lovely bright day. After a wearisome parade in the morning, Macdonald, Harry, and I do the Hudson's Bay store thoroughly and are much disgusted to find we cannot purchase certain furs we earnestly covet, we hearing for the first time the rule of the Company forbidding sales in this country. After lunch we have another of these miserable parades that so thoroughly spoil our chances of doing anything that would take any time and then go to Government House to a garden party. This is rather good fun, all the bigwigs and, better than that, all the pretty girls being on hand and we thoroughly enjoy the unaccustomed dissipation. Lesslie, Hume, Harry, and I dine at the Mulocks', making our appearance forty-five minutes late and not being even scolded. After dinner we unfortunately have to go in for a march out, taking part in a torch-light procession and anything more abominable it has seldom been my ill fortune to assist in. We wander for some hours through Winnipeg mud, merely to afford some slight gratification to the rabble of the city.

SATURDAY, JULY 18TH

Another beautiful day. Harry and I decide not to turn up at parade this morning and instead wander about watching the Winnipeg maidens at their Saturday shopping. We are told definitely that we are to leave this afternoon and spend some time getting our traps together but soon find that this is another false alarm. In the afternoon we go to the Robertsons'[49] and one or two other places, then dine at the club and spend a very jolly evening at the Greens'—a small dance. The young married women predominate but there are some very nice girls and the charming daughters of the house are only too fascinating.

SUNDAY, JULY 19TH

We leave Winnipeg this morning on very short notice, orders reaching us at our morning parade. I am very sorry, as I wanted to see some of the churches, but after all it is time we were getting home. The York and Simcoe Battalion left on Friday, the artillery and Guards early this morning, and the 19th a short time before ourselves. Harry and I, while the baggage is being loaded up, run over to the Mulocks', try to thank them for their many kindnesses, and regretfully say good-bye. We are some time at the station, the city giving us a lunch there and it is nearly three before we leave, homeward bound, amid the hearty cheers of our many Winnipeg friends.

Winnipeg we are all charmed with, the place bright and handsome, and the people most kind. The beautiful decorations (the arches are most fine) make everything look unwontedly gay now, but at any time the city must be goodly to look upon. Some surprisingly handsome churches and public buildings.

About ten we reach Rat Portage and once more have supper at the Rideout. Nothing seems changed.

The same crazy bus, quaint old dining room, flaming chromos, and, one might almost say, the same (only slightly more so) tablecloths and napkins greeting us and the same giggling table maids dispense to the hungry soldiers steaks whose toughness vividly reminds us of our visit of four months ago. It is too dark to see the beauties of this most picturesque place; we do catch one lovely glimpse of moonlit lake and foaming river that makes us long for another and better opportunity of enjoying the wonders of the scenery.

MONDAY, JULY 20TH

We have a delightful night in the Pullman, reluctantly rising about nine when the announcement is made that breakfast will be ready at a station to be reached in ten minutes. This station is Ignace and as we steam in we see the train with the 10th on board slowly departing. Breakfast is not quite ready and when it is we have to feed in relays so that it is past twelve when we start once more. We pass Savanne of happy memory, cross and recross the head waters of the beautiful Kaministiquia, and, after an interesting run through most wild country, reach Port Arthur about five, 430 miles from Winnipeg.

We find that the Montreal Artillery, 10th, Guards, and ourselves, over 1,100 men, are expected to pack in one steamer licensed to carry 450. The Canadian Pacific Railway people, though thoroughly aware of the numbers of the approaching regiments, induced the *Campana* to depart this morning, though she has been specially asked by the government to aid in the transport of troops, and we, to put a few dollars in the pockets of these miserable money-grabbers have to suffer from this most abominable and uncalled for crowding. Harry and I manage to take a short run through the town, inspect one or two shops, get thoroughly well drenched in a heavy shower, and reach our steamer none too soon to get comfortably on board. The men are packed like herrings and goodness only knows how we are to be fed. We start about eight, the night closing in thick and gloomy.

TUESDAY, JULY 21ST

Harry, Hume, and I, who have a cabin to our-selves, wisely sleep till eleven this morning then make a struggle for breakfast. The meal begins at seven and it is often twelve before we get to anything to eat. Dinner begins at two and the last hungry soul gets his second, and only an indifferent one at that, meal about eleven at night.

We are surrounded by fog all day and run at half speed. At times we can scarcely see the length of the ship. About sunset the fog lifts for short time and we find ourselves close into the shore and heading directly for it, quite a narrow escape.

We have little to do today and make thorough in-spection of the ship — the *Athabasca* — a magnificent vessel she is — Clyde-built with all most modern fittings and improvements.

WEDNESDAY, JULY 22ND

We still find ourselves in fog this morning but it lifts about eleven and we find ourselves near the end of the lake. We press on at full speed and soon reach the

Sault, 270 miles from Port Arthur. Here we stay for nearly an hour, not being allowed on shore though. The place is certainly a beautiful, and seems to be a thriving one and the presence of numerous damsels on the wharf (one especially clad in a charming pink gown played sad havoc with our young affections) leads us to think that the lighter social pleasures might here be happily indulged in.

We leave the Sault about two and have a magnificent run of some sixty miles down the St. Mary River. We pass the Shingmonk Home and are heartily cheered by the dusky inmates, meet numerous tugs and propellers, and from all receive lively greetings, and near the mouth of the river we pass the yacht of His Lordship the Bishop of Algoma. On board we discern the portly form of that gentleman himself, his hands upraised as we steam by as if the episcopal benediction were being invoked upon us.

Toward evening we enter upon our run of 250 miles across Lake Huron and safely past the tortuous channel of the St. Mary; our good ship is given her head.

Our meals today are even worse than those of yesterday, the waiters being almost exhausted. Macdonald, Harry, and I are an hour and three quarters picking up various scraps of dishes that enable us to keep body and soul together. We are much amused at the novel way in which the waiters convey orders to the cook; instead of the accustomed "Beefsteak twice" of former days, we now hear shouted forth in tones sepulchral, hoarse "Nine times on your cabbage," "twice on your coffee," and so on.

Thursday, July 23rd

Harry, Hume, and I are sleeping peacefully this morning when a kind friend rouses us and informs us that we are close to Owen Sound. We cry "sucker again" but all the same are careful to poke a head out of our window and find it even so. The pleasant town lies before us and on the dock we are fast approaching is a cloud of white, the sight of which causes strange emotions to thrill us. Soon we reach our wharf, and the joyous shout of the expectant throng, the flutter of the white handkerchiefs, the bright friendly faces, make us realize that at last we are near home. We have a couple of hours in Owen Sound while our baggage is being unloaded and placed in our train and during that time regale ourselves with unlimited and marvellous quantities of lemonade and cake supplied by the citizens and amuse ourselves by going in for most desperate flirtations with the fair daughters of the hamlet.

We have a delightful run from Owen Sound, greeted with cheers at every station, nay, even at every crossroad. With hearts light and thankful withal we see once more the far-off smoke of our beloved Toronto and as our eyes fill fast at the roar of welcome that meets us, our labors, our trials, our dangers, our hardships, are all forgotten and gratitude and enthusiasm alone remain.

Notes

1. Lieutenant A.E. Doucet, a graduate of the Royal Military College, Kingston, was subsequently appointed aide to General Middleton.

2. Margaret Blake was the wife of Edward Blake, former Premier of Ontario, cabinet minister in the federal government of Alexander Mackenzie and in 1885, leader of the Liberal party. Cassels articled in Blake's law office.

3. Mr. Beatty was probably James Beatty, M.P. for West Toronto. Mr. Mulock was William (later Sir William) Mulock, another Toronto M.P. Mulock later became Postmaster General and Minister of Labour in the Laurier cabinet.

4. Major Daniel Hugh Allan, Queen's Own Rifles.

5. Lieutenant Ernest Frederick Gunther, Queen's Own Rifles, was, like Cassels, a young Toronto lawyer in 1885. He eventually rose to the rank of lieutenant-colonel and commander of the Queen's Own. He had a distinguished legal career and served as Superintendent of Insurance for British Columbia.

6. Captain Thomas Brown, Queen's Own Rifles.

7. Augustus Nanton (1860–1925), a young Toronto businessman, had gone to Winnipeg in 1884 to represent the brokerage firm of Pelatt and Osler. He later became one of the most successful financiers in Canada and was knighted in 1917.

8. John Donald Cameron was a Toronto lawyer who had moved to Winnipeg in 1882. He was later a prominent figure in Manitoba politics, becoming attorney-general in 1896. He ended his career as a judge.

9. The Robinson referred to here could have been Christopher Robinson (1828–1905), the leading Ontario trial lawyer of his generation. Robinson could have been in Winnipeg at this time. He represented the federal government in the Manitoba Boundary case in 1884 and was chief counsel for the government in the Riel trial.

10. William (Willie) Redford Mulock (1850–1930), was a cousin of Sir William Mulock.

11. Second Lieutenant Henry Walter Mickle, Queen's Own Rifles.

12. Major Charles John Short had been a member of the permanent force artillery since 1871.

13. Captain A. Hamlyn Todd was the son of the Parliamentary Librarian.

14. There were a number of Whites who took part in the rebellion. The one mentioned here was probably Second Lieutenant George Rivers White, Governor-General's Foot Guards.

15. Superintendent W.M. Herchmer (later assistant commissioner) was one of the original members of the North West Mounted Police in 1873.

16. Lieutenant Colonel William Dillon Otter began his long military career in the militia in 1861 with the Queen's Own Rifles. During the South African War he commanded the Royal Canadian Regiment. He was at various times chief of the general staff and inspector general of the Canadian Militia. During the First World War he was in charge of the internment of enemy aliens.

17. Captain Arthur R. Howard was a former U.S. Army officer working for the Gatling Gun Company as a salesman. He subsequently served as an advisor to the Canadian government on several occasions. During the South African War he served as a volunteer with the Canadian artillery and was killed in action.

18. Following the Frog Lake Massacre, Fort Pitt was threatened by Big Bear's Cree and was abandoned by its North West Mounted Police garrison.

19. Dr. Joseph Walter Lesslie, Surgeon, Queen's Own Rifles.

20. Captain E.A. Nash had been with the Queen's Own Rifles in Toronto until he moved west in 1882. On 24 March 1885 he was made commander of the Battleford Rifles.

21. Captain William Patrick Donahue Hughes and Captain William George Mutton.

22. Lieutenant Colonel Albert Augustus Miller.

23. Dr. William D. Nattress, Assistant Surgeon, Queen's Own Rifles.

24. Superintendent Percy R. Neale was one of the original North West Mounted Police officers on the formation of the force.

25. Lieutenant Robinson Lyndhurst Wadmore had been a member of the permanent force since 1882. He rose to the rank of colonel in 1910 and commanded garrisons in various Canadian cities.

26. Brigade Surgeon Frederick William Strange had previously served with the York Rangers and the Queen's Own Rifles.

27. Lieutenant James Walker Sears, born in New Brunswick, graduated from the Royal Military College in 1881. He served in Egypt with the British Army in 1882. At the time of the rebellion he was attached to "C" Company, Infantry School. He later returned to the British Army, spending most of his career with the South Staffordshire Regiment.

28. Edward Campion Acheson was a student at the University of Toronto in 1885. He was a private and during the course of the rebellion was appointed chaplain to the regiment. His later career as an Anglican clergyman was spent mainly in the United States.

29. Captain Robert William Rutherford, "B" Battery, was born in England and raised in Nova Scotia. He remained with the artillery and later became Director of Artillery (1904) and Master General of the Ordnance (1908).

30. George Exton Lloyd was a private with the Queen's Own Rifles. After the rebellion he became an Anglican minister and ultimately Bishop of Saskatchewan. The city of Lloydminster recalls his association with the Barr colony of the early twentieth century.

31. Major General John Wimburn Laurie was born in England and educated at Harrow and Sandhurst. He served with the British Army in the Crimean War and the Indian Mutiny before coming to Canada in 1861. Laurie volunteered for service in 1885 and was second-in-command, although he outranked Middleton.

32. Lieutenant Henry Brock was born in Oakville in 1859. Like most of the Queen's Own Rifles officers, he attended Upper Canada College. After 1885 he became a successful lawyer and businessman, and a well-known sportsman in Toronto.

He continued his association with the militia, eventually becoming senior Major of the 10th Royal Grenadiers.

33. Lieutenant Charles Hamilton Baird, Queen's Own Rifles.

34. Captain Joseph Martin Delamere was born in Ireland in 1848. He joined the Queen's Own Rifles as a private in 1865 and eventually rose to lieutenant colonel in 1896. He was president of the Canadian Military Institute 1898–1900. In private life he was assistant clerk of the Ontario Legislature.

35. Captain William Campbell Macdonald was a Toronto actuary with a life-long interest in the militia. He was a member of the Queen's Own Rifles until 1892 when he joined the 48th Highlanders, rising to command that regiment from 1900 to 1906. He was president of the Canadian Military Institute, 1901–3.

36. Second Lieutenant Arthur Burdett Lee, Queen's Own Rifles.

37. Captain James McGee, Queen's Own Rifles.

38. Constable F.O. Elliot of the North West Mounted Police was killed in a skirmish between a police patrol and Poundmaker's Cree.

39. Alexander Morris, *The Treaties of Canada with the Indians* (Toronto: Belfords, Clarke and Co., 1880). Morris was a cabinet minister in the Macdonald government and Lieutenant-Governor of Manitoba and the Northwest Territories, 1873–76.

40. Captain Henry Edmund Kersteman, Queen's Own Rifles.

41. Father Louis Cochin, O.M.I., was for a time Riel's confessor prior to the Métis leader's execution.

42. Second Lieutenant James George, Queen's Own Rifles.

43. Major Lawrence Buchan was born at Braeside, Ontario, in 1847. He joined the Queen's Own Rifles in 1872 and remained with the regiment until he moved west in 1881. On the outbreak of the rebellion he joined the 90th Winnipeg Rifles as adjutant. After the rebellion he joined the permanent force as captain and rose to the rank of lieutenant colonel by 1895.

44. Lieutenant F. Campbell, 90th Winnipeg Rifles.

45. William Hume Blake was a former officer in the Queen's Own Rifles. He came west in charge of a shipment of supplies sent to the troops by citizens of Toronto.

46. Lieutenant Colonel Charles E. Montizambert was a Quebecer who joined the permanent force artillery in 1871. Since 1882 he had been commandant of the School of Artillery at Kingston.

47. Superintendent Leif N.F. Crozier was an Irishman who joined the North West Mounted Police in 1874 after serving with the British Army.

48. John McLean, first Anglican Bishop of Saskatchewan (1874–1886) was born in Scotland in 1828. In 1858 he moved to Canada and was curate of St. Paul's Cathedral, London, until 1886. From 1886 to 1894 he was Warden and Professor of Divinity at St. John's College in Winnipeg.

49. The Robertson referred to here was almost certainly the Reverend James Robertson who had been pastor of Knox Church in Winnipeg since 1874. He later became Moderator of the Presbyterian Church in Canada.

Notes on the Suppression of the Northwest Insurrection

■

Harold Penryn Rusden

In writing these few notes of the recent rebellion in Canada, I do not propose to give a history of the rebellion generally. Enough has already been said of that, but very little truth has been written concerning the active work in conjunction with it. This has been kept quiet on purpose so as not to injure immigration; in fact, the whole thing has been kept as quiet as possible. In England people had no idea that an insurrection was simmering until the rebellion openly broke out, but for nearly two years it had been coming to a head. The Indians got restless and threatened revolt long before the halfbreeds were talked of. This was put down by threats, bribes, and perfidy generally; promises never intended to be fulfilled, and consequently laying the seed for more rebellion. The policy in the Northwest seems to have been to ward off an evil by creating an evil. But, however, of that I will speak later, at present I will proceed to the actual rebellion.

As nearly everyone knows, Riel, the leader and instigator, is a French halfbreed, educated at the instigation of Bishop Taché and reared in the Northwest. He received a good education, but was always a useless and an indolent man. In 1870 he incited the halfbreeds around Fort Garry and vicinity to revolt for some imaginary grievance and here showed his vicious and brutal nature by the foul murder of Scott. He marched against Fort Garry with a few poorly armed men, and the Hudson's Bay men, who it is said could

243

have easily held him off, threw the gates open and allowed him to enter and take the whole fort and stores. He also took the whites prisoners and amused himself daily by giving them their death warrant by way of dessert. He held high state here for three months until the arrival of Wolseley, but no sooner did Wolseley come in sight than Riel and his followers picked up traps and skedaddled over the prairie and far away. Subsequently he was paid $5,000 and his wife $1,000, and delicately reminded that his space would be more welcome to the government than his presence.

He then removed to Montana, U.S., where he led a precarious life, whisky-peddling and horse-trafficking, until the halfbreed delegation went over from Batoche to Montana to bring him back to sow the seeds of rapine and murder. He incited the halfbreeds to rise and sent messengers all over the country to incite the Indians to rise and massacre the white settlers. There is not the least doubt that his policy was to murder and plunder, to enrich himself and the fiends under him. He came into the country without a cent and had to be fed by the halfbreeds. He posed as a saint and got the halfbreeds to believe he was sent from heaven to relieve them from the yoke of the white men, but in my opinion, the origin of his presence might be traced to a very earthly institution.

However, his first move after stirring up the Indians was to ransack the white stores in Batoche and afterward those at Duck Lake. At this time Prince Albert, thinking it was time to stop these depredations, sent a body of Mounted Police and volunteers 200-strong, with one seven-pounder gun to treat with them, or protect other property as was thought; but Riel and his followers met them. They engaged and the Prince Albert people were defeated and driven back with a loss of thirteen. The sluggish and criminally indolent government then suddenly opened its eyes and saw what it might have seen months before. Quickly following this outrage, the Indians at Fort Pitt rose and massacred the whites, including two priests, twelve in all and taking two women, (Mrs. Delaney and Mrs. Gowanlock) prisoners. They then ordered the police to evacuate the fort, which they did, and the Indians took the whites prisoner, including Mrs. McLean, her daughters, and some children and other prisoners, twenty-seven in all.

On hearing this, the Minister of Militia immediately started active preparations for a campaign. The 90th battalion Winnipeg Rifles, 314 men; Winnipeg Field Battery, two nine-pounder guns, forty men; were immediately dispatched by train from Winnipeg to Qu'Appelle, the nearest point to the scene of the outbreak, some two hundred miles distant. General Middleton arrived about the 28th of March and immediately started to organize his column to march against Riel. It was unknown what amount of men Riel had, but it was supposed that he might have eight or nine hundred, exclusive of Indians. Middleton's column at this time numbered less than four hundred indifferently drilled and vilely equipped men, and the troops were a source of great ridicule to everyone who saw them. Many of them were clerks who had never slept outside in their lives and some of them even came up in low city shoes to march in. Many had no overcoats. Taking into consideration that March is one of the worst months in the year—cold, snowy, and bitter—a cold that freezes the very marrow in your bones—I think these men showed great spirit to have done the marching and stood the privations they did.

Middleton's first work was to organize transport and, as no resources could be drawn from a barren country, this must needs be a large one. Light two-horse wagons as used by the farmers were procured, some five hundred in number. Afterward there were over two thousand engaged. Having secured these and organized them, he next raised a party of mounted men as scouts. These are men whose duty it is to ride in front of the column and at the flanks, at various distances, from a quarter of a mile to five miles to prevent surprise and to find the enemy, to reconnoiter their position, to draw their fire, or any other work of that nature. There is a good deal of risk attached to it, but it is supposed to be the best position. These men were raised from the young farmers round the country who provided their own horses and, many of them, their own arms. Thirty-two were raised and the command was given to Captain Jack French,[1] an ex-police officer, a reckless, hot-headed Irishman and a soldier down to his boots. These organized, there was still a delay for stores, ammunition and all the innumerable paraphernalia appertaining to a campaign. Until the 5th of April nothing but drilling and organizing was done, and on 5th we received orders to march. I shall now accompany the troops, in my place as scout.

On the night of the 5th of April we received the joyful news to march at seven o'clock on the following morning. The order was received with cheers, for we were all tired of inactivity, although we were loath to leave our comfortable log hut, which did duty as a scouts' barracks. The morning of the 6th broke cold and dreary, with threatened snow, but notwithstanding the bleak aspect of the weather, the boys were all in good spirits and ready for the march. Promptly at 6:30 we were in the saddle and drawn up at the bridge, while the infantry and artillery were forming in the rear. Presently the general's aide came galloping up with orders to advance; then our captain gave the order, "Troop will advance, at a walk, march"; and our little troop moved off—the first to leave Qu'Appelle, the last to come back. No sooner over the bridge than Captain Jack yelled, "double," and away he went, the troop following helter-skelter through mud and half-melted snow, splashing and throwing the mud everywhere. Up the bank of the Qu'Appelle, out of the valley, "Halt," then extending one hundred yards apart covering the advance and flanks of the advancing troops, examining the bushes. The advance throughout the day was very slow, frequent halts retarded our progress, but nevertheless we marched till two o'clock in the afternoon and then halted on a ridge, ostensibly for dinner, but as the weather was getting very bad it was decided to make a night camp. No sooner had we halted, than it came on very fine drifting snow and a high cold wind, which seemed to blow right through our clothes, and many of us were without overcoats. However we endeavored to make the best of things, lighted fires and made tea, and sat down to dinner.

Let me paint the scene as well as I am able, and show you whether campaigning in Canada is pleasure or not! Scene—the top of a bare ridge or hill without any timber and consequently very little firewood to be found about. A cold piercing wind blowing and fine driving snow falling. Altogether a cold dreary day. Groups of shivering soldiers sitting on the frozen ground, their arms piled beside them, endeavoring to gulp down their very frugal meal of hard tack (hard biscuits) and very dry corned beef washed down with tea; then the sentry, marching up and down his beat as if for dear life, to get his feet warm in reality. Further down, shivering horses eating their oats and looking very blue, and lastly (I can't help mentioning it), certain officers of the field drinking whisky in a certain covered van and seemingly enjoying themselves. But then, you know, the liquor prohibition law is in force in the Nor'West, so we could not think of giving it to the men, you know, besides it is not good for them, not even when wounded!

However, after a great deal of trouble, we managed to pitch the tents in the frozen ground and by night things had got into some sort of shape and order. The troops camped in a square and the wagons forming a zareba behind them (a zareba or corral of wagons is formed by putting the pole of one wagon under the back of another and closing them up in a complete circle, making a compact wall). The scouts camped about two hundred yards in advance of the troops, which position they kept throughout the campaign, forming an advance picket two to five hundred yards outside the infantry picket, and doing guard outside their lines.

It fell to my lot to do guard on this particular night, and at two o'clock I was called up to go on picket, and highly amusing it was! No one had taken any clothes off, (nor did anyone get their clothes off for the next six weeks), my boots had frozen solid on my feet, and my rifle was white with frost when I stepped out of the tent and marched out to my beat, out in the cold dreary night. No one can imagine a watch on the prairie who has not seen one. Not a sound disturbed the bleak stillness of the night, the wind had dropped and everything was silent. A few watch fires burned in the camp, but the picket could have no fire. Truly a soldier's guard is a most monotonous duty; every tree or stone seems to take a shape, and we being inexperienced soldiers, a little allowance must be made for our occasional mistakes, as on this particular night while marching around I suddenly saw something move a short distance outside the lines. I halted and looked closer and was satisfied that it was moving. I immediately challenged "Halt, who goes there?" No answer. "Halt, who goes there!" No answer, "Halt, if you don't answer I'll fire!" Still no answer, and as the beastly thing still kept coming on, I lay down flat, not wishing to fire and disturb the camp, who would immediately be turned out if an alarm. Then seeing that the object did not appear to come any further, I crawled toward it, and got within ten yards of it when I suddenly got up and walked back to my beat.

I had not got far when I heard a tremendous "Halt, who goes there?" and listening, I found it came from where I had just left, so I hurried back, and there I saw a sight that made me smile, although only a counterpart of what I had done myself. The scout who was to relieve me, had come the rounds till he had come to this object, and there he was crawling carefully toward it. I got down and crawled after him. Presently he got close enough and got up and laughed, then I walked up to him and told him I had been sold the same way and asked him if he was satisfied it was not a hostile. "Quite," says he, "but let's go back to camp and get an axe and chop it down. I couldn't look that bush in the face in the morning!" My guard now came to an end, and I had the pleasure of going back to shiver in my most execrable government blankets.

Morning broke cold and cheerless. The half-melted snow had frozen solid, and the sloughs and creeks had again frozen over. Everyone was glad for the order to march, so that we might get our blood in circulation. Here the infantry had the pull over the mounted men, for they soon got warm, while we still shivered in the saddle; but toward midday the sun got some sway over the bleak elements and consequently we got a little more comfortable. The order of march was now set so that we could take position every morning without confusion. (I give a sort of sketch here of the column and videttes).

To resume, we camped for dinner at about eleven o'clock in a thick bluff and partook of our usual fare, though our horses came rather short, there being no grass and the transport having run short of feed. Marching again we made a good afternoon and camped about four o'clock, making some twenty miles distance, which for green troops carrying a rifle over back country in bad weather, marching and sometimes dragging themselves through deep snow and water, might be considered very good work. Of course, the troops were tired out coming into camp and were glad to get into their tents. Next morning no orders were given out to march, but shortly after breakfast we received orders to parade at eleven o'clock. At eleven the troops were drawn up and inspected. Afterward the scouts were galloped past the general, or rather charged past, for it was a race. Everyone seemed to put out as much speed as possible and try and get jumbled up with someone else. We were supposed to gallop past in single file, but as the horses were exceedingly fresh and unmanageable; the general must have been rather amused to have seen his scouts careering about everywhere, all over the country, running into each other, and some even getting upset. However, we got past and were dismissed.

During the day "C" School of Infantry came up and took ground in the infantry camp, later on, "A" Battery, two nine-pounder guns. Next morning reveille sounded at five and the troops marched at six o'clock. The weather was better and warmer. All day we marched through broken undulating country, crossing a great deal of water. We passed through many halfbreeds' places, but these either got out of the way or had already gone to join Riel. About 4:30 P.M. we reached Touchwood Hills Hudson's Bay station and

camped for the night. Some of the Touchwood Indians came into camp with the usual protestations of
friendship on the strength of which they begged
tobacco and bacon. They were miserable, dirty-looking individuals, with the same cruel expression of
feature as all the rest of their race.

We passed a quiet night and struck camp in the
morning and marched through rolling and rocky
country very diffiicult to scout. One had to dismount
and force a way through the scrub and was all the
time in imminent danger of getting lost, as nothing
could be seen of the column for hours together. A
good march was made of over twenty miles, which
brought us up to the Salt Plains. That night the
orders were reveille at 4:30 A.M. and march at 5:30, so
as to make the middle of the Salt Plains, a dreary
waste devoid of timber and poorly watered.

The following morning broke cold and forbidding
and we dreaded a march across a bleak plain, but as
the day wore on it got a little warmer and again
shortly after dinner halt it grew cold again. The
country was vile marching, the troops tramping
through water and snow and small creeks, constantly
wet through, at times over knee-deep. Still they
behaved manfully, singing and cheering each other on
and not a murmur and very few fell out of the ranks.
We found the half-way station about five o'clock,
tired and cold. Shortly afterward the troops marched
into camp thoroughly wearied out with a long and
very trying march. So tired were they that many of
the poor fellows could hardly drag themselves into
camp and it must be borne in mind that a soldier's

work is not done when he comes into camp. He is kept in the ranks till the transport comes up, then he has to carry tents and packs, pitch tents, carry cooking utensils, wood, and water, and then a certain number for picket, quarter guard, and sentry. So tired were the troops on this particular march, that we, the scouts, volunteered and did the whole of the pickets and guard for the night. Little acts of this kind create a good feeling amongst troops. They never forgot this act and our captain, who was the instigator of it, was never forgotten by the troops. It was a miserable cold night as were the next three days.

It is needless to describe the rest of the march to Humboldt, as it was all much about the same with very little variety, everything being quiet and no appearance of the rebel scouts. On the 13th we arrived in Humboldt, a small station where we found two Mounted Police, and camped here on the 14th, which was a beautiful day and was a welcome rest for all hands except some of the scouts who were detailed off to escort the general on a reconnoiter. Nothing was seen and on the 15th we marched again and got within thirty-five miles of Clarke's Crossing and camped on a very pretty site overlooking Vermilion Lake.

Next morning the scouts, all but a few lame horses, accompanied by General Middleton, one gun of "A" Battery, and "C" Company pushed on to secure Clarke's crossing. It was a bitter cold day and about the coldest ride we ever had. It blew a gale and snowed right in our faces and, to improve matters, the commissary had forgotten to send any grub for us. Consequently we had no dinner, at which the general swore soundly and sent over some of his own dinner in the shape of a tongue and some ham, which was very welcome and for which we blessed the good-natured old soldier. We arrived in Clarke's Crossing late in the afternoon, very cold and very miserable, but after feeding the horses we managed to find an old hut with some implements and boxes in it, which we speedily chucked out, and installed ourselves therein. It was very cold but a great deal more comfortable than outside, as we had no tents. We came very short of rations again, having only a slice of bread each, cooked by the settlers who were staying at the Crossing. After this frugal meal, we all turned in, that is, as there were about twenty-eight men in all and only room for about half that number, we had to squeeze in like sardines packed tightly one against the other; a very warm mode no doubt, but decidedly not a comfortable one. So tight were we packed that the word of command had to be given to turn around and if you didn't turn you either got unmercifully squeezed, or else got jammed out of your place altogether.

Clarke's Crossing is on the south branch of the Saskatchewan, an isolated settlement on the road to Battleford. There are only three or four houses, a ferry, and telegraph station; the river here is five or six hundred feet wide with high banks and a strong current. The object of securing this place was to open the river for transport and to make a depot; being a junction of the trails from Prince Albert, Battleford, Swift Current, Moose Jaw, and Qu'Appelle and being, therefore, an important point. The day after our advance, the troops marched in and took up a position on the south bank. This was on the 17th of April. Here we had a welcome rest for both man and beast and three or four days were spent making a ferry across river. In this interval the 10th Grenadiers from Toronto, 267 strong, and Boulton's Mounted Infantry, raised in the Territories, joined us and made a very welcome addition. They made a reconnoiter under our captain, as our troop was in need of rest, and while out, came across three of the hostile scouts. They were taken by Captain French and Lord Melgund,[2] supported by Boulton's men, and brought into camp. They were Sioux Indians, one being the son of the old warrior chief, White Cap, who has seen many a fight with the Americans.[3]

On the 20th, after a great deal of trouble, we got across the river being destined to form the advance of the western column, under Lieutenant-Colonel Montizambert and Lord Melgund. After us the troops and transport were crossed over. On the 22nd the scouts were ordered out to reconnoiter the country round and hardly had we left the camp a mile, than we sighted three rebel scouts who immediately made off. They were seen, however, by the whole troop as it was in open country, and the extended scouts and reserve immediately gave chase. Scattering all over the country, regardless of holes or ravines, we tore along, the quarry in sight and giving good chase, being very well mounted. The pace was hard and furious and it was like a very animated fox hunt. The best horses soon got to the front and took the running. Fourteen and fifteen miles of it unbroken were accomplished before the leader got within range. The leader at this time was a young trooper

mounted on a very fine little gray horse. In coming
within range, the rebel scouts drew up and fired at
him, but he, though the bullets struck close to him,
continued on, the while getting out his Winchester
rifle and endeavoring to pump a cartridge into it; but
the machine refused to work, so he threw it back in
the sling and continued on without any arms. At this
time another scout came up, but would not continue
the chase till he had had a shot. He dismounted to
fire and the rebel scouts also dismounted and fired.
They then mounted and skipped again, having gained
a few yards soon after this. They gained shelter in a
bluff, and as other rebels were seen there; our scouts
halted and waited for more men to come up. Captain
French and Lord Melgund came up, and as it was
getting late and doubtful what number were in the
bluff, and as men were seen moving about, decided
not to attack with so small a force of pumped men.

Accordingly we were ordered to retire back to
camp, which was done, and all hands arrived back
tired and hungry, though stimulated by the effects of
their first brush. The hunters growled because they
were not allowed to court destruction by rushing into
a bluff that might have been alive with rebels. After
this little episode everything remained quiet. Pickets
and guards went on and off, the usual humdrum
monotony and discipline of camp life went on. It
began to get very tiresome, everlastingly the same
lazy inactivity. But the night of the 23rd ended all our
grumblings and put the troops in good humour
again. Orders came in to march in the morning at six
o'clock. It was supposed at this time that Riel was

entrenched at Batoche, but it was not known where he intended to give battle, whether on both sides or on one. Fabulous stories reached us of his strength, and it was said that the whole army would be destroyed, that we couldn't possibly cope with them. Frantic stories began to get about and, of course, got greatly exaggerated as they were passed on, unnerving many of the young militia men. The general opinion of the more experienced, however, was that Riel would not fight at all, but run away as he did before.

However we were now under orders to march. Our column, under the command of Colonel Montizambert and Lord Melgund, was composed as follows: French's Scouts in the lead with a draft of men from Boulton's Horse; next Colonel Montizambert, Lord Melgund and officers, 10th Grenadiers of Toronto, Winnipeg Field Battery, and a detachment from "A" Battery. The column on the east bank was led by the remainder of Boulton's Horse, about fifty mounted men under Major Boulton, followed by General Middleton and staff, "C" Company, the 90th Batallion Winnipeg Rifles, and "A" Battery, two nine-pounder guns. All being in readiness on the 23rd, both columns moved off, advancing on both sides of the river within sight of each other. The troops were in good spirits and eagerly looking forward to a brush to try their metal against the rebels. It was expected that they might be engaged at any moment, as it had been reported that Riel was advancing, though generally disbelieved. A good march was made and the weather being good everyone was in good spirits. Toward night a halt was called and camp made, both columns being opposite each other.

The night passed away quickly, and next morning Middleton's column moved out of camp and resumed its march. Our column had to wait for provisions and hay, which Lord Melgund had gone across the river to secure, our troops in the meantime lying about amusing themselves as best they could. Our corps put a couple of old shirts and some rags on the end of a stick and the Grenadiers' band came and played round it as a salute. At about nine o'clock I was sent out to relieve an outpost or vidette, to prevent surprise. I had hardly lit my pipe when I heard shots and, listening, I heard next a volley and immediately galloped in to report. I was sent out in the direction of the firing to discover where it came from, as it was thought to be the Prince Albert Police and volunteers engaged with some of the rebels, as they were supposed to have joined our column about here. However, slipping a cartridge in my rifle and accompanied by another scout, we made down the river as hard as four legs could travel. My partner, having a played-out horse, soon dropped behind and I had the running to myself. I kept on toward the firing, which by this time had become very heavy, the guns being evidently engaged. The heavy boom of the cannon, the whizzing of shells, and the duller boom as the shell burst could be easily heard above the incessant rattle of small arms. Someone was evidently getting it hot. I now saw that the fighting was across the river and half a mile further I came across three horsemen on the opposite bank of the river. I immediately dismounted and prepared to fire in case they should be rebels. I had to shout, "General Middleton," three times before I got an answer, then one of them called out, "Tell Lord Melgund we're attacked in the rear."

Knowing that was a serious business (this was not the case, the officer had evidently misconstrued the state of affairs; Middleton was not attacked in the rear at all), I immediately dashed back to camp to give the news to Lord Melgund, but on the way nearly came to grief. I was carrying a Snider rifle and, being both long and heavy, it was very much in the way galloping through the timber. While passing between some trees the great cannon of a thing swung, caught a branch and swung round off the pommel and caught me a crack on the leg that nearly broke it, so I pitched the thing off and continued on much more comfortably without it. As the government never heard anything about it, I didn't pay for it. However, to continue—as soon as I showed up again one of the scouts, in the excitement of the moment, rushed up to where the scouts were drawn up and told them I was being chased by the rebels. Half the troop immediately dashed off the wrong way to intercept the breeds and I got in in the meantime. I found the troops drawn up ready and immediately made my report, when the whole column moved off, the scouts coming back from their fruitless chase and roundly swearing at the false alarmer. The column now moved down in skirmishing order and halted opposite the scene where Middleton was fighting.

When we arrived he was shelling and the dull whizz of the shells could be distinctly heard and the crashing of shrapnel above the uneven rattle of rifle firing. As Middleton required more support, the scow which had followed us down the river was now brought up and crossing commenced. The guns, accompanied by ten scouts, were first crossed. This was not achieved before midday or later. After the guns, the 10th Grenadiers, all but one company. This left only forty scouts and one company of the 10th to protect a large transport in a country where the breeds might be lurking close to us. It was known that they were not all engaged across the river and toward the afternoon we saw the halfbreeds clearing out in numbers and begged to be allowed to chase them but were not allowed to do so, as we had the river to cross and would leave the transport unprotected.

Toward four o'clock a messenger came across with dispatches. Our column on the eastern bank of the river had marched out of camp in the morning, but about a couple of miles from camp, while the scouts were skirmishing around, a concealed enemy suddenly opened fire and six of the saddles were immediately emptied, but their riders were not killed as at first reported. Two only fell wounded and our men were ordered to let their horses go and take cover to keep back the rebels. On receiving this order our men dismounted, extended in skirmishing order, and effectually checked the rebels from advancing. These men deserved great praise and should have been mentioned and received more notice than General Middleton has been pleased to give them in his dispatch. This was, without doubt, the most gallant act throughout the day. This little handful of men engaged and held in check a force that Middleton with his force could neither dislodge nor get any satisfaction out of.

While Boulton's men were holding in check the rebels, the troops were forming up and soon came up on the double, extended in skirmishing order, and engaged the rebels. Some very heavy firing took place about this time and the nine-pounders were brought up and threw shells across a ravine, setting fire to it and driving the rebels out. Shrapnel shells and case shot were used on the bluffs, but with little or no effect. Later on the guns destroyed with shell some fifty of the rebels' horses, while the scouts were engaged with two companies of the 90th in holding the rebels' front. The rebels had got round and endeavored to turn our right under cover of a prairie fire, which they had lit up to hide their movement. Their advance, however, was seen in time and "C" Company and two companies of the 90th opened a heavy fire on them, which was very heartily returned. Our men nevertheless gradually drove them back down the ravine, the breeds retiring keeping up a brisk fire. They made a short stand in the ravine but shortly afterward ceased firing. It was then found that they had retreated altogether.

About this time the Winnipeg Field Battery came up with the 10th Grenadiers. The battery was engaged shelling the bluffs, the Grenadiers were extended round the head of what had been the rebels' front, and all that was left of the rebels were a few who could not retreat, owing to the guns having taken up a position in their rear. Captain Drewry, with his "A" Battery support, made a dash down the ravine, but was met by a sharp fire and three of his men were killed. He then retired and, had the ground been at all practicable, a charge would have been no doubt successful, but down a ravine, where it was very difficult even to walk, it was a piece of lunacy to say the best of it. The firing had now ceased, except in the ravine aforementioned. Little damage was done after this except a few wounds. The rebels, however, had sent home the fatal missile to ten of our brave fellows and laid out forty wounded.

All through the fighting these untrained and inexperienced volunteers showed pluck and endurance under very trying circumstances, entirely different fighting to civilized warfare, where you can see your enemy, and the excitement gives you courage. In this case you lie down in a bluff and take deliberate aim at a head, or anything you can see, or as is more often the case, lying in a bluff and the bullets zipp, zipp, zipping round you, not knowing where they come from and where to direct the compliment in return. Although, literally speaking, this was not a battle, it served to show that the much maligned and despised volunteer, or rather I should say pioneer-volunteer, is *not* to be despised. Though perhaps not as steady and cool as a regular would be under the circumstances (for an old campaigner would call Fish Creek, as the name of the place is called, nothing but a sharp skirmish), the volunteer still showed the material of a good soldier. The rebels made better shooting than our men, though they wasted a prodigous amount of powder and shot, in some places searching the bluffs with horns of buckshot, as will be seen. The number killed and wounded was heavy considering the small force engaged—some 350 or 400.

On our side the waste of powder and shot was something enormous. What with the nine-pounder shells and the incessant rattle of small arms, you would scarcely credit the small amount of damage done. Only two Teton Sioux Indians were found dead. General Middleton, however, gives account of eleven killed and eighteen wounded from papers afterward found in Batoche.

However, to return, night closing in, the troops were withdrawn to the camp, where the wounded and dead had been previously carried, the teamsters having put up the tents and made the camp for the now thoroughly worn-out troops. Notwithstanding, the pickets had to be doubled and consequently every available man had to take his share of guard, as it was expected that the rebels might try a surprise in the night, a thing Indians are very fond of. No one on the campaign is likely to forget the night of the 25th of April. Everything was in confusion. Food could not be found and supper had to be got the best way you could get it. At dusk it began to sleet and a cold wind got up. By dark it had turned bitterly cold and was snowing. A more miserable lookout could not be possibly conceived. Tired out, cold, hungry, and miserable; on one side of the river the groans of the wounded and dying, on the other confusion, a large transport guarded only by a handful of men who might be attacked, cut off, and destroyed before help could arrive from the already worn-out troops on the other side. All through the long black night the pickets walked up and down their dreary beats in the snow in knots of four, endeavoring to keep warm and occasionally rallying and laughing at each other for their miserable appearance.

At length the long wished-for day broke but brought little or no better weather, in fact worse, for at daylight it commenced to rain cold soaking rain, all through the dreary day. Mounted outposts kept guard over the transport to guard against surprise. Meanwhile a scow was taking the transport across the river to join the main body, but this was slow work and therefore would take up some time. It was a never-to-be-forgotten day. Not knowing when the rebels would come down and endeavor to capture the transport, which was valuable and might have been an easy prey to a well-organized attack; a wet lookout on one side and on another a fatigue party on the other side of the river, digging a last resting place for the boys who had gone to salute the great general. Deeply did our fellows feel for those poor fellows' wives and mothers who were left to mourn for their darlings. It is strange how little men think of death in action. One poor fellow was shot in the head while eating hard tack (hard biscuits), another while laughing and talking to his mate. Many of those slightly wounded returned to their places. Many acts of bravery personally were also noticed in the field and the first of all stands General Middleton, who displayed coolness and courage which did him credit, though he is open to condemnation for his reckless exposure of himself. His excuse is worthy of himself, a brave man as he is. He said, "I had green troops, and what is worse still, green officers, and I had to set them an example," which he did in every way, exposing himself in the most reckless manner, riding amongst the thick of the bullets and seemingly as calm and stoical as if on parade. In fact he always seemed the same, whether on parade or in action. Once he got a near call. A bullet passed through his astrakhan cap, when he turned to his circle and remarked, "That was meant for you, sir."

A little drummer boy, almost a child to look at, named Billy Buchanan, being too small to carry a rifle, amused himself carrying about ammunition for the troops, walking down the line calling out "now boys, who's for more cartridges?" The little lad's coolness and pluck could not but be noticed by even the general himself, for his position was more dangerous even than the troops as he had to keep moving all the time, and the rebels took advantage of everything that stirred to fire at. In the official report he is mentioned last. I think it would have been a great deal more fair if he had been mentioned first, having set such a good example to men far older and more experienced than himself. At any rate he should be mentioned before a craven cur mentioned because he happened to be an officer with a lot of empty prefixes before his name, but who, as every man in the column knows, tied his horse up to a tree and left his sword on the saddle and was afraid to go back and get it and consequently the rebels captured it and bore it off in triumph! There's a nice creature to mention if you like. Captain Peters[4] led his men with pluck and daring, a sort of officer who would not scruple to slaughter all his men and himself, too, if need be.

But to return, the day passed away quietly. The dead had been borne to their last resting place, the last rites said over the soldiers' grave, and the sun went down over a cold cheerless earth. The night was again cold, but no snow or rain. Next morning the weather was a little better so that we were consequently a little more joyous, and began to pluck up spirits in the expectation of soon having another brush with the rebels. In the meantime the work of crossing over the transport was carried on day and night, as it was now decided that the advance would be made in force on the west side of the river. It was supposed that the rebels would be met with next at Batoche, a settlement some thirty miles down the river, being a very strong position and a very difficult one to take, owing to the rough nature of the country and the thick timber surrounding the town. By the night of the 26th the transport had all crossed over to General Middleton's column and about twelve o'clock at night the infantry were crossed, leaving the scouts to watch the banks. Just before daybreak the scouts were crossed, the last of the western column, and very glad we were, for we had not a pleasant position by any means. The forces were now concentrated so that we had a large camp; however, we were disappointed to hear that we should not march for some days, so as to get rid of the wounded and get more supplies that were expected by the steamer, which was coming down the river and might be expected anytime.

Everything was quiet in the camp and the same routine of camp life went on except that the pickets and patrols were strengthened. All the rebels' houses round about, of course, were pillaged, and it was comical to see some of the booty brought into camp. An infantry man might be seen with a small pig under one arm and a squaw's dress on the other, sneaking in through the lines so as not to be seen; scouts coming in with pots and pans tied to their saddles, poultry and other paraphernalia hanging about. One fellow in particular cut a very amusing figure. He had a tin pot on his head, various other cooking utensils hung about his saddle, some ten or fifteen fowls strung round his cartridge belt, several pairs of trousers hung to the back of his saddle, while under his arm he carried a small organ. Looting now seemed to be the order of the day. Everything that could be carried away was taken and the rebel's houses stripped and devastated. We were out mounted during the day running in the rebels' cattle and slaughtering them. Our troop in particular fared very well at this time, as being a scouting corps, we penetrated into the rebel settlement and got quantities of fowls and eggs. On one occasion we took out a wagon ostensibly for hay and passed back through the lines, to all intents and purposes, loaded with that very useful article, but stowed away under the load we had six fine pigs and three or four nice calves on which we had a jubilee.

It was about this time that we got news that Colonel Otter at Battleford had engaged Poundmaker and had defeated him. Later on we heard that Colonel Otter had retreated on Battleford with heavy loss, which was nearer the truth. Taking too small a force into the field, he was forced to retreat with a loss of twenty-six dead and wounded. This was rather a serious check, as it was said that the rebels did not recognize a defeat at Fish Creek and it was to be feared that a little success would lead to a general Indian rising, as the Indians were all at the time restless and only waiting developments to break out and join in the picnic. Had this happened, it would have been a serious thing for our little bunch; in the middle of a hostile country, short of provisions, with our retreat cut off. However our main thought now was to get at the rebs again and give them a severe dressing to revenge the death of our fellow soldiers. About the 30th, all the mounted men, accompanied by the general and staff, headed by French's Scouts, made a reconnaissance to endeavor to find the enemy. We got within four miles of Batoche without seeing the enemy in force. We chased three scouts but they got away in the heavy timber. While advancing we came across a house that had evidently just been vacated by its tenants, for on the stove the kettle was boiling and the table was set for five, meat and bread being laid thereon. The general went in and was going to set to, but being told by his cockney orderly that it was "'orse flesh and the 'orfbreeds was very fond of 'orse flesh," he left it and went out, whereon we scouts went in and devoured the dinner and then upset the china and pocketed everything of any value and many things of no value. At this time the culinary department was rich in utensils, pots and pans by the dozen. Plates were at a discount and every man could boast of a spoon of his own, besides a knife and fork, whereas before two-thirds of the troop had to eat with their fingers. We fared splendidly while in the Fish Creek camp, having quantities of potatoes, fresh pork, veal, and beef, besides fowls and other small delicacies.

But to resume, the reconnaissance was made past a place called Gabriel's Crossing, but as there was no sign of the enemy about it was decided to have dinner at Gabriel's Crossing and then return. We therefore tied up our horses and proceeded to eat dinner, General Middleton mounting on the seat of our old hay rake to eat his lunch in lieu of a soft cushioned chair and mahogany table, and while waiting the unpacking of his lunch amused himself by whistling his favorite tune, "There's One More River to Cross." (I might here mention that this place, Gabriel's Crossing, belonged to a halfbreed called Gabriel Dumont, who was Riel's chief fighting man. A most unscrupulous and bloodthirsty scoundrel, this was the man who did his best to get the council to murder the prisoners then in their hands. The council, however, would not do so. All the houses and buildings belonging to this man were burned to the ground.) After dinner we immediately broke open the doors and proceeded to loot. The place, of course, had been deserted as all the houses had along our lines of march. In Gabriel's house we found a box of cigars, some coins, gloves, and a lot of store goods which we immediately stowed away. In another of his houses we found a billiard table and various articles of civilized furniture. While we were stowing away loot, the general came in and ordered us out. After this we got the order to mount and fall in and the march home was resumed. It is needless to say that we looted the whole way home. All sorts of things were brought in, even to chairs.

About the 1st of May, about one o'clock at night, we were suddenly wakened up by firing from the pickets and were immediately turned out under arms. A small volley was fired by the pickets and it was at first thought to be the rebels coming down, but as the firing ceased and "All's well" was passed down the line, we were turned in again. Next morning the alarm was found to have been caused by a transport officer who was coming into the lines ahead of his transport but who, instead of answering the sentry's challenge, dodged behind a tree and was consequently fired upon. This scared him so much that he lay where he was till morning, when he came in. Several of these alarms were raised but usually they were false alarms to see how the troops would turn out. The wounded had by this time been sent to the rear in improvised ambulance wagons accompanied by an escort of mounted men and a staff of doctors. Nothing now hindered us from advancing but the arrival of the *Northcote* river steamer with supplies and ammunition, which were badly wanted and which we could not advance without.

On the 5th of May in the early morning her welcome whistle was heard in the distance and the troops crowded down to see her come in. As she neared the camp we could see that she had on board part of the Midland Batallion, which was to form a small reinforcement, and when the steamer tied up, our band went down and played them into camp where they were received with vociferous cheering.

Colonel Van Straubenzie,[5] who was to command the infantry brigade also arrived, also an American officer, who brought up with him an American Gatling gun, with a discharge of 1,000 shots per minute, a very handy and complete little weapon. Captain Howard showed some practise with it and the little machine seemed to kick up as much dust as a whole regiment of infantry. This gun can be fired with such rapidity that a man can be shot through the heart and ten bullets can be put in his body before he falls. The *Northcote* was now boarded up and made into a sort of gun boat, without the guns. Thirty-five men of "C" Company were put aboard here and she received her orders to drop down the river in company with the troops.

Everything now being in readiness, on the 6th we received the welcome news to march and on the 7th of May the whole force struck camp and marched to Gabriel's Crossing, which has been before mentioned. The *Northcote* was ordered to remain here, with orders to be opposite Batoche at 8 a.m. on the 9th, while the column struck off the river into the prairie and then struck a line parallel with the river, so as to avoid the heavy scrub and timber on the river road to Batoche. We got within nine miles of Batoche by the evening and Boulton's Scouts made a reconnaissance toward Batoche but, beyond seeing some rebel scouts and putting them to flight, nothing was seen of the rebel forces. It was, however, known that the rebels were in force in Batoche and that they were entrenched in pits round the town, so that we were sure of a brush on the morrow. Very little excitement was manifested, however. In the evening the band played as usual and the troops moved about laughing and talking just as if nothing unusual was happening. Death or defeat never seems to trouble men on a campaign or on the eve of a battle. The troops turned in early so as to get a good rest for the coming struggle as it was expected that the morrow would be a decisive point one way or another.

On the 9th of May reveille sounded at 2:30 and the whole column marched out of camp shortly after three leaving the camp and transport standing, taking only ammunition wagon and ambulance with doctor's staff. Boulton's Scouts, being the strongest corps, were ordered to take the lead, followed by the guns and infantry. Our corps, French's Scouts, received orders to guard the ammunition wagons while on the march and then, as soon as the action began, form a body guard to the general. Nothing was met with till we arrived within two or three miles of Batoche, when we suddenly heard heavy firing in the direction of Batoche and directly afterward the *Northcote*'s whistle. The firing got heavier and heavier and it seemed as if the whole rebel force was pitted against the luckless vessel. She had evidently got to Batoche too early and instead of acting in conjunction with the troops, she got the whole brunt of the rebel fire. At this juncture General Middleton ordered up one of the guns and fired a blank charge as a signal to the boat and then pushed on the advance to assist the boat.

As soon as the first houses were sighted, our corps formed up and with Captain Jack at our head galloped in on the right front of the infantry advance. As we advanced on the road between the river and some houses on the outskirts of the town, we set fire to all the houses and advanced till we came within sight of the church and council house and another large building. The guns were trained and some shells thrown into them. The Gatling gun also threw out a few volleys, but without doing any damage. No volleys answered us and our advance was not met in any way. A white flag was hung out from the church and we advanced carefully but met with nothing. Not a sound did we hear except the firing of the *Northcote*, which the rebels appeared to be following down the river. Advancing up to the church we found the Catholic priests and sister, who put themselves under the protection of General Middleton.

At this point five of our corps came in and reported having been fired on from rifle-pits while scouting round on the extreme right. We now advanced with a gun along a bare bluff toward the river and from the top of the bank we could plainly see the Indian camp and the rebels' houses on the other side of the river, distance about 3,000 yards. Still we met no enemy. A gun was brought up and trained on the largest houses and shells were thrown into them, but doing little damage beyond driving the women out. We could see them making for the bush in dozens and wagons and people driving off. Our troop was now ordered to dismount and cover the guns, extending down to the river and in advance of the guns, they being above us on the bluff while we were down the river bank, some fifteen of us. Several shells had been fired without any response, and we began to think that the rebels had gone, when suddenly, without a moment's warning, we heard a blood-curdling war whoop, followed by a volley from the rebel's rifles as they charged on the gun (they had been lying concealed close to the guns). We heard the gun immediately limber up and retreat and we expected next minute to see the breeds appear over the ridge and our retreat cut off. This the rebels could have very easily done as our little band would not have been able to stand five minutes being exposed to their fire from above. This they would have undoubtedly done, but for the gallant conduct of Captain Howard, who seeing the turn affairs had taken, shoved his Gatling gun within thirty paces of the rebels and turned her loose, grinding the handle fast and furious, oscillating the barrels so as to search the whole of the bluff. The rebels immediately stopped their yelling and firing too and we, who had been thrown into disorder by the sudden and unexpected affair, were enabled to retreat to our horses, which were in rear of the guns. When we got to our horses all we could see of the forces was the retreating gun and Captain Howard with his Gatling gun, to all intents and purposes, fighting the rebels single-handed.

The rebels now opened fire from the other side of the river, and as Howard's position was very much exposed he was ordered to retire. "A" Battery now came up and extended on our right, while we were ordered to take a position on the bluff and prevent the rebels from getting round on our flank. We had hardly taken ground when we were treated to a shower of lead, which we promptly returned. Part of the 90th were extended on our left. Further away on the right we heard of the firing from the rebel pits answered by, I think, part of the 90th and the 10th Royals. The Midland Regiment was in reserve in our rear, Boulton's Horse were drawn up behind the church out of the fire at this time. The Gatling gun dashed about all over the field to wherever the most damage could be done, the batteries were brought up several times to shell houses, but a perfect storm of bullets was directed at them whenever they broke cover, and they were always forced to retire again.

It would be as well to describe the kind of country we were fighting in. Batoche is the capital of the half-breed settlement. A very prettily situated town or village, it is built on both sides of the river and on the east side, that which we were attacking, it is thickly surrounded by timber, deep ravines, and gulches. We had struck their right and attempted to drive it in, but they were too well entrenched and we could not gain an inch of ground. They were so well concealed in their pits in the timber, which is very close, that we could not see them and they took care never to show themselves. We were at this time unacquainted with either their numbers or position, so that for this reason, we supposed, the general did not charge them. It began to get dreadfully monotonous; being down some distance apart from each other, firing at nothing, making guess shots, and hearing the rebel bullets zipp, zipp all round you and the everlasting clack as the bullets struck the trees. It was not the sort of fighting we expected at all. This sort of fighting is very bad for a young soldier. There is no excitement or rush to keep him up, his blood gets cold knowing that he is fighting at a disadvantage and that the enemy knows his position and he does not know how they are situated. Many got nervous, in fact there are very few indeed who can say with truth that they were not nervous during the first day's fighting, although there were very few who showed it.

But to resume, throughout the day no advance was made. We were kept lying in the bluffs and had to be content to take occasional shots at a shaking twig or puff of smoke. We knew that the rebels were not many yards in front of us, also by their firing that they were in much greater force than our corps, as we were only about twenty strong and the firing on this quarter was nearly all directed on us. "A" Battery on our right seemed to be getting a much lighter dose. For nine hours we were kept in this miserable bluff and no support sent to us and no notice was paid to us either. Had we been sent a strong support we might have cleared the bluff and driven the rebels' flank in and so opened the way into Batoche and taken it the first day, for it was taken in precisely this same way four days later as it was afterward found out that this was the key of their position. But perhaps it is as well the attempt was not made, as there would probably have been a greater loss of life to take the position than was lost in the final struggle.

About three o'clock the rebels seemed to have received reinforcements, for the bullets came in doubly as thick. One of the "A" Battery men was hit and directly afterward one of ours. We got orders now to retire as we could do no good and only lose our men. "A" Battery retired to get better cover and at this moment a cry was raised that the breeds were after us and for a moment it looked as if there was going to be a stampede, but it was only for a moment. Though the breeds redoubled their firing and sent in a pitiless hail of bullets, our fellows turned round and took cover for a moment and then again began to retire. The rebels again poured in a volley, and in the thickest of it Captain French was seen coming up the bluff with a wounded man on his back. Another trooper and myself immediately went to his assistance and we carried the poor fellow on a rifle to the stretcher brought down by the ambulance which had been kept busy during the last few hours' fighting.

We were now ordered to take our horses to a more sheltered place as the bullets were singing round them pretty lively. We moved them back close to the church and waited for orders. Whilst waiting, another scout and myself went to the church and saw the wounded. There were at this time two killed and nine men and an officer wounded. The place at this time had a very warlike appearance. Behind the church Boulton's Scouts were taking cover. They formed a picturesque group; some were lying down holding their horses, some leaning on their rifles smoking, others discussing the day's work. About the door of the church the ambulance wagons stood, here and there a stretcher with its sickening blotches of red telling a tale of pain and suffering. Inside the church, the wounded stretched out in a row and the busy doctors doing their best to alleviate the pain of dangerous wounds. In front of the church the Gatling gun spitting out its venom; on the left of the church French's Scouts, mostly lying down in a knot, and between them and the church the Midland Regiment lying down taking cover, while the smoke of a prairie fire the breeds had attempted to light gave the picture a weird and warlike appearance. In fact, for the amount of firing and bullets flying about you would fancy that a regular battle was going on instead of a skirmish, for it could not come under any heading but a hot skirmish and a very unsatisfactory one, too, for we had not gained an inch of ground and, to all intents and purposes, we had not done any damage that we knew of. In fact, to speak the plain truth, things began to look more like a reverse for us than anything else. It was getting late and it became a question of whether we should retire to the camp for the night or bring up the camp and take ground where we were. It was decided to bring up the camp, and it was plain that this was the only thing we could do, as had we attempted to retire to the camp, we should have been harassed by rebel sharpshooters the whole way back. Accordingly, Boulton's Scouts and ours were sent back to bring up the transport. We were glad of the chance to stretch ourselves and also to get something to eat, as we had had nothing since before three in the morning. We galloped back to the camp past the still-burning houses and, arriving at the old camp, we got the transport under weigh with all possible speed and were soon on the way back. It was dusk, however, before we got to where the camp had been located, which was, of all horrors, on a small ploughed field, surrounded by bluffs, and on the left a deep ravine. The wagons were quickly formed into a square zareba, poles inside, which, by-the-by, makes a very good breastwork. The horses were tied inside, facing out, while the scouts' horses were tied in lines facing each other. No tents were pitched except three for the hospital. There were also about seventy head of loose cattle inside the zareba.

It was now getting dark and the Gatling gun and support came dashing in. The rebels, thinking they were retreating, came up the gully thinking to cut them off, but to their surprise they were met by a volley from the zareba on receipt of which they very quickly disappeared. The rest of the troops had already been withdrawn and, after getting supper, or rather scrambling for something to eat anywhere it could be found, all hands were turned to making trenches outside the wagons, though as close to as could be got, extending right round the zareba. All hands were hard at this for some hours until a breastwork had been thrown up all round and a trench to lie in. When this was done the troops, thoroughly tired out, lay down to snatch a little rest with their belts and sidearms on and their rifles close beside them. While this was going on the rebels kept up a dropping fire; firing into the zareba, killing one man and wounding another, besides hitting some of the cattle. They fired at intervals through the night. Our pickets we stationed on the edge of the plain some fifty yards from the zareba and kept firing occasional shots. It was a wretched night and no one on the campaign is likely to forget it. We were depressed and low-spirited, knowing that we had fought all day and lost some of our fellows and had not done any good or gained any advantage. We were receiving the enemy's fire from three sides and it began to look as if they would surround us. We were overcrowded in a small zareba; men, cattle, and horses were jumbled up in confusion. A stampede amongst the stock would have been utter ruin. We were short of provisions and had nothing for our horses, while we were cramped up behind a very primitive earthwork, although we thought nothing of the discomforts of the trenches at the time. All we thought of was how we were going to get out of them. There was only one thing to do and that was to take Batoche. Retreat was both out of the question and unthought of.

The night passed away without anything happening and the sun rose on the morning of the 10th warm and pleasant, and we soon got warmed up after the cold and chilly night just passed through. After a very early breakfast, some of the infantry were moved out but it was very soon seen that the enemy had advanced their position and now held possession of the church. It was also seen that they were in greater number, owing to the fact that they had abandoned the steamer, which had gone down the river out of their reach. During the morning the mounted men were kept in the zareba, while the infantry went out skirmishing. After dinner Boulton's Scouts and French's Scouts were ordered out, but no destination or plan of action was given and it was soon understood that we were on a secret expedition. Accompanied by a friendly halfbreed and an officer of the staff besides our own officers, we struck out as if going away from the scene of action, but when out of sight we turned back and made toward the enemy's rear. By this movement we saw that we were intended to find the enemy's rear and, as the advance was made very carefully and noiselessly—strict orders being given not to speak above a whisper and to keep spurs or other accoutrements from jingling—we came to the conclusion that we were not to be seen by the enemy. We advanced with great care for six or seven miles in a line with the river, taking advantage of all the hollows and occasionally bending down close to the saddle when a knoll had to be passed over. We advanced along the low ground until on our left we saw the opening of a plain. We now altered our course and, under cover of a bluff, struck in directly toward the river and, getting as close to the plain as possible, halted and remained as motionless and as much out of sight as possible, while two men dismounted and crawled on their stomachs as close to the edge of the plain as possible without being seen and took observations. Having satisfied themselves that this was the enemy's rear and taken a sketch of the position, they retired back and we moved off back again.

On the way back we picked up about a hundred head of cattle and some ponies, which we drove off past our own camp. Following the same detour back we arrived in camp without any obstruction in the way of hostiles. Shortly after getting in, the Dominion Land Surveyors' Corps Mounted Infantry came in and joined the troops amidst vociferous cheering. They were a fine-looking lot of fellows, some seventy strong, well mounted and well armed, and formed a very welcome reinforcement to our little band. We could now raise a troop of 150 mounted men. As soon as we got into camp we set to work to strengthen the trenches. The troops had erected some very fine earthwork while we had been out. We now set to work in earnest and there was lots of fun and laughter over the construction of the trenches. Gangs of eight or nine men worked together making each a trench holding the number of men in the gang. The trenches were dug about three feet below the ground and four feet across. About three feet above the earth the top was made flat and a log was laid on it, then rocks were put and another log put on top, with just room enough to put the rifle through, then at intervals there were transverse walls to prevent enfilading. By the evening of the 10th, our position was not only very strong, but almost impregnable to the halfbreed infantry, and we were wishing to heaven that the rebels would attack our position, for had they done so we could have wiped them out of existence. The distribution of the forces round the zareba was as follows: on the extreme right and front, the trenches were occupied by "A" Battery with their guns and support; on their left, Winnipeg Field Battery; next, Boulton's Mounted Infantry; next to them the 90th Winnipeg, French's Scouts with part of "A" Battery commanding ravine and approach; next part of the Midland; next teamsters armed and 10th Royals, Gatling gun, and remainder of Midlands. The Dominion Land Surveyors were put in next to French's Scouts and the 90th Winnipeg.

The night of the 10th closed in without anything of much consequence happening. The guns had shelled some houses and, with the aid of sharpshooters and Gatling, had regained some of the lost ground. Our men during the afternoon had dug rifle-pits on the left bank of the river on our left and amused themselves taking pot shots across the river and down the ravine. Pits had also been dug in rear of our advanced skirmishers, and when they retired at night the rebels were allowed to follow them up, thinking to give them a volley, but instead were met by a volley from the rifle-pits, which drove them back again. The night passed away quietly but when the sun rose on the morning of the 11th we were as far back as ever, if not a little further, for the rebels seemed to be getting confidence, while our men were getting tired of this dead-and-alive kind of fighting. Fighting is all very well when your blood is up, but being on your stomach shooting at nothing visible all day and occasionally seeing your own men carried off dead or wounded, with lots of time to think of your youthful sins and discrepancies, that sort of fighting is neither excitement nor sport. General Middleton made a mistake when he thought that the men were settling down to their work and getting steadier. On the contrary, they were getting exasperated at the check and were getting dissatisfied and restless with this cold-blooded sort of fighting. They had no proof that they had killed a single rebel and a soldier likes to see the fruits of his work the same as any other man. They wanted to charge and, being young and inexperienced soldiers, could not understand why they should not charge, but generals usually know more about the whys and wherefores than privates, so the charge was kept back.

On the morning of the 11th we, that is, French's Scouts, went out on a foraging expedition. We saw no hostiles, but secured a very welcome supply of hay and oats for our horses, which were sadly in want of a good feed. We also secured for ourselves about three dozen fowls and a quantity of eggs and other articles of food from the rebels' houses. When we came back to the zareba, after burning the rebel houses, we found the infantry practising the same tactics, while the guns had been amusing themselves shelling the houses on the opposite bank of the river. Boulton's men with the Gatling gun had been round to the rear and engaged the rebels in a short skirmish and, having discovered their line of defence, returned to camp. We were now settling down to a regular siege life, living and sleeping in the trenches, as no tents were put up. Not even the general had any shelter, barring a hole in the ground behind a nine-pounder. Some of the trenches were got up very elaborately. The trench I did duty in was one of the greatest in the line and rejoiced in the name of Fort Malakoff. The next trench was Fort French and another, Fort Hole-in-the-Ground, Fort Middleton, and various other names were given to the different trenches and, in the same way, the mounted men got called nicknames. Ours being the first in the field, we led off with the cognomen of French's Furious Fighting Fiends, while Boulton's corps had no sooner arrived in the field than they were dubbed Boulton's

Bounding Beauties from Birtle, and the Dominion Land Surveyors' Corps were christened Dennis's Daring Devils.

On the evening of the 11th I dined with a mess of the 90th and had hard tack and canned beef and tea for supper. Considering the novelty of the good cheer, I enjoyed it, you may bet. While prowling round inside the zareba, I had a good chance to steal the general's supper and looked round to see if anyone was looking, but my conscience smote me (it does sometimes), and I refrained when I thought of how he gave us some of his own supper when that horrible animal the commissary forgot to send supplies. The night of the 11th closed in and we were no further ahead than when we first marched. Lord Melgund, who used to call French's corps "my scouts," had left, much to the regret of our corps with whom he was a universal favorite. He would always listen to our complaints and endeavor to rectify them if possible. He was a thorough soldier and a thorough gentleman, a sort of soldier that men would follow anywhere. As long as he was with us we were a petted corps, but when he left and our captain killed we got forgotten and very often left out in the cold, as it were.

Again we passed through a quiet night and when the morning of the 12th opened up we were in precisely the same position, not one inch had we gained in four days. Early in the morning after breakfast, the whole of the mounted men were paraded outside the zareba and shortly after, accompanied by General Middleton and staff, a nine-pounder and the Gatling

gun and headed by French's Scouts, moved toward
the enemy's rear. We moved up to the plain, the gun
was brought into position on the edge of the plain
and immediately commenced shelling the bluffs. The
Gatling gun was also trained on the bluffs opposite,
while the Dominion Land Surveyors' Corps, extended
as support guns, also opened fire on the bluffs. On
the right front, French's corps was now extended on
the right of the guns and lined a ridge running
parallel with the rebel pits and pretty soon drew a
sharp fire from the pits. Boulton's men were partly in
reserve and partly extended on the left. During the
skirmishing a man suddenly galloped out of the bluffs
and rode toward the general waving a white flag. It
proved to be a man named Astley, one of Riel's
prisoners, and he brought a note to the general to the
effect that if he slaughtered the women and children,
he [Riel] would massacre the prisoners, referring no
doubt to the shelling. The general sent back the
answer to put the women and children in one place,
mark it with a flag, and they would not be molested.
Astley took back the answer. Shortly afterward
another of Riel's prisoners came up on foot with a
copy of the same note, but he refused to go back.
Shortly afterward the skirmishers were drawn in and
we commenced to retire back to camp, having, to all
intents and purposes, achieved nothing, but when he
arrived in camp, we soon found that we had done a
great deal and that the plan of action was most
perfect, had it been carried out. Our movement was
intended as a feint on the rebel rear, which served its
purpose in every way. The rebels, thinking they were

about to be attacked in the rear, immediately withdrew a large portion of the force opposed to our infantry front. It was then that the grand assault should have been made, but owing to some mis-understanding of orders, nothing was done and we found the infantry in the same place.

Although there was no firing going on, shortly after we got into camp and while we were at dinner, a party of the Midland and 10th Royals moved out. They marched straight to the same ravine we had held on the Saturday, directly on our front and charged down yelling and firing. The rebels immedi-ately fell back; they could not stand a charge, the first charge made by a handful of the men. They got out of the pits and fell back. The advantage was quickly followed up. The Gatling gun and the 90th were ordered out and "A" Battery and the guns. By this time the rebels were in full retreat. They were panic-stricken and it was a sharp running fight from this out. It was at this time that Captain French, it is sup-posed, thinking his corps would not be called out, left the zareba without his men and joined in the charge. He was ordered back to get his men, but be-ing of a hot-headed, impetuous nature and very excit-able, it was thought his excitement carried him away, and he never came back. Boulton's men were now ordered out and next the Dominion Land Surveyors. Our corps, having no commander, was not allowed to leave the zareba, though one by one most of the troops got out and joined in the charge.

By this time the firing was hot and heavy. Cheer and cheer went up as the rebels got out of their entrenchments and rifle-pits and fled before the advancing column. They ran like deer, every now and then turning to fire. The troops advanced on the dead run, loading and firing without stopping, our men in a tremendous state of excitement and bent on paying off old scores with interest. Before the troops had been out an hour they were all mixed up in a most elegant confusion, the whole line was mixed up one corps with another. Close to Batoche, there was a slight check and the rebels poured in the lead to a pretty considerable tune. This is where they inflicted the most damage on us, but a volley, a ringing cheer, and a rush sent them flying again. They never stopped till they got into Batoche, where they made another stand, but the column, never weakening its pace, dashed on and drove them off again like so much chaff and, regardless of hot fire coming from the bluff in the rear, ran into the town. A company of Royals and Midlands mixed immediately made for a large store where the prisoners were confined. They dashed into the store, broke open the trap door, and hauled the prisoners out, one by one, out of their wretched dungeon amidst ringing cheers. At the same time as the Midlands and Royals entered the store, Captain French at the head of a mixed-up corps of everything bravely dashed across amidst a perfect hail of lead to a large house and shouting to his lads, "Remember, boys, who led you here," he forced open the door and, followed by his men, dashed upstairs, and was in the very act of shoving his rifle through the window to fire when a rebel took deliberate aim at him as he stood and sent a ball through his wrist and into his heart. He fell dead and never spoke a word.

We picked him up and carried him back to camp on a stretcher, which we put in a wagon further up. The capture of Batoche after this had no interest for us. It had robbed us of the favorite officer of the whole camp. It had taken from us a man who, though at times we abused, we nevertheless adored. The life and soul of the camp, he had always a jolly word and a friendly greeting on the tip of his tongue. French was a typical Irish soldier; compulsive, hot-headed, and naturally excitable, as brave as a lion, more fitted to lead a charge than command a column. His death was regretted by every man in the ranks and every officer of the field and it was a bitter blow to his troop when he fell. However, some must lose the number of their mess and I notice that it is generally the best and most useful that go first.

But to continue; though Batoche was taken and in the possession of the troops, the rebels still occupied the bluffs and kept up an incessant sharpshooting fire directed against the troops now in possession of their own stronghold. The troops took cover behind the houses, stables, and outbuildings and here, for the first time, the column seemed to manifest a desire to stay where it was. When a man gets behind cover and gets cooled down it requires something to rouse him again; however, a few fiendish yells set the ball rolling again and merciless showers of lead were again poured into the rebels. The Gatling gun came up and the nine-pounders got into position and, midst the rattle and crash of the infantry, the incessant rattle of the Gatling gun, and the whizzing and shrieking of the shells, the rebels abandoned their last stand and fled for their lives, leaving their town, camp, and everything in our hands. As the troops were tired and the rebels had no doubt had enough, they were not chased. They were allowed to go, which they evidently did, to use an American expression, "they got there with both feet." A hot fire was kept up from the other side of the river during the charge, but after Batoche was taken, this was soon silenced by the guns, which threw shrapnel and case into the rebels and they ceased firing altogether and hung out a white flag. A company was sent over and took the surrender and there only remained a few of the most stubborn rebels in the bush who fired occasional shots, but these gradually fell off and the firing ceased.

Altogether, Batoche and the rebel position was now in our possession and the rebels driven out. They were thoroughly beaten and were flying for their lives. They had left everything behind them. We captured the whole of their camp. The charge was so sudden and the defeat evidently so unexpected that they had had no time to secure or carry off anything. Their stores, ammunition, women and children, and all their camp effects fell into our hands. The firing had scarcely ceased when the *Northcote*, accompanied by another steamer, came up and tied up to the bank by the ferry. The *Northcote* had gone on to Prince Albert and had there joined the other steamer, the *Marquis*, and in company they came back to do what service they could. As soon as they arrived, the prisoners captured who were of any importance were immediately chained and put on board, along with the rifles captured, and put under the Mounted Police guard who were doing duty on the steamer.

The fight was no sooner over than looting began and the houses and camp were very soon stripped. All sorts of things were captured. Among the most useful was the sum of $200 found by one of the troops, Indian curiosities, bead work, Indian coats, and innumerable Indian odds and ends. But the best thing of all and the most needed at the time was a quantity of tobacco and pipes, and a lot of bread foraged out of the camp. It was a very different scene at this time to what it had been a few days previous. There was nothing but rejoicing throughout the whole camp and the discipline seemed to have suddenly got very lax and loose. Everyone did pretty much as he liked. Guards were, of course, mounted at once and a certain number told off for duty. The 10th and Midlands were quartered in the village. All the other troops, scouts, and teamsters soon scattered all over the Indian camp and village and ransacked and pillaged everything. Very little thought was given at the time to the dead and wounded, of whom there were but too many up at the zareba. Too much praise cannot be given to the ambulance corps who acted on this occasion. In their noble work they could be seen throughout the day in the thickest of the fight, picking up and carrying away their ghastly burdens. Though a man very seldom thinks at all about the dead and wounded while engaged, when all is over, if he has any feeling at all, his thoughts must turn with compassion toward those poor fellows who have been less lucky than himself.

Going over the field I was astonished to see the amount of tact and genius displayed in the laying out of the defences and rebel trenches. I heard several old soldiers and old campaigners say that they could not have planned their defence better if they had had a Royal Engineer to do it for them. All round the town from the river back to the river again there was a perfect line of rifle-pits, placed where everything would be most under cover, and would command an attacking force. These pits were about four foot, six inches, deep and were raised about a foot and a half on their front by loose earth. A log was placed on the top and in most cases another log about six inches higher as a head guard while the rifles were fired through the aperture. They were built to hold from fifteen men downward, according to position. After the charge, blankets, meat, and provisions and articles of clothes were found in the pits, so that our surmise that the rebels remained in their pits through the night was correct, their food being carried to them from time to time. Twenty-six rebels were found dead in and round Batoche after the fight, but others were found in the bluffs afterward. Several of the wounded were also found and sent up to the zareba, but the majority of their wounded they carried away as is their custom, thinking that the white men would treat them the same way as they treat wounded white men, *viz.*, batter their brains out. Middleton, in his official report, gives the number of rebels killed and wounded as fifty-one killed and 173 wounded.

By six o'clock all the dead and wounded had been brought in and I went up to the hospital quarters. The dead had been laid out side by side in their blankets. Captain French we had laid out ourselves.

By his side lay another gallant fellow, Captain Brown of Boulton's Scouts. He was shot at the head of his troops and died instantly. He was a very quiet and unofficious officer and very popular indeed with his troops and everyone who knew him. Had he not been killed he would certainly have received honors for his bravery. It is a solemn sight to see the dead laid out for burial after a fight. As a rule men shun them till they are carried out. They seemed to be forgotten in the excitement of the moment. Next I visited the wounded and found the doctors and their assistants so busy and overwhelmed with work that they were glad of even my assistance. I therefore buckled to and helped to carry the wounded from the dressing room to the tents. The patience and wonderful fortitude of the wounded struck me at once. Some of them were suffering agonies and yet would not utter a sound. Others who could literally not keep down a groan stifled it far down in their throats and it sounded doubly painful. I am not a very weak mortal but it took me all I knew to keep from breaking down. I saw one old soldier who had been with Roberts and with Evelyn Wood and in Egypt with Wolseley kneeling by the side of a stretcher on which lay his mate, badly wounded and almost unconscious. His face was a picture in itself. Although wrinkled and weather-beaten and scarred, there was a look of elegance that clearly told of grief for his suffering comrade, while an unmistakable tear stole down his cheek. Besides those in hospital, there were many with slight wounds who merely got them dressed and went back to their batallions. It was late in the night before the wounded were all attended to, in fact, the doctors were at work through the whole night.

Night brought a new aspect, a sense of security and superiority, whereas before the capture we began to think that we were rather inferior to the rebels and were getting decidedly the worst of it. Of the two sensations the latter is decidedly the most exciting. It was a new sensation to turn in without the anticipation of being suddenly called to stand to your arms to repel an attack.

When the town was taken, all the papers and effects of Riel and Gabriel Dumont fell into our hands and amongst them was found a plan of our zareba complete, and also orders to the effect that the prisoners would be massacred at seven o'clock that night and a general attack made on our trenches at a given time that night. All the troops and followers, officers, and everyone else were to be killed to a man and General Middleton taken prisoner and held while they (the rebels) made terms with the Dominion Government. This was no doubt a very healthy program, but, as you see, it didn't come off. If it had I should not be writing this. Riel regaled his followers with some very choice prophesies, which he doled out from time to time, to keep up his reputation of saint. He told them that on a certain day he would darken the sun and if he did not they need not believe in him any more (*vide* Almanac). When the *Northcote* sent up a rocket to us on the 9th, he told them it was a thunderbolt from the Almighty to destroy their enemy. The enemy was alive and well next morning. He also told them that they killed a hundred of the enemy every day.

His new religion was unique in the extreme. Here is an extract as I remember hearing it at time—Riel's gospel according to himself: "And a spirit made itself visible unto me and I spake saying, shall I be wounded? And spirit answering, touched me and said, I think you will be wounded." Another passage said, "And the spirit said, Tommy Ross is anxious to drink a gallon in honor of the movement," and such like rubbish. This gospel is such utter rubbish that it appears to be a perfect farce and if Riel were not such a very religious character it would give one the idea that he had got up the thing for fun.

But to continue, the sun was scarcely up when the rebels began to come in, some with white flags and others with white bands round their arms in imitation of the scouts. They brought in their arms and gave themselves up quietly and with a very crestfallen air. The priests were very actively employed throughout the day acting as mediators for them. They were taken before the general and examined and, if rebels of note, were put under guard and transferred to the steamer. If merely fighting men, they were dismissed, liable to be rearrested if wanted. They all looked intensely wretched and if they had not been such bloodthirsty wretches one might have pitied them. They all had the same tale, "I didn't want to fight but I was made to." Riel and Dumont, their leaders, were amongst the first to clear out. Riel proved himself to be an arrant coward. All the morning of the 12th he was kneeling under a Red River cart praying instead of fighting with his men.

The town and camp and surroundings at this time looked as if a lot of soldiers had been turned loose for a picnic, and some of them had a very comical look. More than half the regiment had secured Indian ponies and were galloping about on them all over the place for the fun of riding, and a comical sight they cut, most of them never having been in the saddle before. Some had secured buggies and were driving about in style. In fact it looked like a volunteer gathering at the seaside. Everything was gaiety and liveliness and one would think these men had never known hardship or privation of any kind, except for their ragged and rather dirty appearance. For be it known, there was no such thing as washing while in the trenches. There was only a very limited supply in water and that was used exclusively for drinking purposes. All day long the rebels kept coming in and giving up their arms. Riel and Dumont, however, did not come in and it was supposed that they had already gone to the protecting arms of Brother Jonathan[6] in preference to so many yards of hemp. Some of the rebels told us that Riel would be safer with us than amongst them, as they were very bitter against him for his cowardice. They branded him as an imposter and a scoundrel and they were not far out.

In the afternoon I went on board the steamers, on one of which they were shipping the wounded and on another the prisoners. It was a stroke of great luck to have this comfortable transport for the wounded. They were carried on board on stretchers and put in a large airy saloon. There is absolutely no motion on these boats, as there is no sea and the engines work noiselessly and without any trembling. They were then sent up to Saskatoon, the hospital headquarters on the river, where they arrived with only one death, whereas had they been sent over rough roads in wagons without springs a distance of some sixty miles, many of them would have died on the road. Going on board the other boat I saw the rebel prisoners. They were packed tight in a sort of half-hold and amidships with a guard of Mounted Police over them and a more horrid, execrable-looking lot I think I never beheld. They looked as if they would not scruple to perpetrate any act of barbarous cruelty. I never saw a nearer resemblance to the brute beast. Some of the most notorious were chained together, others had a ball and chain attached to their leg. It was very mean-spirited, but I could not help throwing them a grin of satisfaction, at which they looked anything but pleasant.

Visiting some of the houses I saw plenty of marks of the previous day's fighting. The windows were all shattered with bullets and the sashes torn up, while ominous great rips and tears showed where the shells had gone through, though they did not seem to have done as much damage as one would have thought, chiefly owing to the shells having passed through and burst beyond, only one house having been blown up by them in the village itself, although several had been demolished outside and across the river. Inside the houses on the stairs and in the rooms were patches of blood, while everything was strewn about in confusion. The furniture was broken up while crockery, clothing, bedclothes, and other articles were strewn about promiscuously all over the shop, to use a slang expression. Some of the houses had been turned into barracks for the troops, who were amusing themselves in various ways. The women and children were all gathered together and put in the center of the village, and their traps and provisions piled around them, while all the rebel stores were sent on board the steamer.

At sundown on the 13th, Captain Brown was carried down to his last resting place accompanied by all the mounted men, while the band played the "Dead March." It was a sad procession as the long line filed out of the zareba, arms reversed, and wended its way deep down the ravine. The grave had been dug down a steep ravine on the bank of the river, in a lonely spot all by itself. The service was read by a Church of England chaplain, and just as the sun dipped behind the hill the coffin was lowered into the grave. It was an impressive sight to see the group of dusty, ragged soldiers standing uncovered round a comrade's grave, some leaning sadly on their arms, some twitching nervously their caps. As the last rites were said over the grave, there was scarcely a dry eye round that sad circle. Each corps buried its own dead. Captain French was put in a coffin and sent to Fort Qu'Appelle to be buried. The total number of killed was nine, and forty-six wounded.

On the 14th we marched out of the zareba and recommenced the march to relieve Prince Albert. The boats had gone back to Saskatoon and early in the morning the whole of the troops marched out of camp, down the river leaving Batoche to look after itself. We had hardly got out when the rebels began to come back again to their houses. They didn't find things as they left them. Along the line of march we came across women and children with white flags, but no men. They had hidden themselves till the troops should pass. We marched to Lepine's Crossing some fourteen miles down the river from Batoche and there camped.

On the 15th infantry troops remained in camp while the mounted men were sent out to scour the country in the hope of finding Riel and Dumont, but in the meantime two special scouts, a halfbreed and another man, left the camp and somehow or other best known to themselves, rode straight to where Riel was. He at once gave himself up and begged the scouts to protect him and not let him be seen by the other scouts, whom he was afraid would kill him. It is a remarkable fact that the rebels were far more afraid of the mounted men than the troops. They seemed to think that the scouts were more like themselves, knowing that the scouts were all men used to prairie and bush work and used to handling a rifle, while they were perfectly aware that the infantry were town-bred and, as a rule, bushmen despise anything town-bred. They thought we were a bloodthirsty lot of ruffins, not to be trusted out of sight of General Middleton, and took care to copy our emblem and tie it on their own arms to show they were not hostile. While skirmishing about in search of prisoners, we captured a quantity of arms and several prisoners, which were sent into camp. We returned again in the afternoon. Riel was brought in by the two scouts, but Dumont the wily had skipped for climes unknown. We wanted to get hold of this gentleman even more than Riel, as he was the military leader and a more bloodthirsty cruel devil could not be conceived, the only thing that kept him from practising his brutality was the fear of some of Riel's council, who were far-seeing to think of the consequences to themselves if they murdered the prisoners.

It was decided that the column should cross the river here and on the 15th two steamers came down the river and crossing was commenced. The whole of the troops were crossed over the river. It was a long and tedious business crossing a large transport over a broad and swift current with very bad banks for embarking and debarking. The troops and transport having all been crossed, the march was recommenced and after a few days' marching we arrived at Prince Albert, where we made a triumphal entry. The garrison troops were drawn up to receive the column as the head of it marched in accompanied by the 90th band. The garrison consisted of one troop North West Mounted Police and several hundred volunteers. The people were overjoyed to see us come in and to hear of the rebels' defeat and capture of Batoche as, up till the capture of Batoche, they had been in a very critical and very unenviable position, cut off from communication with the outer world except by an occasional scout at the risk bringing or taking dispatches to General Middleton. They were obliged to be put under military discipline, every available man doing duty while the supplies were rationed out, while they had the rebels on one side threatening to come down and take the town and on the other side the Indians ready to step in the moment there was any chance of success. Riel's runners kept the Indians in a perfect ferment with lies to the effect that he was giving the whites a wholesale licking and killing hundreds of them and exhorting them to rise and massacre the whites and burn their houses.

Just before coming into Prince Albert we got word that Poundmaker, the Battleford Indian Chief, had captured a transport of thirty wagons on its way to Colonel Otter in Battleford. Prince Albert is a large settlement on the North Saskatchewan. The town is the largest in the Northwest and spread over a great deal of ground, consequently very difficult to defend against an attacking force. What the resources of this settlement are, I don't know. It was formerly a Hudson's Bay fur post, in fact it might almost be called a Hudson's Bay town now. We found that the Hudson's Bay had quantities of things stored, which they brought out to sell to the troops, which they did at most exorbitant prices. Our troop being by far the richest, we soon had a fine assortment of jam and fancy meats and biscuits. We lived in a most extravagant style. We paid seventy-five cents for a little box of Huntley and Palmer's Biscuits with a dozen very small biscuits in it. We ate pastes and potted meats by the dozen at seventy-five cents, a very small tin holding about a mouthful. Preserves were scattered about *ad libitum*. Our tents, of which there were four, vied with each other in getting in the most luxuriant supply of good cheer. In fact this windfall was just as welcome to us as a dinner at the Criterion to a hungry beggar. Hard tack and corned beef becomes very monotonous.

One is liable to get tired of such dry feeding, although we got beef when in Prince Albert.

Two days after we arrived, part of the column got orders to embark on the river steamers, the 10th and Boulton's Horse were immediately put on board, the reason for this being that General Strange, who was in command of the column against the Fort Pitt Indians, Big Bear's band, had engaged Big Bear. The first report came in that General Strange had been beaten and cut up and was flying back to Fort Pitt and that the Indians had captured his ammunition and ten men with it. However, this was found not to be true. Strange had engaged the Indians, who were entrenched on a place called Frenchman Butte, then for some unaccountable reason, just when he had the Indians beaten, he withdrew his troops and retired back on Fort Pitt, leaving some scouts to watch their movements, and sent down to Middleton for reinforcements in the way of artillery. As near as I can find out from questioning Strange's men, the truth was: while engaged in the afternoon, his scouts came in and reported the Indians were coming down with the intention of turning Strange's flank. Wherewith Strange at once retired, not knowing the force of the Indians and not knowing the Indians were beaten. Afterward we found that the Indians reported by the scouts were the women and children clearing out. No sooner had Strange left than the Indians immediately fled, leaving tons of stuff behind them; carts, wagons, quantities of bacon and flour, and camp things besides their camp. Had Strange fired a few more shells, the Indians would have cleared out and left him in possession of the camp and the prisoners who were in Big Bear's hands, consisting of the McLean family—father and mother, three grown-up daughters and several small children—Mrs. Delaney and Mrs. Gowanlock, a minister and his wife, two other families, and other prisoners, making a total of twenty-seven.

The rest of the column received orders to march next morning if no steamer arrived to transport them. A few hours after General Middleton had gone, a messenger came in from Poundmaker to ask the terms of surrender. Middleton was communicated with and his answer was none but an unconditional surrender. He gave Poundmaker three days to come in and if he then failed to come in and surrender his braves and arms, Middleton's troops would destroy him and his whole band. On the 26th of May the remainder of the troops under Colonel Van Straubenzie marched from Prince Albert on the road to Battleford to rejoin General Middleton. The column consisted of French's Scouts, Dominion Land Surveyors' Corps, 90th Battalion, "A" Battery, and the Midlands. We reached Fort Carlton on the second day, where a troop of Mounted Police had been sent to make a ferry or rather repair an already existing ferry. Fort Carlton had been evacuated by the police two months before, when the rebels had marched in, and after remaining in it for a time had set fire to it and burned it to the ground. The day after we arrived a large steamer came up from Prince Albert accompanied by a smaller one, and the work of crossing the transport commenced. Two days were taken up by this work and when all the transport had crossed, they were placed under the charge of French's Scouts and the Dominion Land Surveyors' Corps with orders to make Battleford with all possible speed, while the remainder of the troops were put on board the boats and transported up the river to Battleford.

We moved up along the river in charge of the transport. We saw numerous signs of the enemy, such as fresh tracks, camps, and such like. We had a wet trip up, but arrived in Battleford without having seen any hostiles. We found a very large camp and as we came in the usual amount of cheering was indulged in. We took ground as usual outside the infantry and after dinner took a stroll round the camps. Colonel Otter's command consisted of the Queen's Own Rifles, "B" Battery, Governor General's Foot Guards, Battleford Rifles, "C" Company, some Mounted Police, two seven-pounder guns and a Gatling gun. Battleford is not nearly so large as Prince Albert. The town proper is situated between the North Saskatchewan and the Battle River down in the forks. Previous to Otter's arrival, the people and settlers had been locked up in the town, as the Indians had surrounded the place and put it in a state of siege and were only awaiting a favorable opportunity to attack and destroy the town. On Otter's arrival they had withdrawn to the Eagle Hills, but not till they had killed several settlers and destroyed a great deal of property. On our arrival we found that Poundmaker had already surrendered with his braves and arms to General Middleton who had arrived. He said he would not surrender to Otter because he had beaten him, but when he heard that Middleton was coming after him, after having knocked spots off the halfbreeds, he said he would surrender to the great, big chief. He was promptly put in gaol, along with a lot of his murdering braves, and his arms confiscated. His band had murdered their instructor and several other whites. Poundmaker's excuse was that he could not keep his young braves from fighting.

We got two days' rest here, when the general again shipped all his column of infantry on the steamers and started with all speed to join General Strange. Otter and his command were to be left in Battleford, much to their disgust. French's Scouts, Boulton's Horse, and the Dominion Land Surveyors were joined by a troop of Mounted Police and the whole was put under the command of Colonel Herchmer with orders to reach Fort Pitt by forced marches in the shortest possible space of time. Little or no transport was allowed beyond wagons to carry ammunition and rations. It rained in torrents the first day and we were all soaked through. We made a long march and it was ten o'clock at night before we got time to lie down. Reveille was sounded at one o'clock in the morning again, and we marched till seven, when we halted for breakfast, and marched again till twelve, when we halted again for dinner, and then marched again till late in the evening. It was a very trying march and took it out of both men and horses, especially the horses. However, we arrived within a few miles of Fort Pitt at the same time as the boats and it was decided to camp and unload the steamers. A steamer was sent across and we went on board and crossed over to the troops, but were very disappointed to learn that the Indians had cleared out shortly after our arrival.

Boulton's Horse, the Dominion Land Surveyors, and Mounted Police, a company of the 90th, and a company of the 10th with the general and Gatling gun went out to take up Big Bear's trail and follow him up and force a fight. French's Scouts, or rather the half that remained, and the column struck camp, marched to Fort Pitt, and found there some of Strange's men. Pitt was a Hudson's Bay fort occupied by the Hudson's Bay factor McLean and family and a detachment of police. The police evacuated it and the Indians took McLean and family prisoners and, after sacking the fort, burned it to the ground. I happened to be told off duty with the column carrying dispatches. One half was reserved for this service, while the other half of the corps was doing duty as bodyguard to the general, which provoked the jealousy of the other corps. We moved into camp on a hill overlooking the site of the burned fort and waited developments.

The column organized to pursue Big Bear were still in camp fifteen miles away making packsaddles, as no other transport could be got through the country the Indians had taken. When they finally started, however, they sent back the infantry and, taking only the mounted men and the Gatling, they tracked the Indians through a dense forest, impassable except in single file. They found the bodies of six Indians and one squaw, and from time to time came across Indian goods cast away to lighten them in their retreat. At Frog Lake they saw the graves of the massacred white men buried a few days before by Strange's men. After following them for several days they were brought up by a large muskeg which the Indians had crossed but which our men could not cross with so many horses and, as they were obliged to come back again, on their return orders were sent out to Strange to march his troops out by Frog Lake. Colonel Otter was to march from Battleford and Colonel Irvine from Prince Albert in the direction of Green Lake in the hope of cutting Big Bear off and releasing the prisoners still in their hands, if alive. It was greatly feared that they had massacred them.

Middleton again took the flying column of mounted men and marched to Beaver River, but not finding any trace of the band except a few Wood Cree who had suffered themselves by the other Indians, he returned again to Fort Pitt. While he was away Mrs. Delaney and Mrs. Gowanlock, with one or two others including a wounded Indian, having managed their escape by some means, came into camp and were taken care of on one of the steamers. They told a very sad tale, perhaps the saddest of all. They were both young women, one of them only married a few months. Their husbands, Gowanlock and Delaney, had come up and settle out at Frog Lake, having also something to do with the Indian agency. They were both very friendly with the Indians and were great favorites. It appears when the Indians broke out they had no idea the Indians would hurt them; however, the Indians came down and took them out of their houses, as they said, to protect them. But the Indians went over to the mission and deliberately and brutally murdered the two priests and two other men. They

then took Delaney and Gowanlock, accompanied by
their wives, into the bush and while walking along deliberately shot down and killed Delaney alongside his
wife, whom they dragged away, and she never saw
him afterward. Next they shot and killed Gowanlock
while supporting his wife, whom they also dragged
away, and she likewise never saw her husband again.
They completed their butchery by slaughtering all the
white men, seven or eight in number. Subsequently
these two women were bought by a humane halfbreed
who gave two horses for them and kept them from
harm. Had it not been for this man their fate would
probably have been far worse than death. He finally
brought them in safe to our camp and, I believe, was
rewarded by being arrested as an accomplice.

Shortly after Middleton's return, the Indians,
hunted to death and starving, split up. The Wood
Cree (generally good Indians and in any case the
most humane) got the white prisoners and, not being
able to do anything with them, let them go, giving
them a shotgun and a few pounds of flour on which
they had to reach Frog Lake where Strange then was.
The women and children all arrived in Fort Pitt well
and, though rather ragged, did not look much the
worse for their terrible experience with the Indians.
There was now nothing more to do except capture
Big Bear and his band, which having broken up
could easily be done by the Mounted Police when
they could find out where he was. Riel was captured
with nearly all his councillors. Batoche and the
rebellion were broken up and their arms in custody,
Poundmaker and his choice spirits under lock and

key, all the white prisoners recaptured, Big Bear's band broken up, and the rebellion generally sat upon. Nothing now remained but to concentrate the forces and begin the homeward march.

Strange was ordered in to Fort Pitt and Ouimet,[7] who was in command of the Edmonton column, was ordered into Pitt also. It was some time before they all got in but when they did there was quite a big camp. The following is a list of the most important corps in camp, French's corps coming first by right of being the first and only mounted corps in the field at the first outbreak.

Middleton's Column

Mounted

French's Scouts—Captain Brittlebank
Boulton's Scouts—Major Boulton
Dominion Land Surveyors' Corps—Captain Dennis
Mounted Police—Colonel Herchmer

Infantry

90th Winnipeg Rifles—Major McBean
10th Grenadiers—Lieutenant Colonel Grasett
Midland Regiment—Colonel Williams
"C" Company—Major Smith

Artillery

"A" Battery—Colonel Montizambert
Winnipeg Field Battery—Brigade Major Young

General Strange's Column

Mounted Police — Captain Steele
Steele's Scouts — Captain Steele
92nd Winnipeg Light Infantry — Colonel Smith
1 nine-pounder gun
65th Regiment, Quebec

Colonel Ouimet's Column

61st or 66th Regiment, Montreal
Alberta Mounted Rifles

Colonel Otter was to be picked up on the way
down. The infantry were to embark in steamboats
sent up for that purpose and taken via the lakes to
Winnipeg. A few words about the Fort Pitt camp
may not be out of place. It was a large camp at the
finish. The troops had built large bowers of boughs
for mess rooms, reading rooms, etc., and the camp
got to have a very permanent look. We were over
eight weeks in this camp and it began to get terribly
dreary, even for us who were often sent out with
dispatches. In fact, at one time we were in and out
continually. Concerts, sports, and drill were the order
of the day and carrying firewood, which got to be
quite a serious article, finally. Everyone got terribly
tired of the camp and lived in daily expection of
receiving orders for home, but the long-deferred
orders never came till we had despaired of every getting them. Finally they did come and were received

with exuberant rejoicing. The whole camp was in a state of ecstasy at the prospect of leaving the most dismal holes in creation and getting back into some sort of civilization. The main thing looked forward to, I think, was getting a good square feed. However, very soon after receiving orders, the camp was in a state of rush and bustle. Tents were hauled down and kits packed and very soon where there had been a mass of white tents, there was nothing but piles of baggage. The bowers were set on fire and boxes and barrels piled up and burned. In a very short space of time everything was ready to transport onto the boats. The Dominion Land Surveyors' Corps had gone the day before, Boulton's corps had gone that morning, also Steele's Scouts and the police. Our troop was honored with orders not to leave Fort Pitt until the staff and column had gone down the river.

That evening all the troops had gone aboard and everything was ready to drop down the river. Early in the morning, just as the day was breaking, the flagship, I suppose it should be called, whistled the signal to cast off and drop down the river, and as they pulled out our little band gave them three cheers, in answer to which the general waved his hat. We were astounded to see on what an extensive scale the provisioning had been carried on. The east bank of the river was simply lined with tons of oats and piles of boxes of hard tack and corned meats. There was as much still going to waste and ruin as would feed a regiment for a year. The commissary evidently did not intend that the troops should starve, which they certainly never did, and it must be said to the credit of the commissary that they did their work admirably. There was always plenty of the kind and as long as a soldier gets plenty he has no right to complain, for he might get worse. We had a beautiful trip back. It was just like a picnic. The weather was very good and we had plenty to eat and nothing to do. We passed along the old road back through Touchwood Hills and arrived again in Fort Qu'Appelle on the 19th of July, the last of the column in the field, and a very ragged-looking crew we were, as were all the troops. But as we were particularly hungry, we were not long before we got outside of something very solid in the way of feed. The next day the march was continued and arriving at Troy we were paid off and disbanded. After that dinners and whisky were the order of the day. And throwing off our arms, we once more became civilized citizens again, and that was the end of French's Scouts and the Northwest Insurrection.

Notes

1. Captain John "Jack" French was a former Mounted Policeman who had been one of the original members of the force in 1873. He served ten years before leaving to farm near Qu'Appelle.

2. Gilbert John Elliot, Viscount Melgund, was serving as military secretary to the Governor-General when he was hastily recruited to act as Middleton's chief of staff. He was an experienced military man, having seen action in Turkey, Afghanistan, and Egypt in the British Army. From 1898 to 1904, as the Earl of Minto, he was Governor-General of Canada.

3. White Cap was chief of a Sioux band which had fled to Red River in 1862, after the massacres in Minnesota, to escape the U.S. Army. The Sioux remained in the vicinity of Portage la Prairie until the 1870s when they moved farther west. Ironically, it was only after they took part in the rebellion that they were allotted a reserve.

4. Captain James Peters of "A" Battery was a permanent force officer originally from New Brunswick. Peters was also a photographer whose pictures of the fighting are remarkably good considering the difficulty of the conditions and the crude equipment.

5. Lieutenant Colonel Bowen Van Straubenzie, an English officer, who came to Canada in 1876, was deputy adjutant general of the militia at the time of the outbreak. He commanded the infantry in the Batoche column.

6. Brother Jonathan was a popular nineteenth-century slang name for the United States, rather similar to Uncle Sam.

7. Lieutenant-Colonel J. Alderic Ouimet, commanding officer of the 65th Carabiniers Mont-Royal, was a Conservative Member of Parliament. He became ill and had to return to Montreal before his regiment left Calgary.

INDEX

Index